No Country for Idealists

ALSO BY BORIS FRANKEL

Democracy Versus Sustainability:
Inequality, Material Footprints, Post-Carbon Futures

Capitalism Versus Democracy?
Rethinking Politics in the Age of Environmental Crisis

Fictions of Sustainability:
The Politics of Growth and Post-Capitalist Futures

Zombies, Lilliputians and Sadists:
The Power of the Living Dead and the Future of Australia

When the Boat Comes In:
Transforming Australia in the Age of Globalisation

From the Prophets Deserts Come:
The Struggle to Reshape Australian Political Culture

The Post-Industrial Utopians

Beyond the State?
Dominant Theories and Socialist Strategies

Marxian Theories of The State: A Critique of Orthodoxy

No Country for Idealists

The Making of a Family of Subversives

Boris Frankel

GREENMEADOWS

Copyright © Boris Frankel 2023
Boris Frankel asserts his right to be known as the author of this work.

First published in 2023 by Greenmeadows
P.O. Box 3075, Ripponlea VIC 3185

ALL RIGHTS RESERVED.
Apart from any uses permitted by Australia's Copyright Act 1968, no part of this book may be reproduced by any process without prior written permission from the copyright owners. Enquiries should be made to the publisher.

Every effort has been made to trace copyright holders and any potential infringement of copyright material is accidental. The publisher apologises for any errors or omissions and would be grateful to be notified of any corrections that should be incorporated in future reprints or editions of this book.

A catalogue record for this book is available from the National Library of Australia

Frankel, Boris, author.
No Country for Idealists: The Making of a Family of Subversives.
1. Historical Memoir. 2. Australian history.
3. Soviet society 4. Australian politics and society

ISBN: 978-0-6483633-8-5 (paperback)
ISBN: 978-0-6483633-9-2 (ebook)

Cover photo of Genia, Maya, Boris and Tania Frankel
for visa application, British Embassy, Moscow, 1958

Back cover photo of Abraham Frankel in Kerch, Crimea, 1962

Cover design by Duncan Blachford
Text design and typesetting by Typography Studio

In memory of my parents

Abraham Frankel 1908–1968 and Tania Frankel 1920–1995,

and for my sisters

Genia and Maya

CONTENTS

Preface   ix

*   *   *

1. Unreliable narratives?   1
2. A disturbing voice   15
3. Thick spines: Nostalgia and Political Development   25
4. Surviving the Grodno Ghetto   49
5. North Carlton and the emergence of the non-Jewish Jew   68
6. Family life, politics and Left culture   87
7. St. Kilda childhood under the shadow of the Cold War   112
8. 'Petrov the rat'   146
9. Departing for Paradise   178
10. 'If I could only swim the Atlantic or the Pacific …'   208
11. Soviet life in the raw   223
12. An invaluable education   254
13. We refuse to accept your refusal   273
14. Desperate action   297
15. Freedom and its discontents   324
16. 'ASIO does not concern itself with compassion'   347

*   *   *

Epilogue   361
Select Bibliography   371

PREFACE

Writing for different generations of readers is never easy. Knowledge and memory of historical events or key public players cannot be assumed of the recent past, let alone of several decades ago. I have written this book for a general audience as well as for the next generation of our family – especially Dani, Paris, and Emile – who may find illuminating material in this memoir about their parents and grandparents. In different ways, they too have been shaped by the legacy of these events. A delicate balancing act is always involved in writing about personal and family experiences that are of interest to general readers because these were events that went far beyond the personal.

To add to this complexity, while living in the United States in 1972, I discovered that I had a doppelganger, a Boris Frankel/Boris Fraenkel from Paris who, by coincidence, also published work on leading critical theorists such as Herbert Marcuse. I had to explain to various people in America that I was the Boris from Melbourne and not the Boris from Paris. The other Boris was born in the Free City/state of Danzig (Gdansk) in 1921 after his mother fled the Russian Revolution, the same year that my father and his family left Russia. Like my father, who was stateless for almost half his life, Boris was also a stateless person and moved to France in the late 1930s. He became a militant Trotskyist and recruited people such as former French Prime Minister, Lionel Jospin. Well known for his activity promoting Wilhelm Reich's radical

PREFACE

Sex-Pol ideas to students and others, the rebellious events of May 1968 quickly led to his arrest. After failing to deport him to neighbouring countries, the French government kept him under house arrest for over a year – like in feudal times – in a provincial convent in the Dordogne. We became friends in 1973 and he visited us in Melbourne years later. At the age of 85, on April 23, 2006, Boris committed suicide by jumping into the Seine from the Pont du Garigliano, the highest bridge in Paris. Even in death, people still confused the two of us. Some of the published obituaries for him had my photo mistakenly inserted instead of a picture of the deceased Boris Frankel. Today, it is still an uncanny experience to see our images and publications appearing together in web-based searches. For readers in Europe and America, I wish to state from the outset that this memoir is about the early life of Boris Frankel and his family from Melbourne rather than the other Boris who lived most of his life in France.

I am also reminded of another former stateless person, the Austrian/French radical writer, André Gorz/Gerhard Hirsch, who published his own memoir, *The Traitor* in 1958. A year after Boris committed suicide, André and his beloved partner Dorine committed suicide in a love pact. Back in 1973, André and Dorine had urged me to write about my family's experiences while they were still fresh in my memory. I ignored their good advice for fifty years. However, if I had written this book in the 1970s it would have lacked the reflective knowledge that I acquired in subsequent decades. Additionally, the ASIO and other government files central to what follows, were only made available in recent decades. Hindsight enables me to see that my parents, like the other Boris and André and Dorine, were radical idealists who found no country where their ideas and beliefs were held and valued by most of the population.

Finishing this memoir was easier than finalising the book's title. Various proposals such as: *Memoir of a Rootless Cosmopolitan*; *From Melbourne to Moscow*; *Subversives from St. Kilda*; *Red Herrings*; *Carlton to Crimea*; or *Abe and the Argonauts*, were ultimately rejected. My parents would occasionally refer in Yiddish to people they knew as either a nudnik (meaning nuisance and bore) or a Meshuga (crazy). I also considered titles such as *Nudniks in Melbourne and Moscow* or *Meshugas in Australia and Russia*. However, none of the many serious or humorous potential titles captured the complexity of the issues, events and places discussed in the book.

Finally, I am indebted to various people. I thank Phillip Deery for providing me with additional documents about my family from the National Archives of Australia. Ken Mansell provided helpful clarification about events at Monash in the 1960s. Claus Offe offered similar assistance about the Max Planck Institute in Starnberg. Thanks to Helen and Jack Halliday and the St. Kilda Historical Society for inviting me to make a presentation, 'Recollections of St. Kilda' on December 8, 2022, which informed part of chapters 7 and 15. Special thanks to Peter Christoff for his enduring friendship, his close reading of the manuscript, and advice on editing and selection of photographs. My son Emile and sister Maya also advised on various proposed titles and provided photos. It is a profound sadness that my sister Genia is unable to contribute her knowledge of these events and to argue about my interpretations. Robert Manne was one of the first readers of the manuscript and I greatly appreciate his supportive comments. I am particularly grateful to Duncan Blachford for his excellent book design and typesetting and for his evocative cover design.

Julie Stephens, my partner of the past thirty-five years read everything more than once. We have proved to be an effective working team commenting on and editing each other's writings. She has long nurtured this project, originally sourcing our family files from the National Archives over a decade ago and urging me to write about these extraordinary experiences. Her indispensable support, love and invaluable editorial interventions have made this book possible. Of course, the shortcomings are mine alone.

Boris Frankel
October 16, 2023

1

UNRELIABLE NARRATIVES?

On May 7, 1956, reporters and photographers gathered on board the *Orcades* at Port Melbourne to interview and take photos of our family before we sailed for the Soviet Union via London. Large photos accompanied by inaccurate reports would feature in leading newspapers across Australia. Yet, the distortions in these newspaper reports would prove to be trivial compared to the unreliable narratives supplied over the years by untrustworthy informers and agents working for the notoriously flawed Australian Security and Intelligence Organisation (ASIO). Little did we know on that day in May 1956, that this would be the beginning of seven years of trauma and struggle to return to Australia and reunite our family in Melbourne.

Dictionaries usually define 'subversive' as: "tending or intending to subvert or overthrow, destroy, or undermine an established or existing system, especially a legally constituted government or a set of beliefs." Members of our family would have pleaded guilty to parts of this definition, particularly the desire to subvert or transform existing beliefs and bring about a socialist society. However, we certainly did not engage in violence, incendiary and insurrectionary activity or acts involving secretive, underground pursuits such as espionage. This important qualification was disregarded by Prime Minister Robert Menzies and leading Ministers in his government. The inaccurate characterisation of my parents was fueled by ASIO which continued to maintain over the decades that my father was a 'subversive' and a danger to 'national security'.

Sometimes it is the minor, unknown figures who can reveal much about the political culture, organisational logic and policies of both the Australian and Soviet governments during the Cold War. Although these governments were often depicted in ideological terms as being polar opposites, representing freedom on the one hand, and repression on the other, both in fact shared many common features: mutual ignorance of one another's society as well as bureaucratic, slothful, and compassionless decision-making. Both Australian and Soviet society and their governments presided over hidden or flagrant untruths.

Given the official narrative about our family, one aim of this book is to correct the historical record. It is a social and political history of how my parents came to Australia and how we experienced life in both Australia and the Soviet Union during the Cold War. What follows are both personal memoirs and a collection of vignettes about family experiences set within the context of historical, political, and cultural events. This is a story of memory and forgetting, of civil war, annihilation, and political fanaticism. Yet, it is not just a tale of dreams and deceptions. Importantly, it is also about love and courage in the face of concerted opposition by both the Australian and Soviet governments. Others shared aspects of our family's socio-cultural and political background and involvements. However, to my knowledge, no one else from Australia went through the dramatic experiences I will detail in this historical memoir.

What's in a name?

The fact that our family was regarded with suspicion, probably contributed to the formation of my life as a non-conformist outsider – more often looking in, rather than being fully integrated into and accepted as part of society. Although born in Melbourne at the Bethesda Hospital, Richmond, my name, and background from Russian and

Byelorussian/Polish parents – who met in 1940 after arriving in Australia in 1937 and 1938 – meant that most people assumed that I was not Australian. Before the 1960s, one rarely encountered people in Australia called Boris. Even in recent decades, when giving my name to strangers on the phone or face-to-face, most would invariably apply their Anglo filter, mishear me, and call me 'Morris' instead of 'Boris'. Actually, in popular culture during the period from the 1930s to the 1960s, William Pratt, aka Boris Karloff, was well known for his roles in Frankenstein and other horror movies. 'Boris' was also usually associated with villains in cartoons and television series. As a young child, friends of the family called me Boris Karloff. One even called me 'Boris not Goodenough', a thoughtless inversion of Czar Boris Godunov. Given that I was so often called 'Boris Karloff', when I started school at Brighton Road State School in St. Kilda, and the teacher asked our names, I answered: "I think it is Boris Karloff, but also Boris Karloff Frankel." She then instructed me to ask my parents to write down on paper what my real name was, and to show her their answer the next day.

The recent incident in 2022 of the Queen's Lady in Waiting, Susan Hussey, having to resign for repeatedly asking a British-born black woman 'where she really came from', merely confirmed the racist or culturally superior Anglo assumptions experienced by non-Anglos in the UK and Australia. Instead of being constantly asked: 'how long have you lived in Australia?' or 'which country do you come from?', it was only when I recommenced travelling overseas in the early 1970s, that most people readily accepted me as Australian. However, at home, an Australian Boris was unthinkable. In Europe and America, these two signifiers were compatible, partly because in the 1970s, relatively little was known about the narrow conceptions of Australianness, the exclusion of First Nations' cultures or the waves of mainly white immigrants that had occupied Australia during the nineteenth and twentieth centuries. In other words, the people I met in Europe or North America lacked an obvious presumption about cultural hierarchies in Australia while at home there were clear delineations of who belonged to the dominant social group, who were designated as 'outsiders' and given the label 'New Australians', or Indigenous peoples who were not even recognised as citizens.

While living abroad opened a more cosmopolitan world to me, paradoxically, the longer I stayed away, the more I became aware that Melbourne was home, and that my cultural mannerisms were infused with Australian perspectives, humour, and informality. I am proud of being cosmopolitan and often, in a mocking, self-deprecatory manner, use the anti-Semitic label of 'rootless cosmopolitan' as a badge of honour. However, the truth is that I have always had a deep sense of place. Nonetheless, I continue to harbour a profound dislike of those narrow and exclusive notions of 'home' that are inseparably connected to nationalist prejudice. In this non-nationalist sense, I continue to see myself as a 'non-Australian Australian'.

My immigrant parents taught me to respect the higher ideal of a shared humanitarianism and internationalism. They had already lived in Melbourne for a decade before Arthur Calwell, Minister for Immigration in the late 1940s, coined the term 'New Australians' to describe post-war non-British migrants. Nonetheless, as with many 'New Australians' from non-Anglo cultures, my mother and father found much of the pre-1960s dominant Anglo-Celtic culture alien, parochial, and politically conservative. At a personal level, they experienced a mixture of genuine friendliness and warmth, but also casual, unthinking racism and anti-Semitism.

Throughout most of the twentieth century, European immigrants in Australia encountered what present-day migrants from Asian, Middle Eastern and African countries experience on a daily basis. Contemporary young Australians would not know, unless they heard it from their parents or older relatives, how immigrants were treated as little more than 'factory fodder' and discriminated against as 'wogs' and 'dagos'. The difference today is that most of the factories that employed migrants from the 1930s to the early 1980s no longer exist. Now migrants, especially from non-European countries, are exploited in other sectors, such as service industries or agriculture.

Australian-born locals were generally welcoming and friendly. They were often more accepting of foreigners than citizens in most other countries. Yet, there was also outright hostility and racism which was widely practiced by many employers and social institutions. Intentionally or unintentionally, immigrants were often treated as second-class people by the very same Australians whose own parents, grandparents or great grandparents had themselves been immigrants. Despite far greater social diversity in recent decades, one needed to have experienced what it was like growing up without an Anglo boy's name, such as Tom, Dick, or Harry, or a girl's name such as Margaret, Elizabeth, or Susan, to understand why so many people felt they were not regarded as 'Australian'. I was grateful that my parents had named me Boris instead of Ben-Zion, the Russian and Hebrew names of my grandfather. By contrast, my older sister, Genia (named after her maternal grandmother), preferred anglicising her name and being called Jean as an adult. My younger sister Maya (born in May) preferred the name May as a young child before embracing Maya as she grew older. These 'choices' reflected the changing social and cultural climate of Australia and were more than simply personal.

Levels of acceptance in the larger society should not be confused with how one was treated at the personal level. Both my sister Genia and I were fully integrated into the local kids' culture and played with our friends in the nearby park, streets, and neighbourhood houses. However, my parents' friendships with neighbours and the people they worked with in factories were often superficial. Part of the reason for this is that the topic of conversation rarely got beyond the weather, sport, or local neighbourhood issues, given the deep aversion of many 'locals' to discussing 'religion, politics, and art'. I occasionally heard my parents disparage Australian working-class, laid-back cultural attitudes, especially 'she'll be right, mate'. They were perplexed by the dominant culture that espoused a 'fair go' and yet was riddled with a passive conformity and widespread tolerance of inequality. Equally troubling was a public culture that raised sport above the arts and sciences and maintained a general ignorance of the world unless it had some connection to Australia, especially a war or an Australian in a sporting event.

Anonymity and conflicting cultural priorities

When former Prime Minister, Tony Abbott, said in 2013: "Happy is the country which is more interested in sport than in politics", he was reproducing and celebrating the long conservative tradition from the 1920s to the 2020s which enabled governments to be elected without adequate mass public scrutiny. A largely uncritical media combined with an electorate either minimally involved or uninterested in politics has been a successful recipe for the perpetuation of inequality and injustice. On September 15, 2022, author Richard Flanagan, decried the lack of government support for Australian writers and told ABC radio that in Australia there had been 'a war on the life of the mind' in the past twenty-five years. This was certainly true. What Flanagan omitted to say is that this 'war on the life of the mind' had also been evident for most of twentieth-century Australian history.

Little wonder that my parents found a more attractive and congenial world amongst those preoccupied with alternative cultures and social change. They were self-educated working-class Communists in the Depression years of the 1930s and the war and post-war years of the 1940s and 1950s. Unsurprisingly, they gravitated to local Australian rebels and bohemians. My mother and father's commitment to 'a better world' led them to build friendships and political associations with people from diverse backgrounds. Many of their friends loved sport, but they also recognised that there were far more important social, economic, political, and cultural issues that demanded urgent critical attention.

It is often forgotten that in the pre-digitalised era, most ordinary Australians – whether born here or abroad – could remain relatively anonymous or invisible to their government and community. Many would regard this as a good thing. Yet, the negative side of anonymity is often overlooked, particularly the isolation and loneliness experienced at the personal level. Anonymity also helps breed a passive and compliant citizenry at the larger social level. An active citizenry means that people become known to their community or fellow citizens and not just to their government.

As I will later describe, we were not passive, and members of our family certainly did not remain anonymous. Our faces were splashed over the front pages of newspapers. In fact, our very future would be determined directly and personally by Prime Minister Robert Menzies, the Director-General of ASIO Brigadier Charles Spry, Minister for Immigration, Alexander Downer senior, Minister for External Affairs, R. G. Casey and future Prime Minister, John Gorton, in conjunction with the Secretaries and Deputy Secretaries of their departments and leading Australian and British diplomats.

Despite being repeatedly asked to write about our unique history, I have resisted these requests for decades. There were several reasons. I was too preoccupied with living my life forward rather than reminiscing about the years that our family lived in the USSR. Also, it is all too common for many of us to ignore the complexity of individual lives and reduce them to one-dimensional political or social labels. In my case, it was constraining enough to be automatically pre-judged or pigeon-holed as a 'Russian' rather than as an Australian. I did not want my earlier experiences in the USSR to overshadow or define my life and work in the eyes of others. Privately, I do not deny the impact and formative experiences of these early years in Australia and the Soviet Union. In later years, these experiences in Russia were often talked about by members of our family and close friends. Directly and indirectly, they certainly helped shape not only my political views but also forged aspects of the person I would become.

My previous avoidance of discussing our life in Russia was not equivalent to those who had experienced profound traumas and losses, such as soldiers who witnessed the horrors of war. I have never been afraid of reviving painful memories as I have never really forgotten many of them. Our family certainly went through distressing times. But throughout the difficulties, we also shared many joyous and hilarious moments buoyed by jokes, stories, good books, and music. There was much open argument, heart-to-heart, tear-filled discussions, and solidarity in the face of adversity. The shadow of the Holocaust or Shoah fell on my mother's life and would have indirectly impacted our family in a myriad of ways. This is not the focus of this book, but it may have coloured some of the experiences my mother had when in the Soviet Union, which will be discussed in a later chapter.

Nonetheless, at a deeper psychological and behavioural level, years of surveillance took its toll. We were always alert to the way intelligence agents and other government officials monitored us. Past experiences undeniably helped to develop shades of justifiable and unjustifiable suspicion bordering on paranoia amongst members of our family. The battle against mistrust had to be constantly waged. Learning to love and trust others is a common experience that often prevents people from forming a committed relationship after being hurt by ex-lovers. This form of interpersonal caution or mistrust needs to be clearly differentiated from the mistrust that our family learnt from dealing with governments. Most bureaucracies continue to negatively affect one's life through the exercise of political prejudices, the callous and dehumanising enforcement of authoritarian rules or by sheer incompetence rather than malevolence. In our case, reports based on fanciful or malicious rumours quickly became the 'truth' once registered in written form. These so-called 'truths' were then accepted by subsequent government readers of the files without questioning the original assessment and source of information. They directly contributed to our unnecessary and unjustifiable suffering.

Today, damaging material placed on social media is often directly sourced to the individual themselves, rather than placed in government files by anonymous informants. At least on social media the individual concerned can apologise, reject, or defend views held in an earlier period. With intelligence organisations and their informants, it is quite different. One neither knows what is in your file (until decades later, or sometimes never) and nor does one know what you are accused of doing or thinking. The positive aspect of government files, if one gains access to them many decades later, is that they do contain a record of parts of your life no matter how distorted. They do help to revive memories of past experiences.

Traumas, memory, and 'digging up the truth'

In recent decades, much has been written about the social and cultural roles played by individual and collective memory across the world. It is often said that in contrast to humans, nature does not remember and that the grass growing over a mass grave is no different from grass growing elsewhere. The German writer, Günther Grass, observed in 2001 that: "Whenever we make our plans for the future, the past has left its mark on what we thought was virgin territory; it has set up signposts that just lead us back to what we have already lived through." Yet, he argued, a recollection "is allowed to cheat, to embellish or to pretend, whereas the memory is happy to be seen as a scrupulously trustworthy accountant." (*Index on Censorship*, no.1, 2001, p.63) Little surprise that as we age, "many recollections of all that had long been buried, recollections of childhood, now seem to come closer and often cluster around moments of happiness."

By contrast, Freud and psychoanalytic theory taught us that we are not reliable narrators of our own lives. This unreliability is not because we are dishonest and consciously set out to deceive readers and listeners. On the contrary, it is usually the narrators who deceive themselves by focusing on surface phenomena rather than probing and uncovering the unconscious or hidden memories of their lives. How we present ourselves to others, as well as our capacity to be self-reflective about our relations and experiences is not equivalent to the reality of our lives. There is always a gap between our imagined idealised egos and the unconscious, hidden or barely perceived subjectivity that is driven by and shaped by other motivations, especially fear and desire. Even what is painfully conscious to a person can be written about in a coded manner.

While I will endeavour to write an honest memoir, I do not pretend that my account is either fully transparent or a detailed account of the personal traumas we suffered. This is also not a book of confessions or a 'kiss and tell' settlement of scores characteristic of many autobiographies by celebrities. The contemporary French writer of autofiction, Constance Debré, claims that: "Writing in the first person is always to write about the people you love, and to hurt them in the process. That's the way it is." Yet, instead of leaving a trail of bruised people, I prefer an ethical approach to writing in the first person, even if this means that not all intimate, private experiences are revealed for public consumption. Additionally, this book is not a chronicle of my life up until the present. Rather, it mainly focuses on the years preceding my birth and the twenty-five-year period from 1945 up until about 1970. Like other writers of memoirs, I continue to remember, reconstruct, and relive the past as a never-ending circle of memories, connected threads but also fragmented conversations and experiences that produce a collage or kaleidoscope of images, thoughts, and events. Psychoanalysis teaches us that our past is never something that has passed. Rather, it remains submerged, repressed, curled up, or remains half dormant. At particular unpredictable points in time, it leaps or springs forth in troubling or unexpected ways.

In a 1932 essay, the culture critic, Walter Benjamin, used the old pre-feminist metaphor of the male archaeologist when describing the relationship of memory to the past:

> He who seeks to approach his own buried past must conduct himself like a man digging. Above all, he must not be afraid to return again and again to the same matter; to scatter it as one scatters earth, to turn it over as one turns over soil. For the "matter itself" is no more than the strata which yield their long-sought secrets only to the most meticulous investigation ... And the man who merely makes an

inventory of his findings, while failing to establish the exact location of where in today's ground the ancient treasures have been stored up, cheats himself of his richest prize. In this sense, for authentic memories, it is far less important that the investigator report on them than that he mark, quite precisely, the site where he gained possession of them.
   —'Excavation and Memory', *Selected Writings, Vol.2, 1931–34*

Benjamin's advice is difficult to fully realise. Writing about my family is far more complex than simply finding hidden treasures. Forgetting something is not always equivalent to deliberately burying or unconsciously repressing memories of experiences. Also, contra Benjamin, identifying the precise time or site when and where each one of us acquired specific ideas or became aware of new feelings and attitudes is far from easy. In many instances, it is not even possible. This is because the point or boundary where personal history and collective experiences meet can never be fully untangled. Our psychic life is an interplay between the past and the present, but importantly, it is never outside history.

Few of us can be confident that what we think of as our original ideas were, or are, truly ours alone. Instead, they have been partly forged over time by a whole lot of other people and unknown influences. Disentangling personal from collective memories and the so-called 'present' from the 'past' is therefore extremely difficult. The Italian philosopher, Benedetto Croce, put it well when he observed that "all history is contemporary history". This is because the political and social issues of today usually inform and directly or indirectly help shape the personal priorities that historians, memoirists, or biographers adopt when studying the past.

I have learnt much and relived even more in writing this account of how both my personal history and my family's history intersected with and were framed by larger social and political, economic, and cultural developments. It is very much a dialectical learning process of self-reflection and recognition that questions, identifies, rediscovers, and interprets the past. For instance, as an old man rather than a boy reflecting about my family, I have tried to put myself in my parents' shoes by attempting to reimagine how they confronted obstacles at particular stages of their lives. I have also tried to self-examine earlier periods of my life and the degree to which I was either alternatively sensitive, and attentive, or relatively oblivious to the people and the world around me.

Many readers still devour autobiographies and biographies as if they comprise a static collection of facts and information that will provide a window to the 'truth' of a person's life. My purpose is to try and guard against or be sceptical about producing a reverential, white-washing account or a self-serving confessional outpouring. Conversely, the so-called 'definitive' biography which attempts to exhaustively track down every item of correspondence and interview everybody about the minutiae of a person's life is often no closer to 'the truth' than those adopting less exhaustive methods. One reason why 'the truth' does not reside in digging up every possible detail, to use Benjamin's metaphor, is because many biographers will tend to ignore or emphasise quite different memories and perhaps recall events and experiences that she or he, consciously or unconsciously, thinks will be of greater relevance to an ever-changing audience. It is also due to the false assumption on the part of many a writer that whatever is written down on paper – whether personal letters or official records – is equivalent to the truth.

I often laugh when I read a book review or the publicity for a biography which proclaims its qualities as 'the definitive masterpiece'. Piecing together biographical puzzles is invariably incomplete as the writer has little or no access to the unstated and unconscious motivations and desires behind numerous actions. In this respect, I am reminded of Salvador Dali's obsession with gaining Freud's approval of his surrealist work. In their well-known encounter in 1938, where Dali showed Freud his latest painting, *The Metamorphosis of Narcissus*, Freud supposedly said, "in classic paintings I look for the unconscious, but in your paintings, I look for the conscious."

Like most autobiographies or memoirs, this book contains silences about aspects of personal relationships and embarrassing actions, as well as the desire not to upset the living. My account is not the definitive version of the life of our family or of my life, as this quest would be unachievable. Gabriel García Márquez described it well when he characterised his own memoir, *Living to Tell the Tale* in the following way: "Life is not what one lived, but what one remembers and how one remembers it in order to recount it." However, recounting one's life also depends very much on whether one is looking inwards or outwards and what criteria one uses to compare one's own life with the lives of others. Hence, autobiography is also a project about collective experiences because it is illusory to think of oneself as autonomous. Our so-called exclusively personal memories are never completely detached from social relations and institutions.

Now, that I have finally decided to attempt to recall these fast-disappearing moments in history, more formidable obstacles have to be surmounted. It is not just the constant battle against my own fading memories. Those members of my family who could have helped recall aspects of the past are either dead (my parents) or too ill to remember (my sister Genia), or were, in the case of my younger sister, Maya, too young at the time to be fully aware of many developments. To fill in the gaps, I have relied on a mixture of personal memory, family letters, photos, hundreds of government papers from the National Archives of Australia detailing government intelligence reports, Ministerial and diplomatic letters about our family, as well as other historical and socio-economic sources, and film footage to jog my memory about places, people, and events.

Finally, a brief comment on one of the most influential novels of the twentieth century, George Orwell's *Nineteen Eighty-Four*. One of Orwell's famous themes is the attempt of the Party to erase individuals' private memories. "Who controls the past controls the future: who controls the present controls the past." This often-repeated slogan may be true in fiction or in exaggerated ideological conceptions of totalitarianism. However, it was only partially true of late 1950s

Soviet society which, despite years of terror, had a vibrant subterranean unofficial culture and exchange of ideas as we were to find out for ourselves. Orwell based his insights on the control of the past, such as Stalin's removal of Trotsky and other old Bolsheviks from photos and official historical accounts of the making of the Russian Revolution. Yet, he over-estimated the capacity of governments to control everything, simply because private individual experiences and thoughts are extremely difficult to erase.

Actually, in real life, records of ideas and life experiences can be destroyed without any external political power ordering the cleansing process. Take, for example, our family's memories. In the months before my mother died in 1995 from lymphoma, after having survived pogroms, the murder of her family and many other events, she set about undertaking a radical Spring cleaning in the Winter of her life. Slowly, she destroyed old letters, photos and other invaluable artefacts that were related to her past. I managed to salvage many items when I discovered what she was doing. However, like other people, I have photos in my parents' albums with no names or dates, and nobody left to tell me about these people. Nonetheless, I will simultaneously counter unreliable narratives and will endeavour to do justice to those who are no longer with us. This is a tale about people who tried to change the world but became victims of larger political forces out of their control. It is also a story about courage and resistance to these hostile governments and the impact on the lives of family members resulting from their long struggles.

2

A DISTURBING VOICE

I WILL BEGIN WITH A MEMORY OF SAUL BASTOMSKY WHO was banned by the South African apartheid regime and became my lecturer in ancient Roman history at Monash University in 1966. Saul was a hothead but had good voice control. So loud was his projected voice that he needed no microphone and could be heard clearly at the back of the large lecture theatre. Indeed, Saul had to stand back from the podium so that the students in the front rows did not get headaches. On the positive side, Saul was an engaging lecturer and part of the Monash theatre group which made beneficial use of his capacity to regulate his voice. Yet, it was as a member of a packed audience in the Alexander Theatre on August 1, 1967, that Saul used his voice to powerful effect. The theatre had been opened several months earlier by Minister for Education and Science, Senator John Gorton, a strident anti-Communist, and pro-war hawk who would become Prime Minister in January 1968 after Prime Minister Harold Holt disappeared (presumed drowned) in December 1967. As I will discuss in a later chapter, both Harold Holt and John Gorton had in their earlier Ministerial positions in 1956 and 1960 been connected to our family's departure and possible re-entry to Australia.

It was at the Alexander Theatre that the South Vietnamese ambassador to Australia, Tran Kim Phuong, bravely ventured into the lion's den of Left-wing activism at the height of the Vietnam War.

The university authorities were quite nervous about the ambassador's visit, as Monash was the most radical campus in Australia. Hundreds, and even thousands of students, could be quickly mobilised for protest actions, including the regular occupation of the administration building. Sections of the media had almost full-time postings on the campus given that it was the source of much material for the Right-wing press.

Surrounded by his minders, it was into this highly charged atmosphere that the senior diplomat entered to deliver his propaganda speech to a packed student/staff Monash audience in August 1967. Mid-way through the ambassador's presentation, Saul could restrain himself no longer. With his inimitable capacity for voice projection, the theatre appeared to almost shake and reverberate as Saul thundered in full voice: "YOOOU STAAAND THERE LYING!" The nervous diplomat looked fearful and was thrown off guard by this bombshell of an accusation. He was momentarily rescued by Ken Walker, a lecturer in Politics, who responded by shouting: "Oh, belt up Saul." Ken's response elicited a roar of laughter from the audience which nonetheless made their anti-war views abundantly clear.

It was Saul Bastomsky's intervention that effectively undermined whatever shred of credibility remained of the South Vietnamese ambassador's presentation. After some exchanges with the audience, the diplomat was eventually escorted off campus. His propaganda visit to Monash was designed to counter the announcement by the Monash Labor Club (MLC) a week before on July 25, 1967, to give aid to the National Liberation Front (Viet Cong). This decision was widely condemned by conservatives as 'traitorous aid to the enemy'. On August 3, the Monash Labor Club's news sheet, *Print*, reported the event at the Alexander Theatre and sarcastically commended ambassador 'Mr. Rah Ning Dogg' for "doing such a beautiful job" of exposing himself. Former MLC member, Ken Mansell, laughed as he recently recalled to me that the Monash Labor Club deliberately created a new name for the ambassador to signify that he was a 'running dog' of American imperialism.

The diplomatic visit also aimed to perpetuate the illusion that South Vietnam had invited Australia to help defend 'democracy'. Even the minority in the audience who supported the South Vietnamese regime were unaware that its Embassy in Canberra had a mere token presence. Years later, declassified official documents revealed that increased numbers of Australian troops were sent to South Vietnam on American 'requests/orders' with little or no prior consultation with succeeding South Vietnamese governments or their Embassy.

Voyage of the damned

Like Saul Bastomsky, my father was loud, short, and passionate. However, physically, he had a large chest and was very muscular due to having worked for decades on various tough manual jobs rather than being a sedentary academic. These days, the relationship between a muscular body and manual work has been broken by working out at a gym. It is no longer as easy to locate a person's class position by their musculature or hands. While my father could shout a lot, he was also a former actor in the Yiddish theatre at the Kadimah in North Carlton. With his ability to project and modulate the tone of his voice, Dad also wrote and declaimed poetry, spoke on the political soap box, and was generally the 'life of the party'. What he lacked in height, he more than compensated for in the power of his voice.

Ten years before I began studying at Monash in 1966, my parents, two sisters and I were on the Soviet passenger ship, *Vyacheslav Molotov*. Having sailed from Melbourne in May 1956 to London on the Orient Line ship, *Orcades*, we were now on the second and final leg of our journey to the USSR after a brief stopover in London. The ship was full of tourists as well as a scattering of Russian and Soviet expatriates who were now returning after living in the US, Canada, and Australia. Some, like my father, had left during or after the Russian Revolution of 1917 and the Civil War (1918–1921). Others were either uprooted as prisoners of war and slave labour for the Nazis.

Some fled alongside the retreating German army during 1944 and 1945. The atmosphere amongst the returnees on board was a mixture of nervous excitement, fear of having made a terrible mistake, and anxiety about how the authorities would receive them in what was now a very strange place rather than a familiar country.

The ship was named after Vyacheslav Molotov or 'the sledgehammer' (real name Scryabin), a loyal aide to Stalin, aka 'man of steel' (real name Djughashvili). Molotov had occupied the most senior positions in Stalin's regime from the 1920s to the 1950s and was infamous for many things, including the 1939 Molotov-Ribbentrop Pact (Soviet-German Non-Aggression Treaty) as well as the notorious home-made explosive, the Molotov cocktail. We had already stopped off in Copenhagen, Stockholm, and Helsinki on a scenic trip sailing between numerous islands in the Baltic Sea. In June 1956, as the ship entered the channel that would take us to the Leningrad docks, little did we know about the power struggle inside the Kremlin. A week before boarding the *Vyacheslav Molotov* on June 8, Molotov had himself been removed as Foreign Minister because of his opposition to Nikita Khrushchev's de-Stalinisation policies. After his eventual expulsion from the Politburo in 1957, the passenger ship *Vyacheslav Molotov* was renamed *Baltika*.

Many have asked me how my father could have decided to return to Russia after hearing about Khrushchev's secret speech. Timing, as they say, is everything. Precisely, at the very same time that my father was organising our family's move to the Soviet Union in the early months of 1956, we knew nothing about the simultaneously tumultuous developments in Moscow. In fact, little was known in Australia about the full details of Khrushchev's famous 'secret speech' at the closed meeting of the 20th Party Congress on February 24–25, 1956. The speech caused an uproar amongst Congress delegates and reports stated that dozens of attendees fainted or had seizures and received medical treatment during Khrushchev's revelations of Stalin's crimes. A week later, Khrushchev's speech was disseminated to Communist Party members throughout the USSR.

A DISTURBING VOICE

My father had not read the original Russian text of Khrushchev's speech. On March 3, 1956, an ASIO informer visited our home in East St. Kilda under the guise of someone interested in purchasing recordings of Russian music that Dad had advertised for sale before we departed for the Soviet Union. This unnamed informer (possibly Constable V. K. Fowler of Brighton Police Station) reported on March 9, that mention of Khrushchev's denunciation of Stalin arose during their conversation but "Frenkel stated he believed it could not be because it was capitalist press propaganda." The informer also reported that "large photographs of Stalin and Lenin decorated the living room of Frenkel's home." My father's refusal to confront the reality of Stalin's regime was echoed by many ideologically blind Australian Communists. In late March 1956, the Communist Party of Australia (CPA) paper, *Tribune*, published a brief foreign report of Khrushchev's account of 'crimes and mistakes' committed by Stalin. However, CPA leader Lance Sharkey, like my father, dismissed this and other reports at a meeting of cadres in Melbourne on March 26, as lies spread by the capitalist press.

It was only in the following weeks and months that an English translation of Khrushchev's speech was either sent abroad by Party members and made known to President Eisenhower's administration via Israeli intelligence or, as was perfectly plausible, was deliberately leaked by the KGB. When the full text of the speech denouncing Stalin's crimes was reported on June 5, in the *New York Times* and other leading Western papers, this news was either not seen by us or overlooked. By coincidence, the *Orcades* had just arrived in London on June 4, at Tilbury docks, but nobody from the Soviet Embassy was there to meet us. It was late at night before somebody eventually came to pick us up and drive our family to London. By the time we arrived in London at a hotel in Kensington, it was early in the morning between 4 and 5 a.m. We slept for most of the morning and did not see the morning daily papers that published details of Khrushchev's speech. The next three days were preoccupied with sightseeing in London and arranging the second leg of the journey.

After the short stopover we departed London for Leningrad on June 8 and remained oblivious to the details in the 'secret speech'. Like most others outside the Soviet Union, we were also completely unaware of the anti-Khrushchev demonstrations by Stalin's fellow Georgian supporters that had occurred in Tbilisi on March 9, two weeks after Khrushchev's speech, and two and a half weeks before Sharkey's defence of Stalin. Fearing their loss of favoured status under Stalin, mass protests erupted for days that eventually resulted in dozens and perhaps hundreds of demonstrators being killed or wounded by Soviet troops.

The full repercussions of Khrushchev's de-Stalinisation policies only became felt in Eastern Europe in the summer and autumn of 1956, manifested especially by the revolts in Poland and Hungary beginning on June 28 in Poznan and in Budapest on October 23. By this time, we were already in the Soviet Union. Across the world, Khrushchev's revelations about Stalin's crimes eventually led to mass resignations of disillusioned Communist party members once the veil of Soviet propaganda was torn apart in the latter half of 1956 and subsequent years. Like many other 'true believers', my father had cried on hearing the news about the death of 'Uncle Joe' in March 1953. Now Stalin's 'cult of personality' and crimes against the people were finally being condemned not by the 'bourgeois' or 'capitalist press', but by the leaders of the USSR. What could Communists now believe after being fed lies for decades about the true nature of the regime?

Back to our family aboard the *Vyacheslav Molotov* as it slowly cruised into port. Most fellow passengers were standing on the deck and observing a mixture of drab port facilities, near-empty fields and workers dotted along the foreshore. All at once a mighty voice pierced the quiet, almost sullen atmosphere on board. I will never forget the embarrassment I felt upon seeing and hearing my father continually roaring "PRIVET" ('hello' or 'greetings') as he stood on the bow or foredeck holding a handkerchief aloft and waving his arms. Not one person onshore reciprocated, as they were probably too frightened to speak or wave back. Significantly, no one on board joined my father in shouting out their joy at returning home although a few passengers quietly waved their hands.

The exhilaration in my father's voice was not an act, and the deck of the ship was certainly not the stage in a theatre. Yet, the more my father projected his voice in repeated calls of PRIVET, the more I felt that his excitement and enthusiasm were falling on deaf and incredulous ears. This was the first of many ruptures between what we had imagined of life in the Soviet Union and the reality of Soviet life. Months later after experiencing this reality, it was possible to imagine the reaction of onshore Soviet workers looking at my father's enthusiastic wave and hearing his heartfelt greeting and thinking to themselves: 'who is this madman or innocent fool'? Perhaps they were also thinking: 'you can stick your 'privet' up your arse' or 'quick, turn the ship around and get out of here before it's too late'.

Standing on the deck of the *Vyacheslav Molotov* near my father, I didn't know much about the Soviet Union other than the glowing stories that Dad had told us, supplemented by the glossy Soviet propaganda magazines which we had read over the years in Melbourne. Many ports around the world and their surrounds are ugly combinations of transport hubs and storage facilities. However, the forlorn and grey sight that confronted us as we approached the dock at Leningrad (located outside the old city) was nothing short of depressing.

Before we were accommodated for a few days in a hostel/processing centre near the port, we were mistakenly taken by bus to a hotel with the tourists. Travelling into the city of Leningrad, I became conscious of the many buildings on both the outskirts and closer to the centre of the city that were either damaged from bombing or riddled with unrepaired shrapnel and bullet holes. It is important to recall that when we arrived, a mere 11 years had passed since the end of the war in 1945, the year of my birth.

In Leningrad, half a million civilians had died of famine and persistent German bombardment, including my mother's older brother, Gdalie. It is estimated that up to another million Soviet troops and civilians as well as enemy German and Finnish soldiers died during the 872-day siege surrounding Leningrad, one of the longest, and certainly the largest siege in history. Such was the scale of deaths, that the civilian casualties exceeded the combined casualty list of all other famous atrocities including the bombing of Dresden, Hamburg, Hiroshima, and Nagasaki. In fact, to put the number of victims of the siege in comparative perspective, more people died in Leningrad than the total number of American and British casualties in the entire Second World War.

Despite witnessing the summer white nights and the beauty of the historic city, the sight of war-damaged buildings was stamped onto my first impressions of Leningrad. Coming from war-free Melbourne and not being exposed to the horrors of war except through films and newsreels, the widespread sight of the scars of war triggered nightmares during the following nights. Twenty-seven years later in 1983, I visited the Leningrad memorial museum, the unmarked mass graves, and the exhibition of other traumatic details about the siege. For instance, the tiny size of the rationed daily bread allocation (half of it filled with sawdust) for people performing heavy labour – and half that size for all others – remains with me to this day. Little wonder that with bread, glue and other items only constituting less than ten per cent of the calorie intake needed to sustain life, all pets were eaten, and it was reported that approximately 1,500 people were arrested for cannibalism. Most of those eating human flesh had probably not killed their victims, but were eating people who had already died, whether lying dead in the street or at home. This was in the very recent lived experience of the adults who survived and children my age or older whom we met.

Leningrad was only a transit point on the way to our supposedly new home in Baku, Azerbaijan, an eventful journey along which we would encounter many initial shocks. Stalin had punished Leningrad as the home of rival Bolshevik revolutionaries and deprived it of resources. However, the city proved to be far less deprived compared to Soviet daily life in many other parts of the USSR as we were to shortly discover. As our family watched my father's emotional solo performance in embarrassed and detached silence, the anti-climactic entry into the Soviet paradise only fuelled our doubts and fears and a growing sense of dread. If we were already disheartened by the drab onshore sights even before we had landed, what would the rest of the country be like and what would become of us?

My mother had publicly shared my father's Communist beliefs that their children would have a better future being raised in a socialist society. Privately though, she was far from enthusiastic about going to the Soviet Union. In reality, as we later discovered, she did not want to leave Melbourne and had argued and pleaded with Dad not to go. However, the only other alternative, in the face of his zealous commitment, would be to split up the family. This desire to keep the family together forced her hand and she reluctantly agreed to join him. Remember, the 1950s was a pre-feminist age when most married women followed their husbands. Despite being born in that part of Poland which later became part of the USSR as Byelorussia (now Belarus), my mother harboured no joy about leaving Australia. Russia was neither her former home, nor a country which offered enticing prospects to start a new life all over again at age 36, after living as an adult in Melbourne for almost two decades. Her anxiety was not helped during the brief stopover in London after a chauffeur at the Soviet Embassy had told her that she was a fool to go and to live in the USSR.

Mum, my sister Genia and I may have been visibly disappointed at the onshore sights, but we had little invested in upholding a glowing but false image of Soviet life. As a 'housewife' who still believed in Communism, Mum was nonetheless much less involved directly in Communist or Australia-Soviet Friendship Society activity after she had children from 1943 onwards. While she occasionally attended Communist-organised meetings or social functions, lack of childcare prevented her from enjoying a full public life. By contrast, Dad remained publicly active. It was therefore doubly difficult, painful, and disillusioning for him to confront the reality of Soviet life. He was forty-eight years old and had fanatically believed in the Soviet system for decades. It was not simply a matter of encountering inferior material conditions to those which we had enjoyed in Australia but something much worse, involving the total collapse of his ideals.

Would my father have changed his mind about returning to the USSR if he had known and fully digested the consequences of Khrushchev's secret speech? I do not know. Upon arrival, it took my father only a week to begin uttering serious doubts and a further week or two to confirm that he had made a terrible mistake in returning to the country of his birth. Importantly, the gap between reading criticism of a regime and seeing the reality of Soviet life is not only immense but two entirely different experiences. What I do know, however, is that my father was already experiencing misgivings in London after he heard that the Russian chauffeur at the Soviet Embassy warned him via Mum not to return to the USSR.

On board the *Vyacheslav Molotov*, there were other shocks. Dad had engaged in heavy drinking with other Russian passengers. During one of these sessions, the head waiter asked him where he was going, and Dad replied that he was travelling to Baku to live with his sister. The waiter then suggested that he would buy goods in London and Dad could sell them in Baku and they would divide the profits. My father was shocked by the revelation of the presence of black markets in the Soviet Union. His concerns were heightened when a female steward begged him for cigarettes for her son only to find that she was selling them on the Leningrad wharf soon after arrival.

Despite these misgivings, my father never did things in a halfhearted manner. He had always committed himself one hundred and ten percent to beliefs or activities. This is why he shouted 'privet' with such enthusiasm. Dad's whole personal identity and belief system were associated with the 'workers' state'. Sadly, the resonant power of my father's voice was little match for the devastating, deflating, and intimidating experiences he was shortly to begin to suffer.

3

THICK SPINES: NOSTALGIA AND POLITICAL DEVELOPMENT

LITTLE DID BABY AVRAHAM FRANKEL (ALSO SPELT 'Frenkel' by Russian and Australian governments) know that he would end up living in Australia. Dad was the youngest of four children born to Ben-Zion and Ester Frankel on January 26, 1908, in Kerch, Crimea. Seven years earlier, the Commonwealth of Australia came into being and what today remains a controversial date, was only declared Australia Day for all states in 1935. Prior to this, January 26 was Anniversary Day or Foundation Day in New South Wales marking the arrival of the British colonising fleet in 1788. First Nations peoples have long protested this date and the first 'Day of Mourning' was held by the Australian Aborigines League and the Aborigines Progressive Association in 1938, by coincidence, the year my father arrived in Australia.

In the thirty years between being born in the Czarist empire and setting sail for Fremantle, a series of momentous events would help shape the life of young Avraham (Hebrew) also known as Abraham, Abe, Abbie (English formal and colloquial) or Abram and Abrasha (Russian diminutive). The Russian Revolution, the Great Depression, the rise of fascism, and the ongoing conflict in Palestine all had a profound impact on my father's ideas and life chances.

By coincidence, when our family moved from Carlton to St. Kilda in early 1951, many of the local streets such as Crimea, Inkerman,

Redan, Malakoff, Raglan, Nightingale and Cardigan Streets, or Alma and Balaclava Roads were named after places, battles, or people in the Crimean War of 1853–6. The incorrectly translated spelling of Sevastopol as Sebastopol Street was another link between the St. Kilda of our family and my father's origins in the Crimea.

In recent years, Kerch and Crimea have featured prominently since Vladimir Putin's takeover in 2014, the invasion of Ukraine in 2022, and the explosions on the strategically vital Kerch bridge. The propaganda war over whether Crimea was either historically Russian or Ukrainian is not the Crimea that my father and his family knew and experienced. Until 1917, the largest ethnic grouping within Crimea was the Tartars at 35% of the population, followed by Russians at 30% and Ukrainians at only 11%. The Tartars were descendants of Central Asian and Mongolian peoples and had lived in Crimea for at least nine centuries. Both Ukrainian and Russian nationalists conveniently ignore this fact. The region was also populated by various other cultural groups who generally lived peacefully with one another in the Czarist empire, except for the pogroms against Jews. One such pogrom occurred in Kerch in July 1905, three years before my father was born. A few months later, following a proclamation from the Czar, pogroms broke out in 660 towns in present-day Ukraine and Crimea with numerous assaults and over 800 Jews killed.

Well before the Tartars, the area had been colonised by the ancient Greeks whose archaeological ruins still can be found in Kerch and surrounding places. In the nineteenth century, Crimean beaches and resorts became a holiday playground for the Russian middle class and aristocracy, famously captured in Anton Chekhov's 1899 story 'Lady with a Dog' set on vacation in Yalta. Following the 1917 Revolution, Crimea and the Black Sea continued to play this role as a holiday spot during Soviet and post-Soviet times. However, during most of the life of the USSR, Kerch and surrounds were a part of the Crimea that were off bounds to foreign and many Soviet tourists for a range of strategic and industrial reasons.

Crimea was also an area rich in produce, especially fruit and vegetables. It was the Tartars who were particularly skilled producers and heavily involved in growing the rich annual harvests of fruit and vegetables until the Civil War. My father would often tell us of the wonderful apples and stone fruit that he would eat when he was a boy. The Kerch Strait, connecting the Black and Azov Seas was particularly rich in fish. My grandfather, Ben-Zion was a fish curer who made a living smoking and marinating Kerch herrings. I particularly remember my father describing these herrings of his boyhood as having thick, fat spines and were some of the tastiest in the world. Consequently, whenever I eat a herring in Australia, The Netherlands or Denmark, I always look at the thickness of its spine.

Beginning in 1918, the Civil War would change Crimea. The savage conflict between Red Bolshevik forces and White anti-Bolshevik armies (supported by Britain, France, Germany, America, Japan, and even some Australian soldiers), resulted in numerous alternating occupation armies and governments between 1918 and 1921. In town after town, village after village, the victorious occupying army would summarily execute 'enemies' however defined, and pillage, rape, and commit other crimes before being driven out, only to see the whole cycle of abuse and terror begin anew with the next group of victorious soldiers.

Crucially, had the Bolsheviks been defeated, it would have dramatically altered world history during the twentieth century. Yet, the Civil War remains poorly understood in countries such as Australia. A case in point is Geraldine Doogue's August 7, 2022, interview with Sir Antony Beevor on ABC Radio National about his book *Russia: Revolution and Civil War 1917 – 1921*. Doogue appeared unaware of the complex political, economic, and cultural causes of civil wars and asked Beevor whether the savagery on both the White and Red sides was due to something in the Russian DNA. Not only was this a simplistic and offensive question based on Doogue's failure to recognise its quasi-racist or eugenicist assumptions, but she also disregarded the fact that those involved in the Civil War were not just Russians and invading foreign troops. Rather, several other national/ethnic groups, such as Ukrainians, those from Baltic regions, the Trans-caucuses, and future Soviet Asian republics also fought in this large conflict. Her question was akin to asking whether Hitler's atrocities were due to 'something in the German DNA'.

Doogue was not alone. There has long been widespread ignorance about Soviet history amongst the media and the so-called 'educated class' in Australia. Between 1993 and 1995, Helen Darville/Helen Demidenko was awarded three top literary prizes for her anti-Semitic hoax novel, *The Hand that Signed the Paper*. The so-called 'authentic migrant voice' was nothing of the sort. Instead, it revealed how little people knew about the Ukraine and a so-called 'Jewish Bolshevik conspiracy', thus enabling the literary judges and many readers to be so easily fooled.

Despite being backed by heavy foreign government support, the disparate White armies during the Civil War were fundamentally disunited over their political goals. One of the worst offenders of White terror was General Symon Petliura, head of the Ukrainian National Republic (1918–21) who either directly initiated or did nothing to stop hundreds of pogroms of Jews resulting in the deaths of between 100,000 and 200,000 Jews and infinitely more Jewish victims of rapes and assaults. Having escaped with other anti-Semitic butchers, he was eventually assassinated in Paris in 1926 by the anarchist poet, Sholem Schwartzbard, who, at his highly publicised trial in 1927, said that he had killed Petliura to avenge the deaths of hundreds of thousands of slain Jews. Despite Schwartzbard's confession, the jury sympathised with his action and found him not guilty.

The overwhelming incidents of violent attacks on Jewish communities were carried out by White armies. However, about ten to twelve per cent of attacks were also carried out by Red Army troops even though key commanding officers such as Leon Trotsky and Béla Kun were Jewish. Anti-Semitism was culturally deeply ingrained in the Czarist empire and continued to thrive in post-revolutionary USSR.

In 1920, the White forces' stronghold in Crimea was defeated by the Red Army which then unleashed the 'Red terror' under the direction of Béla Kun (or Kohn) the former leader of the 1919 short-lived Hungarian Soviet Republic. Kun had moved to Crimea and became one of the leaders of the Red Army that oversaw the summary execution of approximately 50,000 White prisoners who had surrendered to Red Army forces. Tens of thousands of civilian supporters were also executed. Many escaped by ship to Constantinople, including former Czarist generals Denikin and Wrangel. The new Czar of post-Soviet Russia, Vladimir Putin, in 2005 authorised Denikin's daughter's request that her father's remains (following Denikin's death in the US in 1947) be transferred and reburied at the Donskoy Monastery in Moscow. The journey from Czarism to revolution, followed by the rise and fall of Soviet power and the emergence of a new hybrid authoritarianism using Czarist symbols and religion – but neither restoring Imperial nor Soviet power – was thus complete.

The destruction of pre-revolutionary Kerch

At the end of 1973, I worked briefly at the Max Planck Institute for the Study of the Living Conditions of the World of Science and Technology in Starnberg. The Institute was close to where the body of Ludwig II, the 'mad' King of Bavaria and lover of Wagner's music was found in Lake Starnberg in 1886. The co-director of the Institute was leading philosopher and social theorist, Jürgen Habermas. He and his secretary, Frau Petras were both familiar with my family's name. She followed a long German tradition of spelling it with an umlaut over the ä – thus enunciated or written as Fraenkel. This overcame the inconsistent spelling in English or Russian of 'Frankel' or 'Frenkel'. No longer was I associated with Boris Karloff as my name was no longer alien and misspelt or mispronounced, as it was in Australia and Russia.

Habermas's secretary also told me stories of how as a young woman she flew with her family and other tourists to Nazi-occupied Ukraine for holidays. This image of a playground in the East, in the midst of a brutal war, gave me a small glimpse of Hitler's notion of living space or 'lebensraum'. Gaining vast additional territory was not just for vital economic and natural resources. 'Lebensraum' also meant space for some privileged Germans to relax before 1943 when the push to drive them out of the Soviet Union gained momentum.

The Frankel's of Kerch were probably of south-western German origin (Franconia) and their predecessors belonged to those earlier generations of Jews who moved eastwards during the eighteenth and nineteenth centuries. Like thousands of other Jews, the Frankels had migrated to various parts of the Czarist empire and probably spoke Yiddish before eventually acquiring Russian or Polish as well. My grandparents had been well settled in Kerch and had raised three sons and a daughter while enjoying a comfortable although not privileged or wealthy lifestyle.

Sister Nusia, Mother Ester holding Abraham and brothers Misha and Nahum 1911, Kerch.

They were essentially a small craft-based family centred on grandfather and his eldest son Misha smoking fish and earning enough to keep the family fed and housed. All was to change during the Civil War. It was the seizure of food and the disruption of food production and distribution by succeeding White and Red armies of occupation that led to widespread starvation. Due to the desperate and intolerable conditions of war, combined with rampant, violent anti-Semitism, in 1920 my father's family decided to leave Crimea for Batumi on the Black Sea near the Turkish border.

A decade later, Stalin's collectivisation of private farms had a lasting disastrous impact on agricultural production. Rather than take their livestock and assets into collective farms, a civil war broke out in the Soviet countryside between 1929 and the early 1930s. Millions of livestock were slaughtered, or crops burnt by many peasant owners who refused to surrender their property to Soviet forces. The ensuing famine, especially in the Ukraine and Kazakhstan, and the mass killings and deportation to the Gulag, was a human and agricultural catastrophe. Such was the scale of the disastrous policy – disruption to food production and millions dying of starvation – followed by the havoc of war beginning in 1941, that it took about thirty years or until the late 1950s for Soviet livestock numbers to return to pre-collectivisation levels in 1928. As for peasants and their families, the main human casualties of collectivisation, they were permanently lost to the Soviet regime as they could never be restored physically, culturally, or politically to their former condition in 1928.

In Crimea, an additional calamity came during the Second World War when Stalin ordered the mass deportation of hundreds of thousands of Tartars (including those serving in the Soviet armed forces and their families) because a minority of Tartars collaborated with the Nazis. There were plenty of other nationalities (including Russians and Ukrainians) whose members also collaborated with the enemy, but they weren't deported *en masse* because this would have been impossible. The Tartars suffered the notorious act of ethnic cleansing long before the term was made popular in the 1990s. This forced deportation resulted in the social and economic transformation of Crimea after 1945.

Being located on the strategic Kerch Strait, the city of Kerch and surrounding areas was the site of three German invasions and four counter-offensives against Soviet troops. Due to superior German fire power and incompetent political interference by Stalin and his political commissar Lev Mekhlis, who rejected the strategic advice of General Koslov, tens of thousands of Soviet troops were needlessly massacred by German forces. The Germans succeeded in destroying three Soviet armies and hundreds of thousands of people were killed or taken prisoners of war. Shocking atrocities were committed by the Nazis, including the massacre of more than seven thousand civilians at the nearby village of Baguerovo in 1941. Their mutilated bodies were dumped in an anti-tank ditch that was one kilometre long and four metres wide.

Having suffered the violence and calamities of civil war, famine, collectivisation, and more famine, it was the devastation of the Second World War that constituted the final nail in the coffin of the old Crimea and Kerch. Across the USSR, twenty-seven million people had been killed or died from hunger and various war-induced causes. More than twenty thousand cities, towns and villages were destroyed, and vital industry and infrastructure lay in ruins. No other country had lost so many people or suffered such catastrophic losses. A third famine was to befall populations in 1945/47 when disrupted food crops in war-ravaged land, heavily mined areas and other dysfunctions and disasters saw people forced to eat insects and rats in order to survive. Unsurprisingly, the romanticised Crimea of my father's memory and experience had disappeared by the time he returned with his family in tow to Kerch in 1956. It was no longer the Crimea of abundant harvests and thick-spined herrings.

Our first accommodation in Kamysh Burun (also called Arshintsevo) south of Kerch, was in a single room in housing blocks built by German prisoners of war on the site of one of the many horrific battles of 1941 and 1942. The room where the five of us lived had no running water and we had to carry buckets of water that we pumped from a nearby well. Gradually, we were to hear the first-hand accounts of the shocking hardships that local Soviet citizens had lived through in the decades between Dad's departure in 1920 and his return in 1956.

Unforeseen consequences of the Civil War

Reluctantly, my grandparents decided to leave Kerch in the midst of violence and famine in 1920, before the calamities of the 1930s and 1940s but during a time of extreme hardship, nonetheless. Family photos show the gaunt faces of my grandparents suffering from hunger and malnutrition.

Arriving in Batumi from Kerch, 1920

They first went to Batumi, a town acquired by Russia from the Ottomans which is now a large Georgian resort city on the Black Sea coast. Before the formation of the Soviet Union in December 1922, Dad's family left Russia in 1921 and headed for Constantinople where they lived and worked for two years. Constantinople was the transit city for many people fleeing the Russian revolution and civil war. The target goal was Paris which would become host to White emigres as well as become a base, like Berlin, for Bolshevik spies and dissident socialists, such as Trotskyists. My father's family did not follow the path to Paris.

In the same year they left Batumi, the Cairo Conference of 1921 saw the British and French carve up the old Ottoman empire and establish mandates over Palestine and other territories. The legacy of this colonialist carve-up was to play out in the loss of millions of lives throughout the 20th and 21st centuries up until the present day. Instead of going to Paris, the Frankel family travelled through these artificially created countries of the Middle East. My fifteen-year-old father together with his parents and two older brothers Misha and Nahum, eventually settled in Tel Aviv in 1923. Dad was seven years younger than his brother Misha. From Constantinople, Misha had actually travelled ahead of the rest of the family and had organised accommodation and the setting up of their small family fish curing business in Tel Aviv. The notable absence was my father's sister Nusia who was eleven years older than him. She remained in the USSR with her new husband who was also called Misha. Eventually, she and Misha moved from Kerch on the Black Sea across the Caucasus region to Baku on the Caspian Sea. From here she maintained contact with my father over the following decades and it was Baku, rather than Kerch, that would be our first destination after arriving in Leningrad in June 1956.

There is one other noteworthy connection to the Civil War that was to have unexpected consequences for my family in future years. In 1919, Trotsky had formed a military alliance with the forces led by Ukrainian anarcho-communist, Nestor Makhno, who sought independence from first the Whites, and later the Reds. This alliance not only helped defeat the White armies in Ukraine and later Crimea during 1919–1920, but also enabled the Red Army (minus Makhno) to drive out the Whites across the Ukrainian/Polish border as it proceeded to march across Poland. Having been part of the former Czarist empire, recapturing Poland from anti-Bolshevik regimes was regarded as legitimate by the Bolsheviks. In 1920, the Red Army almost took Warsaw until an alliance of Polish troops under Józef Pilsudski and Ukrainian forces led by Symon Petliura achieved what religious Poles called the 'miracle on the Vistula' and drove the Bolsheviks out of Poland. Pilsudski's Polish nationalists were feared by sections of the Soviet politburo during the 1920s, as the Poles had long claimed that Ukraine belonged to Poland. It was thought that Pilsudski, with help from the British, could possibly invade while the Bolsheviks were still very weak. Historically, there had never been a well-established independent Ukraine. Other neighbouring powers well before Vladimir Putin had claimed that Ukraine was always theirs and not a separate country.

In the constantly changing borders of what today is Poland, Belarus, Ukraine, and Lithuania, lay the city of Grodno (or Hrodna in present-day Belarus). It is here on May 16, 1920, that my mother Tauba Lubitsch (spelt Lubicz in Polish) was born to mother, Gitel (or Genia) and father, Samuel. Like other surrounding towns, Grodno had either been occupied or claimed by the Germans, Russians, Byelorussians, and Lithuanians between 1918 and 1920. The defeat of the Red Army by the Poles at the battle of Grodno in July 1920 two months after my mother was born, saw the city remain as part of Poland until its forced annexation by the USSR following the 1939 partition of Poland by Hitler and Stalin.

Various occupying armies marked the year of my mother's birth. Had the Bolsheviks not been defeated, then Mum would have been raised in the USSR and would have been unable to emigrate to Australia. From being born 'Tauba' or 'Tanie' in Poland, my mother would become 'Tania' in Melbourne, a Russified version of 'Tanie'. She had left her family in Grodno in March 1937 and following her arrival in July 1937, would later marry my father in Melbourne in 1941.

If my father had no idea that his birth on Australia Day would later connect him to Australia, my mother was equally surprised that her name would decades later become dinky di Aussie. In the late 1930s, 'Tania' or 'Tanya' (pronounced with a soft 'a' as in 'taa'), was a rare name in Australia. This changed after Russian immigrant (formerly living in China), Tania Verstak, became Miss Australia in 1961. Thereafter, Tania (often pronounced by Australians with a harsh or even guttural 'a' as in 'tan' or 'van', became a popular name for baby girls. Many parents naming their daughters in subsequent decades probably eventually had little idea of its Russian and Slavic origins.

In the same year that my father departed Kerch for Batumi in 1920, my mother was born and being raised in Grodno. Tania and Abe, not their given names at birth, would be what they were later called in Australia. The fact that they would meet and get married in Melbourne was, of course, unimaginable in 1920. Even more remarkable was that in returning to the Soviet Union in 1956, their fate, and mine, was linked to the successor state of the Czarist empire, two vast and now defunct historical states that had once embraced both Kerch and Grodno.

From one civil war to another

When my father's family escaped the horrors of the Russian civil war and sought refuge in Constantinople, they did not expect to find themselves two years later eventually settling in the British colony of Palestine that would itself soon be engulfed in another escalating civil war. During the 1920s and 1930s, a growing conflict developed between the rapidly expanding Jewish population that wanted their own state of Israel, and the wishes of the existing majority of Palestinian Arab residents who resisted this new colonisation. This was the context of Palestinian life within which my father developed his secular Left-wing Jewishness. Initially, fifteen-year-old Avraham, my father, worked alongside his father and brothers smoking fish in their little factory in Tel Aviv. It was a small family concern that did not employ workers and barely managed to eke out a living. Slowly the family had to adjust to their unfamiliar environment in the midst of rising political and social tensions.

In the 1990s, the late Patrick Wolfe, a friend who died much too early, developed a systematic analysis of 'settler colonialism'. What linked 'settler colonial societies' such as Australia, the US, and Israel, Patrick argued, is that their white colonial foundations rested upon either the myth of terra nullius as 'nobody's land' or the barest, begrudging recognition that First Nations peoples or Palestinians had been a constant historical presence and continued to live there. With Palestine, the situation was different from Australia in that the land could not be initially invaded and claimed by using military force and border wars, as was the case in the US and Australia, particularly during the eighteenth and nineteenth centuries. Instead, the Zionist movement had to legitimize its claims to *Eretz Yisrael* or 'land of Israel'. Other scholars such as Gary Fields in his book *Enclosure: Palestinian Landscapes in a Historical Mirror*, showed how language, archaeology, and cartography would prove to be powerful instruments in the highly contested 'Hebraicizing' of the Palestinian landscape.

Avraham at back with father, Misha, mother and Nahum, Tel Aviv, 1928

The adoption of Hebrew as an official language by the British authorities was the first step in this trajectory. From being an almost dead language or one principally used either by religious practitioners, scholars or small Jewish enclaves in the Ottoman empire, Hebrew was transformed into the vernacular, a quasi-secular, colloquial language of the Jewish population in Palestine. The Zionist movement abandoned German as its high official language and adopted Hebrew.

Yiddish continued to be spoken by Ashkenazi Jews in Europe and new settlers in Palestine, but Hebrew gradually evolved in the period between the 1920s and late 1940s to become Israel's official language.

Secondly, archaeology took on a nationalist agenda in that European Jewish and local Zionist archaeologists set about uncovering antiquities and the remains of buildings that linked ancient Israel to places in contemporary Palestine. Thirdly, a new nationalist cartography was developed by 'Hebraicizing' the names of places, a tactic that infuriated Arab Palestinians and was resisted by British authorities who wished to maintain sovereign control over naming territory. This same process of renaming places and removing evidence of Indigenous culture had been carried out in Australia between 1788 and the early twentieth century and in other colonised countries such as India. Slowly but surely, the carving out of a claim for the 'land of Israel' first required the renaming of the landscape as if Palestinians were invisible before their actual physical removal took place in later decades.

Six years after arriving in Palestine, my grandfather, Ben-Zion, tragically died in 1929. His sons continued to smoke fish in Tel Aviv and Dad would later carry on this traditional craft in Melbourne in the period 1953 to 1956. While his older brothers would get married, start their own families and retreat into the private sphere, my father would pursue his public involvement in politics and culture. From the late 1920s until 1938, he also did manual jobs in Tel Aviv, Haifa, and other places. These included working on construction sites, road works, performing agricultural labour and whatever other work he could find during the Great Depression. The opportunity to study medicine was denied to him due to lack of income to finish high school. My father belonged to a generation that suffered from either mass unemployment or precarious, short-term work. I imagine he would probably have been surprised to see the return of widespread precarious work in Australia after the brief improvement of working conditions between the 1940s and late 1960s.

THICK SPINES: NOSTALGIA AND POLITICAL DEVELOPMENT

The development of a Palestinian radical

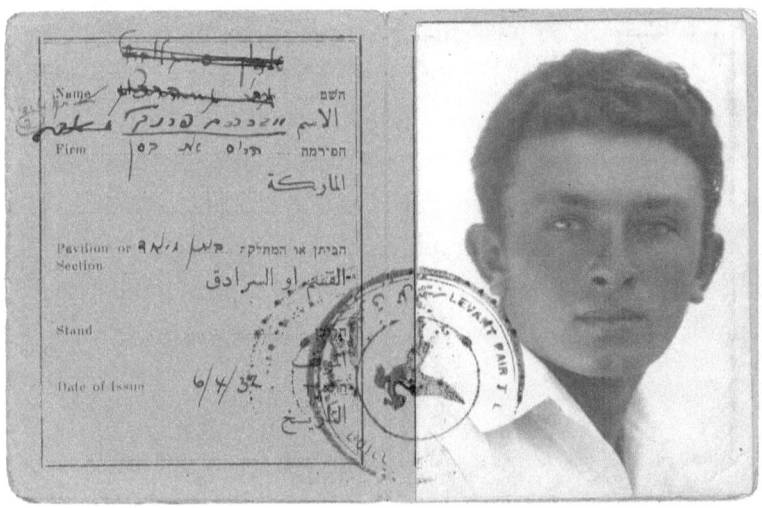

Avraham Frankel, British Palestine colonial identity card, 1932.

I always got the feeling that Dad's attitude to Palestine was quite conflicted. On the one hand, he wanted to be close to his family and friends and also help shape the future development of Palestine in a direction that was neither Zionist nor the cultural conservatism and anti-democratic practices of Arab leaders. On the other hand, he also desired a larger social environment like what he imagined revolutionary Russia to be or the richer cultural offerings of European cities. Instead, he lived in a parochial British colony that was sub-divided by such incompatible political agendas. It was during the highly volatile 1920s and 1930s that my father became actively involved with Communist and other Left anti-Zionists. Not only was he politically active, but this activism also fuelled his autodidacticism. He was an avid reader, wrote poetry and took a strong interest in broader cultural issues such as theatre, music, philosophy, and various social activities that went beyond the narrow confines of Palestinian Jewish concerns.

Whether Socialist or Communist, there was a belief amongst radical movements during the 1920s and 1930s that a new post-capitalist society should be built by people combining the head and the hand.

Many Zionists had themselves been influenced by earlier socialist and communist traditions that rejected alienated labour and believed that the full-rounded person should take pride in the toil of labour as well as developing their mind through the arts, science, and community activity. A common attitude in the 1920s and 1930s – shared by Left and Right movements across the political spectrum – was that a healthy body through sport and exercise also helped build a healthy society. One photograph I have of my father shows him lifting weights on the beach in Tel Aviv. Others show him in theatrical poses or labouring with other workers on roads and in fields.

1930 – stylised portraits of a young man with an uncertain future.

Palestine was not exempted from the harsh effects of the Great Depression. The grim economic situation was compounded by the British presiding over persistent violent conflicts between the local Arab population and the new Jewish settlers. In 1929, the year that Dad's father died, there was an Arab revolt that would continue to boil over into the 1930s. It was the combination of the Communist critique of capitalist economic failures and a rejection of imperialist colonisation that underpinned his Leftwards move during the 1930s.

Various jobs saw my father labouring alongside Arab workers. Dad told me that the Great Depression made him more politically conscious of the need for worker solidarity across class rather than just ethnic and religious lines. For many young people of his generation, Soviet Communism became increasingly attractive as an alternative to dysfunctional capitalism with its high unemployment, poverty, and inequality. While he had left Russia as a teenager, my father was a romantic and inspired by what he saw as the attempt of the Bolsheviks to build socialism in the USSR. Little was known about the horrors of collectivisation of agriculture and Stalin's mass purges during the 1930s. There were a few reports from people such as Gareth Jones and Malcolm Muggeridge about millions dying during the famine caused by establishing collective farms or reports of mass purges and Stalin's show trials. However, Jones and Muggeridge were roundly condemned or dismissed by Communist Parties and prominent intellectuals, church figures, artists and other 'fellow travellers'.

In contrast to the violent anti-Semitic White armies that partly caused his family to leave Kerch, the Soviet Union represented the enlightened forces fighting against a crisis-ridden capitalism and the new dangerous threat posed by Hitler and other fascists. In this highly polarised political climate, Dad's eyes and ears were closed to any criticism of Stalin and the USSR. One of his former girlfriends in Palestine during the 1930s, Nadia, was an active Communist and returned to the USSR. I have wondered whether she also became another victim of Stalin's repression, as did other leaders of the Palestine Communist Party (PCP) who went to the Soviet Union.

Beginning with its roots in Czarist Russia, the mainly Russian Jewish immigrants who eventually formed the two separate strands of communism in Palestine, united as the PCP in 1923. From being a predominantly anti-Zionist party made up of Jewish members, Moscow ordered the PCP to become an anti-imperialist Arab-orientated Communist party. This was an unrealistic if not absurd political strategy, as David Ben Gurion and other Zionist leaders were clearly far more popular amongst Jewish settlers. Many of the original Jewish Communists left the Party until an influx of new members joined in the 1930s.

Near Tel Aviv, 1932. Avraham 5th from left holding his arm around Arab comrade.

The PCP could never counter Zionism amongst Jews by becoming predominantly Arab-based. This is because attracting large numbers of new Jewish members would be extremely difficult if Arab Palestinians continued to be seen by the majority of Jewish settlers as their largest immediate threat. Similarly, on the Arab side, the tiny Communist movement had little influence amongst the prevailing mixture of religious and politically conservative leaders and their adherents. The latter were just as much anti-Communist as they were anti-Zionist.

There was also the major problem of the attraction of prominent Arab leaders to Hitler's anti-Semitism and rising fascist movements. The Moscow-controlled Communist International (Comintern, 1919 to 1943) was a history of disastrous near-uniform strategies imposed on national Communist parties that were highly inappropriate for the specific social conditions that local Communists faced. Despite being torn between Zionism and Stalin's orders to expand amongst Arab populations, Dad's idealism depended on the illusion of somehow overcoming the reality of the intransigent positions of both Arabs and Zionists that underpinned the deepening civil war.

As a radical internationalist, my father was part of the Jewish membership that tried to build links between the minority of Palestinian Arabs and Jews that favoured peaceful co-operation rather than separate states. He joined other Arab and Jewish activists who tried to form their own cross-cultural collectives that were similar to the Kibbutz movement but minus their exclusive Jewish membership. The traditional group photos of the period show my father with Arab and Jewish activists labouring away on the land or in other collective work situations. Being a Communist in Palestine, however, was not only a distinct minority position but also quite dangerous as the civil war escalated. Any Palestinian or Jew could be killed by conservative Arabs if found fraternising with the enemy. A common punishment for men was to have their penis cut off and then have it stuck in the mouth of their dead body.

Politically, the Arab Palestinian revolt between 1936 to 1939 was motivated by the need to pressure British authorities to give Arab Palestinians their own independent state and counter Jewish settler claims. Violence was also carried out by Jewish paramilitary organisations such as Haganah. Tactically, it was Ben-Gurion who argued that Jews should not engage in violent reprisals against Arabs for fear that in a brutal civil war Jews would still be too weak to win.

Within this context, radical Jews such as my father were often socially ostracised by Zionist Jews for associating politically with Palestinians. Dad told me that he campaigned against Ben Gurion in the 1930s because of his narrow nationalist policies. As leader of Histadrut, the General Federation of Labour movement, from 1921 to 1935, and then as head of the Jewish Agency, Ben-Gurion became the de facto leader of Zionist Jews in Palestine between 1935 and 1948, before becoming Prime Minister of Israel. The Histadrut had been influenced by socialist ideals and represented over 75% of Jewish workers. It attempted to service and protect all facets of a worker's life, both on and off the job. Eventually, after 1948, it became one of the largest employers next to the government of Israel through owning multiple co-operatives and enterprises. Little wonder that Bob Hawke, as newly elected leader of the Australian Council of Trade Unions (ACTU) in 1969, and also a fervent Zionist, proceeded to adopt some of the policies of the Histadrut. These policies included the entry of the union movement into retailing and other ventures, but they failed as there was little loyalty amongst Australian workers to patronise ACTU-owned outlets.

On becoming Prime Minister in 1983, Hawke no longer used Histadrut as a model but instead embraced neoliberal policies. This initiated what became the eventual gutting of the Australian labour movement by the end of the 1990s and early 2000s. It remains a shadow of its former self. The Histadrut was also severely weakened by neoliberal policies which saw many of its union-owned enterprises privatised and its provision of health and other services closed. My father never lived to see the dramatic transformation of both the Histadrut and the Australian labour movement. Unlike Histadrut, most Australian unions had largely confined themselves to workplace issues and the ACTU had historically lacked even coherent social democratic policies, let alone a socialist strategy. The ALP/ACTU Accord of 1983 was a feeble agreement that had only a slight similarity to Histradut's earlier historical social policies. Unfortunately, the ACTU traded away key aspects of working conditions in return for a weak Medicare and a few other crumbs.

When my father opposed Zionism in the 1930s, Ben-Gurion was a so-called 'moderate' compared to Ze'ev Jabotinsky who was a hard-Right nationalist. Both, nevertheless, favoured the 'transfer' or removal of Palestinians from the British mandate. Only their methods differed. The hard-Right nationalists openly rejected any compromise with Palestinians and pursued an aggressive military solution. This hard-line tradition has dominated contemporary Israel's policies since the old socialist Zionists were defeated decades ago.

At the very least, Stalin's zig-zag policies must have caused political confusion if not anger. Jewish Communists were first told to submerge themselves in an anti-Zionist Arab Communist Party in the late 1920s and throughout the 1930s. And yet after 1945, Communists were now told to support the Zionist goal of a new Jewish state of Israel. In recent years, I wondered how Avraham felt about his years struggling against Ben-Gurion in the 1930s only to see the Soviet Union negate this activity by being so actively pro-Zionist between 1945 and 1953 simply because Stalin thought that Israel as a socialist society would weaken British imperialism in the Middle East.

When my father was alive, I was either too young or too involved in my adult life to have this conversation with him. What was clear, however, was Dad's failure to dissent from Moscow's ever-changing policy directives. It was certainly a sign of his blinkered loyalty and defence of the Soviet Union up until 1956. My father's informal education and political formation was affected by Palestinian life characterised by vibrant debates between Zionists, Communists, and other socialists over how to construct a new socialist society. His anti-Zionism was based on a rejection of an exclusive Jewish homeland, as he believed that all people living there – whether Arab or Jew – should help construct a more equal and self-managed society.

From Palestine to Perth

In 1938, a combination of political and personal factors led to my father leaving Palestine for Australia. People rarely emigrate from their home countries if they are happy. As mentioned, with increasing violence in Palestine, plus dire economic conditions, and a lack of prospects for someone who was neither a Zionist nor an Arab, Australia suddenly loomed as a new opportunity. Other opportunities, such as studying in Europe were blocked by a lack of money. There were also entry obstacles to higher education institutions in various countries. At this time, he desired to return to the USSR. However, he had insufficient funds, and his sister was unable to sponsor his return. This obstacle proved to be a lucky break that probably saved him from either dying in the Gulag or being killed in the war. Given how forceful he was in expressing his opinions, he would have been easily targeted by the Soviet secret police had he gone to the USSR in the 1930s.

By chance, a distant relative from Tel Aviv, Moshe Kritchevsky, had migrated to Perth in 1928 and anglicised his name to Morris Crewe. Morrie arranged for Dad to travel to Fremantle on the ship called Largs Bay and helped him find work in Perth. The National Archives list 'Avrham' (a misspelling of Avraham) Frenkel, nationality Palestinian, arriving in Fremantle on October 7, 1938. When I first read this entry from the archives over a decade ago, it was an initial shock to see him listed as a Palestinian. After all, Jews had not been called Palestinians for seven decades. It was, however, a logical and accurate label that depicted not just Palestine as a British colony, but also harked back to an idealised yet completely unrealised world of potential harmony between Jewish and Arab Palestinians, the very joint homeland that Dad had championed. A shared Palestine remains a vastly different imaginary from the nationalist hatreds that characterise the contemporary reality of Israel and occupied Palestinian territories.

My father never set foot in either Palestine or Israel again, and after 1938, he never saw his mother and brothers and their own growing families. Even though the rest of Dad's family did not share his radical politics, they maintained loving relations via letters. What made my father socially and politically active is difficult to pinpoint. Perhaps it was an interest in exploring ideas or his burning sense of social justice. Maybe it was due to his opportunities as a single person to seek out new friends and social groups that led him onto radical political paths. Whatever the reason, his political formation as a critic of capitalist imperialism had already been well formed before arriving in Australia. Dad would no longer be heavily preoccupied with Palestine as in the 1930s. Instead, he would shift his concerns to helping to promote Communism in Australia.

Perth was a small city with limited prospects. Dad planned to establish the craft of smoking fish taught to him by his father and brothers, but there was no opportunity to do so. He then got a job labouring for a building construction company and worked in Perth for almost fourteen months before coming to Melbourne in early 1940. Although he spoke Russian, Yiddish and Hebrew, his knowledge of English did not mean that he could easily understand Australian accents. One day on a building site, the foreman mumbled: "you do that too". All Dad heard was: "too, too too" and thought that the foreman was playing some game with him. So, my father gesturing with his hand close to his mouth as if he were playing the flute, responded in a musical voice: 'to toot, too.' This infuriated the foreman who yelled: "YOU DO THAT TOO OR YOU'LL GET THE SACK!" Another 'lost in translation' incident occurred months later when my father had a sore throat. He asked the messenger boy, who went out daily to get the workers their lunches, if he could buy him some sour lollies to suck. Not having any small coins, Dad gave him a pound note which was more than a third of a man's weekly wage. Back came the messenger boy an hour later carrying a giant package. 'What's this', my father asked. "You asked for saveloy sausages" the boy replied, so I went to the butcher shop and here they are."

Overall, the contrast between Palestine and Perth was dramatic. Palestine was multiculturally vibrant but suffering from intense political conflict. Perth was dominated by Anglo reserve, a sleepy, parochial, and conservative city in the late 1930s. Being politically argumentative, Dad soon fell out socially with his few contacts in the immigrant Jewish community. From having a network of social and political friends in Palestine, Abe now found himself relatively isolated as a single man. Melbourne beckoned as it was a larger city with a more vibrant Left-wing political and cultural scene. At the beginning of 1940, he moved to Melbourne. Had he settled down in Perth, our family would never have come into being as he would never have met my mother.

It was not long before his gregarious personality saw him involved in many political and social activities in Melbourne, including acting at the Kadimah Theatre. A few months after he arrived in Melbourne, Prime Minister Menzies made the Communist Party an illegal organisation in June 1940. Communist activists still opposed the war between Britain and Germany as an 'imperialist war' due to their loyal but often reluctant defence of the Soviet-Nazi Pact. One year later, when Hitler invaded the USSR in June 1941, Communists went from being banned as traitors, to local heroes. They became the most vociferous pro-war party in the country. Dad threw himself into a range of political and cultural activities – from protest demonstrations, attending the Yarra Bank to listen to political talks, to labouring away on the renovation of the new Australia-Soviet Friendship House in Flinders Lane which eventually opened in 1944. He also taught Russian classes at this centre and generally promoted the Soviet Union and workers' rights at every opportunity. Avraham the Palestinian would now become Abe the Melbourne activist. Instead of promising to marry Rachel as the popular song '*Abie my boy*' would have it, Abe would meet Tania and a new chapter in our family's life would begin.

4

SURVIVING THE GRODNO GHETTO

A KEY MOTIF OF ANTI-SEMITISM IS THE ASSUMPTION that Jews have money. The opposite was the case for millions of Jews who lived in the countries and territories formerly constituting the Czarist and Habsburg empires. Dire poverty and persecution either drove large numbers of Jews to emigrate to America and other countries, or become revolutionaries, form trade unions and fight for civil liberties and other reforms. Not for nothing did Hitler rant and rave about the 'Jewish-Bolshevik enemy'.

My mother was the only member of her family to survive the Holocaust, apart from her older brother who died in the siege of Leningrad and became a victim in another way. Grodno was my mother's home city where approximately forty per cent of the inhabitants were Jewish. While there were many synagogues, my grandmother, mother, and her brothers did not attend any of them as they were not religious. However, Mum's paternal grandmother was a deeply religious person. When she later came to live with her daughter-in-law and three children, there were many arguments and clashes over the failure of her grandchildren and their mother to observe Jewish holidays and rituals.

Despite growing up in what was officially Poland from 1920 to 1939, little had changed for Jews in Grodno when compared to life under the Russian Czar. In 1928, my maternal grandfather died from stomach cancer when my mother was eight and her brothers Gdalie and Mordechai (Motek) were eleven and six years old respectively. My grandfather, Samuel Lubitsch, had been a self-employed, small scrap metals merchant who barely made a living. When he died, his wife Gitel (Hebrew) also known as Genia (Polish), and their three children were reduced to impoverished conditions. Grandmother Genia worked as a seamstress for sixteen to eighteen hours a day, but her income was too little to properly feed and clothe the family.

Father, Samuel Lubitsch, Grodno, 1916.

Hence, my mother's life was formed by harsh poverty and the need to combine schooling with supporting her mother. She told me that they had no running water and had to bring water from the outside well. Bathing was done once a week at the public bath house. There was a wooden stove, but they couldn't afford heating for most of the time and the walls of their small apartment were often damp during the wintertime. As a young teenager, Mum had to cook on a small kerosene stove for her brothers and grandmother while her mother was away working. Lacking fuel for cooking, it was often cheaper to take a pot of food to the nearby baker who would put the neighbours' cooking utensils into his big oven for a tiny fee and have the food cooked or warmed up. When my great-grandmother was unable to survive on her own, she became another mouth for my grandmother

Genia to feed and to look after in the 1930s. It is often forgotten how widespread tuberculosis and other threatening illnesses were due to poverty. Life-expectancy was cut short by malnutrition, poor housing conditions and unemployment.

Genia Lubitsch/Lubicz Grodno, 1939

The film actor and director, Ernst Lubitsch, was my mother's second cousin. His father Simon Lubitsch had been born in Grodno before Ernst was raised in Berlin. Ernst's relatives in Grodno were proud of his fame which only increased when he went to Hollywood in 1922 and began directing films over the next twenty-five years with many stars such as Mary Pickford, Maurice Chevalier, and Greta Garbo. Mum's relatives in America, possibly also Ernst Lubitsch, would regularly send money and parcels to help support her family in Grodno. Although her grandmother wanted her to go to a Jewish school, my mother's parents couldn't afford it and she was taught by nuns at a Catholic school. The parents' committee at the school also provided her and other poor students with a pair of boots, rye bread and chicory.

The fusion between government and religious education in conservative pre-1939 Poland was quite extensive. Jews were often excluded from key professions and institutions and were forced to become either small self-employed merchants or work for low wages. Only a minority were wealthy. Hence, a Jew could not identify with Poland or think of themselves as a Pole, for this would have meant identifying as a Catholic. Interwar Grodno had a mixed population of Poles, Jews, Byelorussians, Lithuanians, and Germans. Deep-seated anti-Semitism was not the only form of cultural strain and conflict in Grodno. There was also tension over the Polishisation of Byelorussian culture and discrimination against other minorities. Overall, the level of compulsory education for all students was low as millions of Poles did not go beyond primary education and large numbers of people, especially in rural areas, were illiterate.

Bundist and Catholic influences

As mentioned, it is not just that Mum and her mother Genia and brothers were not religious, but they were raised in a Bundist socialist milieu. The socialist Bund was a recognised force amongst the interwar Jewish population in Poland. It regularly won a majority of Jewish votes in dozens of towns. Before the revolution of 1917, the Bundists had rejected Bolshevik strategies, especially their attempt to dominate and control other socialist revolutionaries in Czarist Russia. These divisions would only intensify in the 1920s and 1930s.

During summer holidays, Mum would go to the Bundist camp organised by the local Bund labour movement for poor kids. She loved all the organised activities in the forest camp which was a welcome relief from the poverty she experienced at home in Grodno. Later, in Australia, she attended the big camps (a mixture of politics and leisure) organised not by the Bund – because they were small in numbers – but by the Young Communist League and Eureka Youth League in the areas close to Barwon Heads, Healesville, Cowes and elsewhere. In Grodno, her family also knew a number of Bundists and Communists who had been arrested or were in jail. While grandmother Genia was not officially a member of the Bund or Communist Party, she shared their socialist and anti-fascist cultural values and political opposition to Right-wing Polish governments.

My mother loved school and was an excellent student. She was an avid reader and if not for her family's poverty, would have pursued her formal studies much further. The photos of her in school uniform at age fourteen show her proudly squatting in the front row on one bended knee. However, like most Jews and other minorities in Poland during the 1930s, she encountered limited educational and job prospects. Formally and informally, most young, poor working-class Jews faced a bleak future.

With the partition of Poland by Hitler and Stalin, Grodno became part of the Byelorussian Soviet Republic. Despite harsh conditions and poverty, there were far more opportunities for further education in the USSR compared with the restrictions in Poland. Three years after she departed for Melbourne in 1937, her older brother went from Grodno to Leningrad to study. Less than two years later, he was caught in the siege and perished there either from starvation or killed by Nazi bombardment.

Brothers Motek and Gdalie, Grodno, 1938.

Decades later, Mum recognised the influence that the nuns had had on her in regard to particular social and moral issues such as abortion. For example, she took on board aspects of conservative Catholic teaching. From being initially opposed to abortion, it was not until the early 1970s that she changed her views and became pro-choice after agreeing with feminist campaigns. My mother would help make the garden in the first women's refuge in Melbourne run by feminists. On the other hand, her experiences of living in Catholic Poland made her a staunch anti-clericalist. The alignment of the Church with anti-socialists and anti-Semites made her detest the conservative religious forces of her day. Mum's atheism was not based on a deeper philosophical critique of metaphysical thought. Rather, it was a fusion of anti-clericalism directed at the institutional practices and abuses of the Catholic church and other religions. It was a familiar critique of religion that relied on science and empirical evidence as the way forward to enlightenment.

Class photo 1935, Tauba/Tanie third from left, front row.

In Grodno, it was her Catholic school uniform, rather than God, that saved Tauba's life. Pogroms had long been a feature of life in the region. Any trivial incident could easily spark violent attacks on Jews.

In 1935, another pogrom broke out which led to Jews being killed, wounded, and savagely beaten up. Rampaging mobs roamed the streets looking for Jews to kill, properties to loot and smash up as well as to carry out other violent abuses. On the first day of the pogrom, my fifteen-year-old mother was on the way home from school with her school friend. Two Polish men accosted them with knives looking to kill Jews. Fortunately, one of the attackers restrained the other from stabbing my mother and her friend by pointing to their Catholic school uniforms and saying to leave them alone as they were not Jews but Catholics. After getting home safely, Mum and her family, like most Jews in the city, hid at home and feared going out during the following weeks.

By contrast, there was one section of Grodno where my mother told me that 'tough Jews' confronted the mob. This section of the city near the Niemen River was populated by Jewish coachmen and blacksmiths who took their irons and hammers from their workshops or wooden posts from their horse-driven wagons and chased the mob away. Six years later, however, even these 'tough Jews' were helpless to stop the Nazis from rounding up most Jews in the city for mass extermination. It was one thing to defend Jews against local pogromists with limited hand-made weapons and tools, and quite another thing to stop a military machine with an industrialised plan for ridding a whole continent of Jews.

Departure for Melbourne

Unlike my father's family escaping the horrors of the Civil War in 1921 by going to Constantinople and Palestine, my mother did not have any desire to go to Palestine even if this had been an available option. In the Grodno ghetto, by the time she had finished primary school and a few years of high school, it was already clear that the combination of family poverty and lack of opportunities for young Jews in Poland would not improve.

Her father's sister Sarah had married Samuel Strelec and they had emigrated from Bialystok, Poland, in 1929 and set up a small clothing factory in Flinders Lane, Melbourne. With her mother's approval, it was arranged for sixteen-year-old Tauba to have her fares paid and be sponsored by her aunt and uncle to come and live and work with them in Australia. If this worked out well, the idea was for other members of Mum's family to also join her in Melbourne in the following few years. When she left Grodno in March 1937 there was still snow on the ground. Tauba, soon to be Tania, would turn seventeen on the way to Melbourne. While she was incredibly sad to leave her family, Mum did not think at the time that she would never see her family again. Nonetheless, she must have shown the courage and determination characteristic of her later years, to set out as a teenager to a completely unfamiliar and very distant country.

Her first stop was Warsaw for four days where she would join several other Jews on the long journey to Australia. Here she was processed by an organisation familiar with arranging international passage for emigrating Jews. They were first deloused, or fumigated with chemicals, a widespread practice for poor Jews whether they had lice or not. After four days in Warsaw, she travelled by train to the Baltic port of Gdynia where she boarded a ship that would travel to the French port of Le Havre via London. From Le Havre she proceeded to Paris where Mum and others from Poland would reside for six weeks waiting for her cargo/passenger ship, the *Commissaire Ramel* to arrive in Marseille.

My mother talked about her stay in Paris for years to come. After the small city of Grodno, Paris was a dramatic contrast and left such a positive impression on her that she would have preferred not to have gone to Australia and instead to have remained in this exciting city. Yet, if this desire had been fulfilled, it is highly likely that she would have been rounded up by the Nazis a few years later.

Paris in the Springtime of 1937 was another story. Not only was it a city with millions of people, full of significant places to see, and contemporary cultural offerings, but it was also a city where socialist politics were on full display. Germany and Italy were under the rule of Hitler and Mussolini, while Spain was in the midst of a savage civil war. By contrast, since May 1936, French Socialist, Leon Blum, led a Popular Front government made up of the Socialists, Communists, and others. One year later, my mother witnessed the largest Left-wing march of workers she would see for the rest of her life. May Day 1937 brought out what she thought to be more than a million workers. Reports at the time put the turnout at several hundred thousand people marching together and representing the different industries, occupations, and affiliations affirming the *Front Populaire*. Whatever the correct figure, the sheer size of the celebration was a breathtaking experience that she would never forget. Unfortunately, later the *Front Populaire* was weakened by internal divisions and external opposition.

Aboard the Commissaire Ramel, on the way to Australia, June 1937.

For a seventeen-year-old coming from a provincial town in Poland, the journey from France to Australia was an eye-opening experience. Her love of the range of tropical plants, monkeys and other animals on their stopover itinerary stayed with her for the rest of her life. She remained a devoted plant and animal lover. However, soon after the *Commissaire Ramel* departed Marseille on its voyage to Noumea via the Panama Canal, the political divisions troubling France were to become evident on the ship. Several of the crew were openly anti-Semitic and expressed hostility to Leon Blum's government. The three women and thirteen men from Poland in my mother's group of immigrant Jewish passengers had strained relationships with the ship's crew. Tensions developed as the ship sailed through the extremely hot and humid weather of the Panama Canal and across the Pacific Ocean. In an era before air conditioning, the small cabins were stifling. The group from Poland had never experienced such weather and were also upset by the inferior quality of the food served to them on the ship. Mutiny was brewing in the minds of several of the members of this group.

At one of the stops in the Pacific, a few of the passengers in her group decided to go on a hunger strike until the food improved. To aid their rebellion, they secretly smuggled into their cabins branches of bananas which they had purchased onshore in order to maintain their sustenance while giving the appearance they were on a hunger strike. Unhappily, their plan misfired. Being unfamiliar with bananas, especially whole branches of the fruit, they did not calculate on the sweltering heat in their cabins accelerating the ripening and rotting process. According to Mum, within little time, flies and other insects swarmed in the cabins and it was impossible to remain inside.

The captain was furious and threatened to remove them from the ship before they arrived at New Caledonia if they caused further trouble. Forced to accept the captain's terms, the rebellious passengers had to put up with the ship's conditions for the remaining portion of the ship's journey to its destination in Noumea. From New Caledonia, she and the other passengers travelled to Sydney on the *Pierre Loti* which also had pro-Nazi French crew members. Indeed, after the war broke out, the crew of the *Pierre Loti* were detained in Sydney. The local Sydney French population, which was heavily pro-Free French under General de Gaulle, were very unhappy to have these pro-Vichy crew members in Sydney.

After arriving in Australia on July 3, 1937, Mum and her new girlfriend from Poland, Lil, proceeded to travel by train on the slow journey from Sydney to Melbourne. Both she and Lil knew only a few words of English. Watching the large empty country from their train window, they overheard two nearby passengers deep in conversation and constantly uttering the words 'oh, golly', 'golly gee' or simply plain 'golly'. Each time Mum and Lil heard these words they began laughing until this developed into fits of unstoppable giggles. The word 'golly' means naked in both Polish and Russian, so they thought that either English was a funny language, or that the two passengers were incessantly talking about something sexual. Remember, my mother had gone to a strict Catholic school where there had been a total ban on any topics to do with sexuality.

Tania and Lil Melbourne, 1938

A year later, one of Mum's boyfriends called Bert, took her on a scenic drive to the Dandenong Ranges. Stopping on the road for a pee in the bushes, Bert said to Mum: "you wait in the car as I'm just going to see the dicky bird". Not yet understanding slang and thinking that she would miss out on seeing an exotic Australian bird, Mum immediately cried out: "Oh Bert, I want to see the dicky bird too!"

It was Sunday, July 4, 1937, when my mother arrived from Sydney at Spencer Street station. She was met at the station by her aunty and uncle who proceeded to drive with Mum through the city on their way home. "Are we in Melbourne?", she asked in disbelief. When told that this was the centre of the city, she was shocked as everything was closed and the Sunday streets were deserted. After Paris, she could not believe that Melbourne was even a city.

Young Communist League camp, Barwon Heads, 1937,
Tania 7th from left, 2nd row.

The following day, her aunt took her to the hairdresser and had her long hair cut short before being taken to their factory where Mum laboured for the next year. Not only did she have to work in the factory for reduced wages (in return for having her fares to Australia paid), but she also had to cook for her aunt and uncle and clean their house. This unhappy beginning to her life in Melbourne ended as soon as my mother learnt sufficient English to enable her to leave her relatives' house and employment. She eventually found a new place to rent with one of her friends as well as another job as a machinist in a clothing factory. Being a young politically and socially engaged woman, she could now develop new friends at the Young Communist League where she attended meetings, discussions, and a range of social activities. As a single vivacious woman, she also had a number of boyfriends before meeting my father in 1940.

In a recorded interview in 1984 with my friend Jan Bourne, who was doing a project on women's lives and changing attitudes, Mum told her about some of her beliefs and behaviour when she was a young woman. When she married, she was still a virgin and she had only engaged in kissing and heavy petting. Like many others of her generation, my mother regarded having intercourse as too risky because pregnancy was a much bigger threat in an era of backyard abortions. There was also a widely practiced taboo on unmarried people living together and having premarital sex.

Although she dated my father for over eighteen months before getting married, both of my parents went out with other boyfriends or girlfriends in the initial period. They were a handsome, well-matched couple and as the romance blossomed, Mum said that she decided that Dad was the person she wanted to be with. Tania and Abe shared a great deal in common, whether cultural interests, politics, or a network of friends. She was cosmopolitan in her thinking and had a thirst for knowledge. The fact that he was twelve years older than her, gave my mother a sense of security. Because she had lost her own father as a young girl, the wider life experience of my father also attracted her. In the 1984 audio interview, Mum said that Dad met many of her romantic and social needs as a partner as well as fulfilling the additional role of being something of a father figure. The war was in full swing by the time they married on December 26, 1941.

My parents must have either exuded an optimism about their ultimate future together or wanted to share as much time with one another before the war reached Australia. How else could one explain people getting married less than three weeks after the Japanese attack on Pearl Harbour and the victorious Nazi forces not only capturing most of Western Europe but also cutting through the Soviet Union all the way to the outskirts of Moscow and Leningrad.

Annihilation, and the anxiety of not knowing

Mum's personal happiness in Melbourne was overshadowed by her growing concern for her family in Grodno from late 1939 onwards. This worry turned into desperation as all news from her mother or brothers ceased arriving from mid-1940. Prior to this, she still received letters in 1940 but after German advances combined with the banning of the Communist Party in Australia from 1940 to 1942, all news from home abruptly stopped. The predecessor of ASIO, the Commonwealth Investigative Branch (CIB) seized all letters from the USSR which was regarded as an 'enemy state'. During and after the war, my mother appealed to the CIB to release any mail held from Grodno or Leningrad. These applications were denied by the CIB which was an authoritarian organisation run by dehumanised bureaucrats lacking any concern about victims of war.

Tania's brother and mother, last photo from Grodno, 1939.

After Hitler's invasion of the Soviet Union on June 22, 1941, Grodno was one of the places quickly captured. It was only after the war that my mother learnt of the fate of most of the Jews in the city. Rounded up into one of the two areas consisting of 15,000 and 10,000 Jewish residents, her mother, grandmother, younger brother, and all other relatives, were either murdered in the city or transported to Treblinka or Auschwitz between late 1941 and 1942/3. Meanwhile, her older brother was also out of contact due to the great siege of Leningrad. She had been unable to arrange for her other family members to come to Melbourne given her own lack of funds after she had left her aunt and uncle's place in 1938. Over a year later, the situation had deteriorated with the Nazi-Soviet Non-Aggression Pact. As Grodno became incorporated into the USSR, all possibility of leaving the country was denied even if people had the financial means to travel.

Several years after the war, my parents met a recent arrival from the displaced persons camps in Central Europe. We called him 'Chaim the Partisan' and he now worked in Melbourne as a taxi driver. Chaim had lived in Grodno but escaped with a small group of other Jews to become partisans in the surrounding forest. He told Mum that he had seen a member of the Jewish council or Judenrat, a man called Schulkes, sell out the other Jews in the ghetto in return for the Germans sparing his own life. This was extremely distressing news for my mother to hear, even though Chaim did not know exactly when and where Mum's family was killed.

It is important to remember that Jewish councils in each town or city were instructed to organise fellow Jews for either labour required by the local Nazis, or for transportation to the extermination camps in an orderly manner. Any Jew disobeying orders was subject to immediate execution. During the first twenty years after the Shoah, there were two main criticisms of Jewish councils. The first was based on various accounts or rumours told by survivors that members of these Judenrat had sold out their fellow Jews for material gain and personal survival. The second main criticism came from political analysts, such as philosopher Hannah Arendt, who claimed that Jews were poorly served by their leaders. Had they not co-operated with the Nazis, then the ensuing chaos and misery confronting Germans – who needed to industrially co-ordinate thousands of disorganised communities – may have resulted in fewer than the four-and-a-half to six million Jews being shipped off to the death camps. Notably, it was this accusation that caused more outrage among Jewish leaders than Arendt's comments about the 'banality of evil' during the Adolf Eichmann trial.

While recent historical studies have not invalidated Arendt's arguments about the chaos that would have ensued had the Judenrats not co-operated with the Nazis, they do cast doubt on Arendt's figures. It is now estimated that almost half of the approximately six million Jews killed never saw the inside of a sealed train or the gas chambers. Instead, Himmler created four special groups consisting of 3,000 fanatical SS Nazis who accompanied the German armed forces. In the first year of the war in Eastern Europe after June 1941, more than 1.5 million Jews were killed at a myriad of locations, as these four elite SS Einsatzgruppen (special operations) rounded up local Jewish residents and murdered them by shooting, bashing, burning alive and other brutalising acts and massacres. By the time of the Nazi defeat at Stalingrad in February 1943, eighty percent of Shoah or Holocaust victims had been mainly killed by either the Einsatzgruppen or in the gas chambers.

My mother had been an avid reader of most of the books about the Shoah, from accounts of specific death camps to survivors' histories and analyses of the slaughter inside and outside the camps. What ultimately enraged her at a very personal level, was the fact that several years after she had read Arendt's 1963 book, *Eichmann in Jerusalem*, she discovered that the new owner of the block of flats in which she had rented an apartment since 1960, was the person called Schulkes that 'Chaim the Partisan' had accused of selling out the Jews of Grodno. This had all the ingredients of what could have been a dramatic morality play or film.

Despite me cautioning her to first speak to Schulkes to see whether he actually came from Grodno before she made wild accusations, Mum immediately went to the Australian Jewish Welfare Society to denounce this so-called treacherous being. She demanded that action be taken and that the Jewish community in Melbourne needed to know that this man was enjoying a wealthy post-Holocaust life based on selling out thousands of Jews in Grodno. The people at Jewish Welfare advised my mother that she couldn't besmirch the reputation of a person without any evidence other than hearsay that this was the same Schulkes that Chaim had spoken about. On their suggestion, a meeting was arranged for Mum to meet Schulkes so that she could ask him about his personal history. I also attended the meeting, but little was established other than Schulkes saying that my mother had confused him with someone else and that he had no role in organising for Jews to be sent to the extermination camps. Although his age and other facts fitted Chaim's profile, nothing more could be done to confirm whether she was right or wrong.

Mum continued to fume over the matter for years to come but was half-heartedly pleased by what she thought was the *karma* associated with the block of flats that Schulkes had purchased. It had been a bad investment. Following the drought in the late 1960s, our rented flat and the three other flats in the block of four began to crack very badly. I was living overseas when Mum had to eventually move out as the building became dangerous. First, the roof and ceilings had to be propped up with beams until the whole block at 20 Mary Street, St. Kilda had to be demolished.

Many years later, with the advantage of numerous files posted on internet sites, I looked up the extermination of the Jewish population in the Grodno ghetto. I found a document on the trial entitled: 'The People vs. Kurt Wiese and Heinz Errelis Accused of Murder, Verdict and Judgment, Cologne District Court, Federal Republic of Germany June 27, 1968'. Weise and Errelis were the surviving Gestapo officers in charge of extermination at Grodno and Bialystok and received life sentences. It is not clear how long they spent in prison.

One of the witnesses testifying against the accused was a person called Boris Schulkes. It stated that he now lived in Victoria, Australia, and that 'attorney Schulkes' had been a member of the Judenrat that had to deal with Weise and Errelis. It was Weise who had punched Schulkes several times in the face over an incident. The trial report gave no indication of how 'attorney Schulkes' had survived the liquidation of the Jewish ghetto between 1941 and 1943. Was this the same Schulkes that 'Chaim the Partisan' had accused? If so, did he sell out the Jews of Grodno to save his own life? It is doubtful that we will ever know.

After the Nazis occupied Grodno, German troops looted Jewish homes and Jews were evicted from their apartments. They were then segregated into two ghettoes. The Judenrat organised the forced labour imposed by the Nazis. One ghetto housed approximately 15,000 'skilled workers' in the crowded Shulhof area or 'synagogue quarter'. The other ghetto was on the outskirts in an area called Slobodka consisted of 10,000 'unproductive' Jewish people. One year later in November 1942, the liquidation of the ghettos began. The Slobodka ghetto was destroyed, and all residents were sent to their deaths in Auschwitz. It is likely that Mum's grandmother and possibly her mother were amongst those in the first group that were either killed in Grodno or sent for extermination whilst her younger brother may have been classified as 'skilled' and held within the other ghetto.

According to Nazi sources, between November 1942 and February 1943, 44,049 Grodno Jews were sent to Auschwitz and Treblinka extermination camps, which included 23,272 people from neighbouring villages and towns around Grodno. In one operation during January 1943, 11,600 were sent to Auschwitz where 9,851 were immediately gassed and 1,799 put to work. About 1,000 'skilled workers' were also sent to Bialystok in March 1943 and 180 were hidden by Gentiles until Soviet troops liberated them in July 1944. Perhaps Schulkes was amongst the 'skilled workers' sent to Bialystok or one of those who were hidden by non-Jews?

Mum belonged to the minority that luckily left before the horrific years of mass extermination. Although she was not a direct victim of Nazi annihilation and brutality, the loss of her family affected her deeply over the rest of her life. Carrying this loss, she was a victim in another way.

In March 1993, two and a half years before she died, I arrived home one afternoon to find the police at our home. My partner Julie was in hospital recovering from just having given birth to our son Emile the previous day. My sister Genia opened the door and told me that Mum had been shot in the street on the way to do her daily shopping with her trolly pusher. "What!" I exclaimed in disbelief. When I visited Julie in the hospital later that evening and she asked me if there was any news, I nonchalantly joked that there was nothing to report except that Tania had been shot!

Apparently, someone hidden from view in a nearby house was firing an air gun. Mum was shot with a pellet in the leg and as more shots were fired, she ran bleeding to warn a mother with a baby in a pram walking about ten metres behind her to quickly turn around and run for her life. As it transpired, the physical injury was minor but could have been much more serious if she had been shot in the head. Genia came over and called the police, but they could not find the culprit. They filed a report, instructed her to get medical attention and then suggested that she lodge a claim for victim's compensation. Being shot in suburbia was not a common experience for most residents.

About a year later after filling in a victim's statement, she was requested to appear before a magistrate at Prahran Court. I also accompanied her. Asked if she would like to say anything to the Court before he made a ruling, Mum told the magistrate in her inimitable East European accent:

> As a Holocaust survivor, I'm a complete wreck. Since the shooting,
> I haven't been able to sleep a wink for months.

She was a memorable, one-of-a-kind character. I quietly half-laughed to myself as I watched Mum, with tears in her eyes, lay it on thick. Yet, I also knew that she had suffered for decades as the only survivor of her family and that the psychological scars were infinitely deeper and more painful than the shotgun pellet wound in her leg. The magistrate awarded her $12,000 in compensation, but no monetary figure would have been able to compensate my mother for the loss of her family and the trauma she endured.

5

NORTH CARLTON AND THE EMERGENCE OF THE NON-JEWISH JEW

Before they met in Melbourne, my parents came from different currents of Left Jewish political culture. My mother grew up within the culture of the Bund in Grodno and my father developed his politics as part of the Communist movement in Palestine. Mum gave two accounts of their meeting in 1940. In one version she saw him perform at the Kadimah theatre and talked to him after the play. The other version is that my father noticed my mother reading the Victorian Communist newspaper, *Guardian*, on a tram and struck up a conversation with her. Either way, after eighteen months of going out together, they married on Boxing Day, December 26, 1941.

Although an atheist, my father had promised his beloved and religious mother before leaving Tel Aviv in 1938, that if and when he would ever marry, he would get a rabbi to perform the ceremony. He tried to fulfil his promise, but being unemployed in December 1941, he was shocked when told by the local rabbi's assistant (who visited him at his lodgings at 405 Station Street, North Carlton) that it would cost between seven and ten pounds to perform a simple service. Promise or no promise, this was more than double what most people earned in a week, let alone an unemployed person. Dad was outraged and asked him to leave. He and Mum then got married at the Registry Office in Queen Street, Melbourne.

NORTH CARLTON AND THE EMERGENCE OF THE NON-JEWISH JEW

Young couple Melbourne, 1941

After my parents married, they soon moved from their separate rented places in Rae Street, North Fitzroy and Station Street, North Carlton into their new rented place at 317 Canning Street, North Carlton. Our family lived there until the end of 1950. North Carlton was a suburb that during the 1930s and 1940s had been labelled 'Little Jerusalem'. At home, my parents mainly spoke English and Russian with some Yiddish sprinkled in between. As internationalists and modernists, they decided not only to reject a religious upbringing for their children but also regarded Yiddish as unimportant for their children to learn. This was a conscious decision on their part despite both being involved at the Yiddish cultural centre, the Kadimah. Their relationship with Yiddish was ambivalent. It was a language they had grown up with, but they also saw it as affirming a too restrictive cultural identity that would soon be replaced by modern languages. As an indication of her worldview and politics, my mother actually began learning Esperanto as the lingua franca of international communication that crossed national borders.

While they enjoyed the company of their Jewish friends, they were future-orientated and regarded Yiddish and local members of the Socialist Bund as clinging to a 'museum culture' that would eventually die out, especially in countries such as Australia. My parents were certainly not assimilationists in the sense of denying their Jewishness or wishing to become Anglo-Australians. Instead, they respected both secular and religious Jews who wished to practice and preserve their cultural traditions, just like the cultural practices of other migrants. But they instilled in their children the desire for a form of secular, multicultural internationalism that would one day end racist and cultural discrimination, thereby transcending particular narrow cultural identities, including faith-based religious identities. After we began attending primary school, Genia and I would listen and be involved in their discussions about their cultural values and political beliefs. They neither forced us to learn Yiddish or Russian in Australia, nor were they opposed to us learning these languages had we chosen to do so.

The North Carlton 'ghetto'

North Carlton of that time has been variously romanticised by former residents as a Jewish ghetto or village shtetl. While Melbourne was a city full of disadvantage and inequality, it did not have ghettos in the European or American sense. Our neighbours were Italian, Lebanese and Anglo. Like other immigrant groups who congregated in particular suburbs before moving elsewhere, East European Jewish residency in North Carlton was transitory and briefly reached its peak between the mid-1930s and early 1950s.

Several thousand Jews lived in an area bounded roughly by Lygon and Nicholson streets on the east and west, and between Lee Street Primary School in the South and Princess Hill School in the North. There was a range of Kosher butchers, cake shops, delicatessens, drapery stores and bread shops that catered for East European tastes. Most Jews living in Carlton and Brunswick were working class (white or blue collar) or self-employed and came from Russia, Poland, and other parts of Eastern Europe. They worked in the surrounding factories and offices in the city, Brunswick, Fitzroy, Collingwood, and other inner Melbourne areas. In the 1930s, middle-class Jews lived in St. Kilda and East Melbourne and had arrived during the 19th Century or before the First World War. By contrast, those in Carlton lacked established connections and often had a different relationship to their Judaism. This was reflected in the dominant language of Yiddish, regardless of whether they were fluent in English, their political views, or their country of origin.

Tania on the right in a clothing factory, 1940

Mum and Dad used to attend the Kadimah theatre in Lygon Street near the Melbourne Cemetery. The David Herman theatre started in 1940 and was led by leading Yiddish actor Rachel Holzer who left the dangers of anti-Semitic Poland in 1938 and came to Melbourne in April 1939 with her husband the dramatist Chaim Rozenstein. Together with director Yankev Waislitz, they recreated many of the Yiddish classics as well as new plays in the 1940s and 1950s, including a few that my father performed in during the early 1940s. Yiddish theatre mixed religious and spiritual themes including many secular plays about the joys and troubles experienced by both urban and rural Jews. The Kadimah was a non-politically affiliated Jewish cultural centre where mainly secular or not very observant Jews – whether Bundist, Communist, Zionist, or other political currents – congregated to meet friends, attend the theatre or community functions, and also use the Kadimah's library.

The writer, Arnold Zable, whose family came to live in Canning Street several years after our family had arrived, painted the scene inside the Kadimah where excited visitors met friends in the foyer. As Arnold relates, the bells rang and rang for people to take their seats in the theatre, but these were usually ignored by acquaintances deep in conversation or argument. The Kadimah eventually moved to Elsternwick in 1968. The white building was converted into a community centre for Italian immigrants from the beautiful islands off Sicily and renamed Eolian Hall. Perhaps the most prominent descendent from these islands was B.A. Santamaria, whose parents came from the island of Salina and settled in Brunswick.

My parents' generation of Carlton Jews later dispersed to Caulfield, Kew, Malvern, and other suburbs, as many had 'saved their pennies' and moved from factory work to opening small businesses or investing in real estate during the 1950s and 1960s. Mum and Dad did not follow this path of embourgeoisement. They believed that both mental and manual labour were highly valuable. Hence, they neither became petite bourgeoisie nor moved into business, let alone developed large corporate entities like the Smorgon conglomerate, which originally started with a Kosher butcher shop in Lygon Street, Carlton. Instead, Mum had been a machinist in various clothing factories but after we were born, was unable to do paid work due to the lack of childcare. Dad had laboured in a timber yard as well as in factories doing electric welding, making textiles and other jobs. His wages were insufficient to pay the bills and our family was evicted from our rented house in Canning Street at the end of 1950 for failing to pay the rent.

The early 1950s were far from the mythological affluent boom times for millions of low-income people. It was only with the help of my mother's aunt and uncle that in early 1951 my parents managed to find a small house to rent at 12 Godfrey Avenue, East St. Kilda.

Although they still maintained contact with friends in Carlton, it was especially via the weekly delivery of meat from Polonsky's butcher shop in Rathdowne Street or attending the screening of Soviet films at the 'Bughouse' in Faraday Street, that Carlton continued to feature in our family's life. Polonsky's butcher shop had developed a delivery service for a growing number of ex-Carlton emigres now residing across the river. The meat cuts and bones for soup were wrapped in paper bundles tied up with string. I remember that these bundles had a distinct non-Anglo European smell compared to local Australian butcher shops.

A defining feature of the Jews in Carlton was that they were predominantly secular. After 1945, the majority of Jews – whether Communists, Zionists or supporters of Labor were in favour of establishing the state of Israel. Only the Bundists were consistently anti-Zionist. Importantly, even though Stalin had been anti-Zionist for decades, for cynical strategic reasons he strongly supported the founding of Israel to help weaken British imperialist power in the Middle East. Not only did the USSR throw its weight behind the vote to give Israel its own state, but Stalin secretly aided Israel by sending arms to Israeli forces via Czechoslovakia. It is often forgotten that Donald Trump's controversial decision to move the US Embassy to Jerusalem on the 70th anniversary of Israel's founding in 2018, was preceded long before in December 1953 by the Soviet Union becoming the first state to recognise Jerusalem as Israel's capital. However, within the next year, the rise of Arab nationalism witnessed the Soviets switching their support to Egypt's president, Gamal Abdel Nasser, and other Arab states. All these *realpolitik* manoeuvres on the part of the USSR may not have eliminated the hostilities between Communists and Zionists. Nonetheless, Soviet wartime sacrifices in the fight against fascism and support for Israel did make Communists less unpopular with Zionists at the Kadimah in the 1940s and early 1950s.

On the other hand, the historical animosity between Bundists and Communists was transferred from Poland to Australia. Bundists had suffered during Stalin's purges and were critical of Jewish

Communists who were blind followers of Soviet policies. Moreover, the news about a new wave of anti-Semitism in the USSR during the late 1940s and early 1950s undermined the favourable reception of Soviet support for Israel amongst Australian Jews and alienated a majority of both the non-Communist Left and conservative Jews from Communists.

Notably, the Jews in Carlton were also quite unlike the relatively recent growth of more inward-orientated ultra-orthodox and patriarchal Jews with their black coats and hats and subordinated wives and girls in present-day Caulfield, Elsternwick, Ripponlea, and East St. Kilda. Many secular Jews fear that these fundamentalists are causing anti-Semitism with their ghetto-like practices. Indeed, the larger secular, Jewish community, call the fundamentalists 'frum' in a pejorative sense, meaning hypocritically pious or holier-than-thou. It is ironic that in the period from the 1920s to the late 1940s, Carlton Jews – the parents and grandparents of present-day 'non-frum', and predominantly secular Jews in Melbourne – were also disliked and looked down upon by established Anglo-Australian Jews. The latter were hostile to the Carlton Jews not because they were 'frum', but because they were also perceived to be too alien, and radical, and it was thought that their presence would fuel anti-Semitism.

Apart from well-known Australian Left-wing authors and intellectuals, most non-Jewish residents of Carlton would not have witnessed the vibrant community activity inside the Kadimah. Later, it became an attraction for people from other parts of Melbourne to come to Acland Street St. Kilda on a Sunday to visit Café Scheherazade, and the various cake shops. These cafes were a more public expression of Eastern European cultures from the 1950s. Thousands of single, lonely migrant men arrived in Melbourne and gathered after work or at weekends at their respective cultural clubs. They were similar to the mainly male guest workers from southern Europe who met at railway stations in northern European cities to see fellow countrymen. Unlike imported migrant workers, many post-1945 East European Jews arrived as sole survivors having lost their families in the mass extermination camps. After *kaffee und kuchen*, dozens of Jewish men would stand in Acland Street to meet their friends and debate politics and other issues. This scene reached its peak during the 1960s and 1970s but then declined during the 1980s and 1990s as age thinned out numbers and the various strands of socialist politics also lost their influence.

Anti-nationalism and the Non-Jewish Jew

As mentioned, my parents had a conflicted relationship to 'Jewish culture' which not only influenced the way they raised their children, but also helped shape both their anti-Zionism and my later political development. Before 1948, one could partly understand the logic behind Zionism which argued that Jews needed their own state to protect themselves against pogroms, centuries of victimisation and the recent mass extermination. Unfortunately, the narrowly focussed political project of a Jewish nation-state depended on the myth of a common 'Jewish culture'. Creating a secular nation-state that is not based on religious institutions while still deriving its legitimacy of place from ancient Judaic religious culture is why present-day Israel has always been torn between entirely different conceptions of identity, faith, and purpose.

The nineteenth-century Zionist conception of Palestine as "a land without a people, for a people without a land" paralleled the European colonial treatment of non-Europeans as inferior and expendable. Israel could not be created without displacing others from their homes. Even the 1930s proposal of the Freeland League to set up a Jewish home for seventy-five thousand refugees in the Kimberley region in Western Australia, or the 1940 Nazi plan to forcibly remove all European Jews to Madagascar, would have involved displacing Indigenous peoples.

My mother knew the artist Yosl Bergner who was not only the same age as her but also arrived in Melbourne from Poland at the same time that she did. They mixed in similar Communist and Communist-front circles in Melbourne. Bergner's father, who took the pen name, Melech Ravitch, was a leading Yiddish writer who eventually settled in Canada. Earlier, he came to Australia in 1933 to investigate the feasibility of the Kimberley Plan. It was his son, Yosl, who after arriving four years later, lived in poverty in Parkville and other inner suburban slum houses which he painted in works such as '*House backs, Parkville*' in 1938.

Bergner also recognised something familiar about the huddled appearance and cowered physical demeanour of marginalised and mistreated Aborigines in inner Melbourne suburbs such as Fitzroy. He was the first artist in Australia to paint urban Indigenous people not as proud people on their traditional lands but as a people humiliated, weakened, and oppressed (see for example, his painting *Aboriginals in Fitzroy*, 1941). Indigenous people were constantly harassed by police, suffered from malnutrition, and were forced to live in rat, bug, and lice-infested slums. Like Jews in Poland, they experienced deep-seated abuse and discrimination. Developing this linked theme, between 1941 and 1946, Bergner painted Aboriginals in Melbourne and Jews in Poland.

Another link between these different forms of racism and oppression was William Cooper, a Yorta Yorta elder, who led a deputation in December 1938 to the German Consulate to protest the Nazi persecution of the Jews during Kristallnacht. Bergner also mixed in similar circles to Indigenous activist, Bill Onus, who had lived in Fitzroy and was close to the Communist Party. In May 1946, eight hundred Indigenous pastoral workers in the Pilbara walked off twenty-five stations in protest at the shocking treatment they were receiving from the owners. Onus produced a play about this strike for the Communist New Theatre. He battled against all forms of a quasi-slave system where Indigenous people were tied up in chains in Western Australia or suffered apartheid at cinemas in Melbourne and were only permitted to sit in the front rows of the stalls while whites enjoyed the comfort of the upstairs balcony.

Despite associating with Communist artists and critics such as Noel Counihan, Vic O'Connor and others, Bergner only stayed in Melbourne for a decade before moving to Israel in 1948. My parents though, were not attracted to either the Zionist goal of a state in the form of Israel or to a so-called autonomous city and region for Jews set up by Stalin called Birobidzhan near the Chinese border. Instead, they wanted an internationalist solution where anti-Semitism and racism were eliminated, thus enabling Jews to live alongside non-Jews as citizens anywhere across the world regardless of country.

By contrast, Stalin's notion of a 'Jewish homeland' located in distant Soviet Asia was dressed up in the 1930s as a new attractive quasi-national home supported by various Jews from Argentina to Canada. In reality, Birobidzhan was a complex, thinly veiled anti-Semitic project designed to either effectively get Jews out of European areas of the USSR or to give the appearance that Stalin was not like the raving anti-Semite, Adolf Hitler, but was giving 'rootless cosmopolitans' (anti-Semitic code for Jews) a Soviet home. Stalin had long been an anti-Semite and anti-Zionist as his political enemies within the Party were predominantly Jewish Bolsheviks such as Trotsky, Zinoviev, Radek and others who were purged. Karl Radek joked: "What's the difference between Moses and Stalin? Moses took the Jews out of Egypt; Stalin takes them out of the Communist Party." During the 1930s, some Jews in Europe such as Austrian novelist, Joseph Roth, believed in 1935, that Zionism and Nazism also shared Stalin's goal of wanting to get Jews out of Europe. This was before Hitler embarked on the 'final solution'.

Having suffered from Stalin's later persecution of Jews in the late 1940s and early 1950s, Birobidzhan never became the dominant location for Soviet Jews that Stalin had hoped for. After Poland was partitioned in late 1939, many Jews from Grodno and Eastern Poland escaped Hitler's forces and moved to the USSR. Despite being sent to Soviet Asia beyond the Ural Mountains and experiencing very harsh conditions, most survived the Nazi Holocaust and lived to tell their stories. It is highly ironic that Stalin saved more Jews than any so-called democratic leader, as the US, Australia and other parliamentary democracies closed their doors to most Jews trying to flee the Nazis.

In 1990, my anti-Zionist Jewish friend from Boston, Paul Breines, published a book called *Tough Jews* which explored the historical evolution of three stereotypes of Jews: the weakling, the gentle Jew, and the emergence of tough Jews. Although Paul focussed on the changing image and role of Jews in American culture, many of his insights also apply to other countries, including Australia. The image of the pre-1939 timid, sickly, and poor urban Jews in Eastern European ghettos fearful of being beaten up and killed by anti-Semites, was replaced by Western affluent, nerdy but gentle or weak Jews from New York to Melbourne. Woody Allen, the bespectacled, neurotic schlemiel, became emblematic of a type of hypochondriac, 'weak Jew' compared with the tough, so-called neurosis-free Israeli paratrooper, bronzed kibbutznik or Mossad agent.

Paul rejected the contemporary political outcomes that flowed from the desire to develop 'tough Jews' at the expense of humanitarian and caring feelings for all people. In any case, the reality of the category of the 'tough Jew' remains double-edged. One edge is a harsh, no mercy, militarised crackdown on any group that threatens Israel's security and interests. The other, is the precarious and fragile future of 'tough Jew' Israel, still dependent – although to a lesser extent – on American military and economic support. No country, no matter how 'tough' can be fully independent in a world of interdependent resources, trade, geopolitical power struggles and extremely fragile environmental conditions. Israel's toughness will be sorely challenged in the next twenty years when renewable energy futures will lead to America no longer needing to protect undemocratic, fossil-fuel petro-states in the Middle East and thereby also possibly jettisoning Israel in the process.

Looking backward at the 1930s and 1940s, my parents' experiences led them to espouse a form of Jewishness that the historian Isaac Deutscher would, years later in a famous 1958 talk, call 'the non-Jewish Jew' (published with other essays on Jewishness and Israel posthumously in 1968). Deutscher was raised as a rabbinical student in Poland and later became a Communist and then a Trotskyist. He is best known for his three-volume biography of Leon Trotsky published between 1954 and 1963. Historically, Deutscher's life (1907–1967) spanned a similar period to that of my father (1908–1968). Both died far too young. Apart from sharing similar critical views of Zionism, they followed quite different political trajectories as my father remained a Stalinist up until 1956.

In 1958, Ben Gurion had asked 51 leading Jewish thinkers in Israel and the diaspora 'who is a Jew?' Should Israel accept the religious definition of a Jew as someone either born of a Jewish mother or a convert to Judaism? Ben Gurion personally favoured a broader secular rather than religious definition of a Jew as he believed that nation trumped Judaism. This division between religious and secular definitions of Israel continues to bitterly divide the country. In 1958, Deutscher went beyond Ben Gurion's secular notion of Jewishness linked to Israel as a nation state. It was Marx, Freud, Einstein, Rosa Luxemburg, and Leon Trotsky, argued Deutscher, who all espoused universalist ideas that transcended the narrow cultural confines of the various Jewish ghettoised communities as well as the larger anti-Semitic Christian and capitalist societies in which they lived. Therefore, these pioneering figures advocated forms of knowledge and action that would challenge parochial, irrational, and prejudicial philosophical, cultural, scientific, and political forms.

The greatest long-term tragedy that would befall the Jews after two world wars based on nationalist hatred and conflict, was the establishment of a historically obsolete Jewish nation state. Deutscher did not mean a future tragedy in the form of another holocaust. He understood why the turmoil in Europe drove Zionists to seek their own state, but he predicted that it would only be a matter of time before the long historical cultural contributions made by Jews in the diaspora would be replaced by a narrow and aggressive nationalism similar to that which flourished in most other nation-states. This prediction not only proved to be correct, but sixty-five years after his analysis, even Deutscher underestimated how Right-wing and militaristic Israel would become.

Despite a significant minority in Israel advocating progressive ideas, the tragedy is that a majority of Israel's Jews have lost much of their identification with oppressed groups and their former support of progressive social causes. The same is true of most Zionist supporters in the diaspora such as Australia. Apart from a Left-wing minority, they are no longer at the forefront of progressive causes to end discrimination, poverty, and injustice, as they once were in the pre-1960s. In fact, there is a familiar syndrome amongst fervent Zionists and their organisations that reminds one of dogmatic Communists adhering to whatever changing line the old Soviet Union adopted. Instead of old Communists praising or criticising people for their pro- or anti-Soviet views, many Zionists in the diaspora now see and judge every person and every policy only in terms of whether it is pro- or anti-Israel.

The conservatism of Australian Jewish official bodies goes back decades. It is worth remembering that with the onset of the Cold War in the late 1940s, liberal and conservative Jews began to worry that many Jews linked to the Communist Party were causing anti-Semitism. Prominent pro-Moscow line people within the politically divided strands of the Jewish Council to Combat Fascism and Anti-Semitism, such as Norman Rothfield, Sam Goldbloom and Judah Waten, consistently and uncritically defended the Soviets against charges of anti-Semitism. Yet, for decades up until the 1970s, the Soviets either played down or ignored the Jewish Holocaust in the Soviet Union as they argued that the Nazis had killed other non-Aryans as 'sub-humans' and not just Jews. Moreover, following the removal of many Jews from their jobs in a range of Soviet institutions between 1948 and 1952, Stalin's anti-Semitism led to the announcement in *Pravda* (January 1953) of a 'Doctors' plot' consisting of nine mainly Jewish doctors falsely accused of trying to kill and sabotage Soviet leaders. Luckily, Stalin's death in March 1953 ended further public attacks on 'cosmopolitans'. After a visit to the Soviet Union in the same year,

Norman Rothfield declared that there was no anti-Semitism in the USSR. Such naïve and blindly loyal views were also echoed by my parents. Three years later, they would be shocked at seeing the extent of anti-Semitism pervading everyday Soviet life.

Back in 1950, Sam Goldbloom and a friend disguised as plumbers entered the showers at Bonegilla migrant camp. The Australian government had significantly boosted the intake of German migrants which had alarmed many Jews because they were afraid that former Nazis would be included and thereby proceed to stir up more anti-Semitism. Goldbloom wanted to confirm if reports of ex-SS hiding amongst migrants were true or not. He photographed a number of men with tell-tale plastic surgery marks under their armpits and reported this to a meeting in Melbourne.

Despite these important anti-fascist acts, rather than maintain democratic pluralism within the Jewish community, the Victorian Jewish Board of Deputies (VJBD) was more concerned to appease Menzies' Right-wing government. The VJBD succumbed to McCarthyite Cold War hysteria and expelled the Left-wing Jewish Council to Combat Fascism and Anti-Semitism in 1952 as a so-called threat to Jews should a third world war break out! That the VJBD would worry more about Jewish Australian fellow travellers and Communists rather than a new world war based on nuclear weapons was a telling revelation. The conviction in 1951 of Americans Julius and Ethel Rosenberg of spying for the Soviets, and their execution in 1953, contributed to the VJBD's anti-Communist hysteria even though Left-wing Jews in Melbourne were not spies. A year later, the Petrov Affair and the hunt for the so-called Soviet spy ring in Australia would dominate national politics.

To be put in a situation of having to choose between Australia and the country of one's birth or one's parents' birth is the invidious and false choice that has long faced many migrant communities. The old chant of 'go back to where you came from' was particularly directed at Communists or other dissenters and overlooked that most were born in Australia. My parents taught me that blinkered nationalist options and identities – Zionist or Australian and also Palestinian nationalist or Australian nationalist – only created more deep-seated problems. These positions or ideologies diminish compassion and tolerance and ultimately close down debate. This is the opposite of the internationalism in which I was raised.

However, Dad and Mum were not genuine internationalists until after living in the Soviet Union. Like other true believers, they often conflated the promise of internationalism with the narrow Soviet version of Communist internationalism. Up until the early 1960s and before the Sino-Soviet split, many Communists assumed that internationalism first required an uncritical defence of the Soviet Union against threats from capitalist powers. It was only after experiencing life in the USSR that my parents recognised that any genuine humanist internationalism is incompatible with blind loyalty to a single country, whatever its name or ideology.

While my parents and others such as Isaac Deutscher were all raised in pre-war Jewish communities, my sisters and I were brought up as non-Jewish Jews. We were made fully aware by our parents of how Jews had been oppressed and victimised for centuries. Moreover, it didn't matter, they told us, whether one was religious, or a secular Jew fully assimilated into the country in which one was born, whether Germany or Australia. Our parents taught us never to deny that we were Jewish, even if we were not religious, or had no clear, so-called 'ethnic' characteristics and did not practice any explicit Jewish culture.

Yet, once you take away Yiddish culture, or any religious affiliation, or an identification with Israel, there are no so-called 'ethnic' or biological similarities between Jews from Ireland, India, Morocco, or Sweden. After all, being a Jew is not just a matter of how people self-identify or understand their origins and existence. Rather, this identity has also been externally imposed and remains inextricably related to how the larger society stereotypically labels or defines Jews. The Soviets deliberately and absurdly defined Jews as a nationality and ignored that there were Russian Jews, Armenian Jews, Ukrainian Jews and other Soviet Jews from Latvia to Azerbaijan. In Australia, government officials still subscribed to race theory in their categorisation of Jews. On May 13, 1960, and fifteen years after the liberation of the extermination camps in the Third Reich, W. M. Phillipps, ASIO Regional Director, A.C.T., wrote to ASIO Headquarters about my parents: "The man concerned is Abraham Benzionovich Frankel. He is a Russian by birth and a Jew by race. In 1938 he migrated from Israel to Australia where he met his wife Tania (also Russian by birth and a Jew by race)." Apart from the mistakes concerning the non-existence of Israel in 1938 and the fact that Mum was Byelorussian rather than Russian, he and many others defined Jews not as a religion or a cultural/ethnic group but rather on ideologically and biologically spurious grounds as a 'race'.

No wonder our parents always told us that regardless of how assimilated or secular the Jew is, if fascists or others want to persecute you, they will always find some superficial reason such as name or family tree or else quickly invent a conspiracy to justify their hatred. We experienced anti-Semitism even though from the 1960s onwards, we did not seek to be part of Melbourne's predominantly Zionist community organisations. Unsurprisingly, one learns to develop a powerful radar for both crude and subtle forms of anti-Semitism, just as most black people know when somebody is racist in either covert or overt ways.

My mother still had ties to her Jewish background in Poland and Australia. Although anti-Zionist, she still wanted to keep in touch with Jewish politics and cultural activities in Australia by reading the weekly *Australian Jewish News*. The Melbourne Jewish Welfare Society was also immensely helpful to her after returning to Melbourne in 1960. By contrast, my self-identity as a 'non-Jewish Jew' is related to being an atheist, having no particular interest in Israel compared with other countries, not speaking Yiddish, never seeking a Jewish partner and regarding Jewish cooking or Jewish art with the same level of interest as I have for other international cultural achievements.

For decades, I have also deliberately disengaged from the political quagmire of Israel/Palestinian relations. I mention my long refusal to engage with the question of Israel's future because of an event that took place in April 1988. Exactly twenty years after my father's death, the Left-wing group, Australian Jewish Democratic Society (AJDS) invited Justice Marcus Einfeld, President of the Human Rights and Equal Opportunities Commission, to speak on human rights and the treatment of Palestinians at their annual dinner held in Kew. Einfeld was an arrogant man whose significant public service and career ended in self-made tragedy after he was issued with a $77 speeding fine in 2006. When caught lying about the so-called driver of his car (who had been dead for a number of years), Einfeld was subjected to a long-drawn-out legal saga with serious political overtones. He was sentenced to three years jail in 2009 and stripped of all titles and honours.

Back in 1988, a friend invited me to hear Einfeld speak at the AJDS annual dinner, and I half-heartedly decided to go. At the function, I listened to Einfeld discuss human rights abuses all over the world for about one hour with barely a single word mentioned about the plight of Palestinians. He then sat down, refused to take questions, and abruptly departed leaving the stunned and disappointed audience of about 160 guests dismayed and angry. Some members of the audience discussed whether he had been nobbled in his refusal to speak in detail about Palestinians. I was then unexpectedly asked by the organisers whether I would like to be on a panel to discuss the issues ignored by Einfeld. Having refused for decades to waste my time discussing the hopeless issue of Israel/Palestinian politics with either the largely conservative Jewish population of Melbourne or the small, Left-wing minority, I foolishly agreed to this request.

The AJDS convened a meeting at the home of former Labor Minister, Moss Cass, in Carlton. An audience of about fifty to sixty people listened to the panel consisting of prominent human rights lawyer, Ron Castan, children's author, June Factor, AJDS activist Les Rosenblatt and me. Monash University academic, Philip Mendes, was a young twenty-two-year-old when he joined AJDS. Years later, he authored an article describing the forum at Moss Cass's house as 'a fantastic open discussion'. However, commenting on me, Mendes declared:

Frankel was annoying and seemed to go out of his way to offend the audience. He began by saying that he had never previously bothered attending a Jewish function because he found most Jews right-wing and was disgusted by the State of Israel's collaboration with right-wing regimes across the globe.

Perhaps Mendes was in denial and shocked over my factual description of Melbourne's formerly progressive but now largely conservative Jewish population? He was not the only person upset about my remarks. Others who were moderately Left-wing but staunch supporters of Israel, also stood up and denounced me.

Ironically, within Israel, there is a much more vibrant and open democratic debate about contentious issues than among Australian Jews or within the non-Jewish Australian media. My remarks would not have been unusual in Israel. Over the subsequent thirty-five years, the hopeful views expressed by other panellists at Moss Cass's house regarding a future peaceful and tolerant Israel/Palestine were rendered utterly utopian by the Right-wing policies pursued by Benjamin Netanyahu and his allies.

Despite having no connection to Melbourne's official Jewish community, I do not wish to deny the rich cultural contributions made by faith-based communities. When our son Emile was born in 1993, Julie and I both took a year off work in turn to look after him at home. Finding a place for him in a good childcare centre was not easy after he turned two years old. All the good places in the St. Kilda/Elwood area were full and others with vacancies were little more than inferior quality child minding rather than pre-school learning centres. However, there was a place at the Jewish kinder located behind the Elwood synagogue. I was very reluctant to send Emile there as I feared that they would inculcate him with Zionist propaganda. Thankfully, they agreed to admit him, despite his mother not being Jewish, and gave him a Hebrew name, Lior, meaning light. Emile spent two years there and was given wonderful care and education by Morah Ruth and her Russian assistant Betya who were both very loving towards the kids.

We used to sing songs such as 'Who built the Ark, Noah, Noah' that Emile and the other kids sang joyously. As to Zionist propaganda, I had little to fear. One day, Emile came home and told us: "Israel had his birthday (Israel's national day) but, you know what, he didn't even come to his party."

6

FAMILY LIFE, POLITICS AND LEFT CULTURE

My mother was twenty-three when she gave birth to my sister Genia in August 1943. Dad was thirty-five and as he was not an Australian citizen, he was not conscripted into the armed forces. This enabled my parents to live together as if it were peacetime, even though civilian life in Australia functioned under all kinds of wartime measures and restrictions. Genia was conceived at the time of the greatest battle of the Second World War which was decisive in turning the tide of the war. The battle for Stalingrad had commenced in mid-1942 on the southern Volga. Soviet forces defended the city to stop German and allied troops from advancing to the rest of the USSR. It was an epic battle with enormous military and civilian casualties exceeding a mind-boggling two million dead, and countless wounded or captured as prisoners.

At the beginning of the battle, Stalin had refused to evacuate civilians and issued Decree number 227 to his troops: 'Not One Step Back'. This was another example of the merciless character of the war. Like the 'punishment battalions' made up of prisoners from the Gulag sacrificed on the front line, a bullet in the head awaited any Soviet soldier who dared to retreat at Stalingrad. Similarly, Hitler's command to 'stand and fight' was eventually disobeyed by General Paulus. During the bitter winter of 1942/43, Paulus and twenty-two other generals finally surrendered on February 2, 1943. Only ninety thousand frozen and starving German troops, were the remaining survivors of their 330,000 elite sixth army. It would be another two years of fighting with millions of casualties before Hitler was finally defeated.

In Carlton, the news of the Soviet victory at Stalingrad was greeted by my newly pregnant mother and expectant father with immense joy and celebration. The Japanese bombing of Darwin and northern Australia (on February 19, 1942) had caused fear to spread through Sydney and Melbourne that the distant war was fast approaching home. Across Melbourne, practice drills, blackouts and the construction of bunkers became more common. Dad and the neighbours dug trenches in nearby Curtain Square Park. Trenches were also dug further down Carlton at the Exhibition Building in the Carlton Gardens. By January 1943, the possibility of a Japanese invasion had receded, so victory at Stalingrad was doubly welcomed.

The thought of bringing a child into a world where Melbourne was no longer seemingly as isolated or as safe as a year ago must have frightened my parents who had either escaped from civil wars or had lost contact with family members in Grodno. To add to the tension, nearby Royal Park had been converted into a large American base for troops called Camp Pell. This base was used to transfer troops to Pacific war zones further up north. The Camp became notorious for two main reasons. First, an American soldier, Eddie Leonski, created terror in Melbourne in 1942 after three women were strangled and others managed to escape. Twenty-three years later, I worked with a woman who was one of Leonski's victims but fortunately managed to flee and evade being murdered. Leonski was eventually caught after an eye-witness parade of 15,000 troops at Camp Pell. He was court marshalled and hanged at Pentridge on November 9, 1942. In the 1970s, by coincidence, the painter, Albert Tucker, moved into a house directly opposite us in St. Kilda. Decades earlier, he had painted 'Memory of Leonski' in 1943. This was one of the most disturbing images from Tucker's work that he created during the war. It featured a naked woman's body with an American flag next to fingerprints that had prised open her vagina while a dove tried to escape from a giant hand above her body. These aspects symbolised Australian male and female relations disrupted by imported Americanised sexuality due to the war.

During the late 1940s and early 1950s, Camp Pell transformed into a prominent site of inequality and poverty in peacetime Australia. Instead of American soldiers, it now became a slum dwelling for thousands of poor people suffering from a shortage of public housing and public services. Although Camp Pell was demolished in 1956 and Royal Park returned as a sports and recreation area, this site on Wurundjeri land was never restored as a Kulin nation ceremonial, meeting, healing, and trading place.

If Camp Pell was a key part of the allied war effort in Melbourne, there were other camps or detention centres during the Second World War that most Australians were either unaware of or knew little about their inmates. These were the camps for people who were born in Germany, Italy, and other enemy countries or were Australian-born but had German or Italian names. They were rounded up regardless of their pro- or anti-fascist political views or how long they had lived in Australia. A person's name alone was grounds for discrimination and internment. One morning in 1942, the police arrested my father on his way to work. They thought he looked like an 'enemy alien' who had escaped from one of these detention camps. After questioning and holding him for a few hours, he insisted that they call his boss and explain why he would be late to arrive at work that day.

Communist family life

Between starting to go out together in 1940 and the birth of Genia in August 1943, my parents had what they described as full and exciting times together. Despite the war and factory work, life for my parents as young Communists after working hours was one of social gatherings, campaigning, supporting the war effort (after June 1941) and many other activities. From being regarded as enemies, bohemians and outsiders, the Soviet Union and the Communist Party now became immensely popular. It was during these war years that tens of thousands either joined the Party or were strongly supportive of its ideas and policies. My parents had Communist friends who joined the army and visited them on leave. The war was simultaneously disastrous in terms of loss of life and destruction, but also a unifying force that saw people pulling together in a manner that was genuine and transcended government propaganda.

Young Communists at Canning Street Carlton, 1942. Len Dowdle 2nd from right front row, and Abe and Tania above him, 2nd and 3rd from right.

Before entering her third trimester of pregnancy, my mother had been working at Sackville's clothing factory in Queensberry Street making uniforms for Australian troops. Like most mothers of her generation, she knew little about giving birth or how to look after a baby. Instead of widespread education, women had rules to obey. It was a rigid and unenlightened era. At the Bethesda Hospital in Richmond, for example, she recounted how frightened she was in the maternity ward. The matron instructed her that she would not put up with any screaming and that if Mum did so, then matron would come and slap her across the face.

Apart from minimal advice at the local baby health centre, Mum had no mother to advise her on how to look after my sister Genia. Dad worked long hours to earn money but washed nappies on the weekend and did a little housework. He made a small loom at home and began weaving fabrics for clothes. Dad also made a bassinet which was rather bulky and crude but served its purpose as a cradle for both Genia and for me, after I was born. Lacking money, he became skilled at crafts, an approach currently admired by ecological degrowthers advocating simple sustainable alternative lifestyles to capitalist consumption.

However, like most men of his era, Dad was hardly a feminist. Mum recalls how unhappy she was alone at home with no support during the day and having to learn how to look after a new baby with barely any time to go to the toilet, let alone get sufficient time for herself just to relax, read or get some much-needed sleep. She was particularly upset at the end of 1943, when Dad told her that he had been invited to a New Year's Eve party and, because babies were not welcome at night-time parties, left her alone with four-month-old baby Genia at home. She experienced a miserable entry to 1944. My father, like most Communists at the time, adhered to conventional patriarchal values concerning the roles of women at home and a puritanical dislike of make-up and commercial fashion which he labelled 'bourgeois'. Despite his lapses in care that flowed from conservative conceptions of gender roles, they were a good couple for most of the time and were certainly very caring and loving parents.

Our place was also regularly full of visitors, especially Communist Party member friends, as well as Russians and East European Jewish émigré acquaintances who attended lively parties, discussions, or just popped in for a meal or a drink. Left bohemian friends were often present to share with my parents their love of literature and classical music. During the 1940s and early 1950s, my parents mixed in cultural circles that were Communist Party front organisations promoting a new array of Australian artists and authors who would become household names in years to come. At the time, a love of the Russian classics (Tolstoy, Dostoyevsky, Pushkin, Gogol, Chekhov) or contemporary Soviet writers such as Gorky, Alexei Tolstoy, or Sergei Yesenin, attracted young people in Melbourne interested in the arts.

It is not widely recognised that in the absence of government support, the Communist Party had done a great deal to promote new Australian writing and revive old authors such as Henry Lawson as part of the 'people's culture'. My parents had first-edition copies of books by Alan Marshall, Judah Waten, Eric Lambert, Frank Hardy, and others associated with the Australasian Book Society and Melbourne Realist Writers. Bill Wannan was the secretary of the Book Society and published collections of Australiana stories, folkloric yarns, and ballads, copies of which we had at home. Later in the 1960s and 1970s, my sister Genia became friends with abstract expressionist artist Ken Whisson who then became a frequent visitor at our place. We also got to know Bill Wannan's daughter, Paula, who was in a relationship with Ken. Instead of an artist's garret in Paris, Ken lived an austere life above a garage in St. Kilda. For decades he struggled to paint in an Australia that was terribly slow to recognise his talent. In 1973, my sister Maya made the only film available about Ken and his art.

Although Ken was not a social realist, he was influenced by the stirring of radical politics and art in the 1940s which also expressed itself in workers' theatre, film, literature, and visual arts. Being involved with artistic work that challenged the old stuffy bourgeois world of fawning, colonial Anglo-Australian institutions gave my parents and their friends a sense of hope and momentum. It was not just a case of adhering to Communist propaganda. Following the Great Depression and conservative governments and cultural practices, my parents genuinely believed that they were at the forefront of an exciting world that would not only defeat fascism but would also help construct a new society based on workers' rights, greater equality, and an enriched cultural future. Present-day generations unfamiliar with the 1930s and 1940s would find it surprising to learn how the formerly politically isolated Communists prior to June 1941, now became legitimate and at the centre of Australian social and political life after Hitler invaded the USSR. Public concerts featured Russian classical music, folk songs, and Red Army marching songs. Leading politicians, judges, academics, and other institutional figures jostled each other to become supporters of the Australia Soviet Friendship Society as part of the war effort.

For my parents' generation, the struggle for socialism was inseparably linked to self-education, a love of the arts and a rejection of injustice and discrimination. However, it is difficult to know what new Party members understood by the term 'communism' as many were attracted to join due to the USSR now being a wartime ally. Communist ideas were subordinated during the war years to a broad 'people's war'. By 1943, Stalin had not only closed the Communist International (Comintern) set up by Lenin in 1919 to promote world revolution, but also abandoned the *Internationale* as the Soviet Union's anthem. In its place was a patriotic national anthem extolling the Great Patriotic War and Stalin's leadership. Eventually, it was adopted by Boris Yeltsin and Vladimir Putin as the Russian national anthem with new lyrics that omitted any reference to the USSR.

With the onset of the Cold War in 1946, Communists once again became undesirables. This process, however, took a couple of years to re-establish itself as Party membership was still relatively high after the influx of 'Red Army' recruits and post-war militant union activity kept Communists at the centre of politics. The pivotal point came with the election of the Menzies government in December 1949. Anti-Communist attitudes accelerated as the Coalition government tried to put the country into a cultural deep freeze. It took until the late 1960s and early 1970s for censorship of books, films, and the arts to be gradually challenged and removed.

Similarly, many ideas and Communist practices that were dominant before the late 1960s were also criticised by the non-Communist New Left as being far too conservative. This was especially true of issues ranging from the treatment of women through to all kinds of practices affecting sexual, environmental, and authoritarian organisational matters. Another Carlton Jewish resident that my parents knew was young Zelda Orloff who married Charlie D'Aprano. Zelda was eight years younger than Mum and also worked as a machinist in factories before joining the Communist Party in 1950. In 1969, Zelda famously chained herself to the doors of the Commonwealth Building in support of equal wages for women. She left the Communist Party in 1971 after getting little support for her campaign against sexism. The CPA was soon to overhaul its policies and treatment of women. However, the Party that my mother and Zelda experienced during the 1940s and 1950s, despite its progressive rhetoric, was still a hierarchical, patriarchal organisation stuck in a pre-feminist, dark age.

Peeing in North Carlton

Canning Street, Carlton, was a broad street with a nature strip running down the middle where children could play. As others have described, there were many horse-drawn carts and wagons, including the ubiquitous iceman who was an essential service delivering blocks of ice for the icebox in the era before electric refrigerators. Water troughs for horses marked many Carlton streets, especially main streets such as Lygon and Rathdowne Streets. Every suburb, including Carlton, had at least one dairy and milkmen delivering milk, plus bakers with the smell of fresh bread, and other assorted trades and deliveries.

I was conceived in a period of optimism when the war in Europe only had a few more weeks to run and the Japanese were in major retreat across the Pacific. By the time I was born a week before Christmas 1945, the war had been over for more than four months. My mother said she had become a more experienced mother by the time I was born after looking after Genia for more than two years. However, when I was about six months old, Mum had a stressful argument with her aunt who had sponsored her immigration to Australia. She was a twenty-six-year-old having to cope on her own with a toddler and new baby while my father earned a basic wage labouring in factories. Her response to this argument with her aunt was compounded by the earlier trauma of hearing the news that none of her family in Grodno had survived the Nazi death camps. Mum was so stressed that she lost her breast milk. She tried giving me bottled baby formula, but I refused to suck the bottle. For the next period of time, I had to be spoon-fed a few times daily which was a laborious ordeal that my parents and I had to go through.

Father and son, 1948

Apparently, as a toddler and pre-schooler, I was up to all sorts of unconventional behaviour for the conservative times. The neighbour would often shout to my mother: "Boris has taken all his clothes off in the street outside the front gate". We also had a few cats at home, and I would sit them up on stools pretending to be a hairdresser, as I proceeded to try to cut off their whiskers. Genia and I hated having our hair washed when we were pre-schoolers. On more than one occasion, we would have our hair and bodies all covered in soapy suds in the bath only to wriggle out of our Mum's or Dad's hands and run out to the backyard and crouch under the pine tree which was full of cobwebs and spiders near the back fence. This was a place where our parents had great difficulty reaching us.

When I was three, my father was in the back yard one summer's weekend. Because of the heat, he had taken off his shirt and singlet and was bending down doing some gardening. Suddenly, he felt this stream of very warm water on his back and turned around to see me peeing on him and laughing away. This symbolic Oedipal 'killing of the father' angered Dad but he also eventually laughed and warned me to never do that again. My father's reaction was much less authoritarian than Freud's father's reaction to his son's rebelliousness. At the age of seven or eight, Freud had deliberately urinated in the bedroom of his parents. Not only was his father quite angry but he also exclaimed to his wife: "That boy will never amount to anything."

Unlike Freud, my relationship with my father was one of deep love and friendship. Our connection was characterised by the usual admiration and respect of a child for their father but very importantly, there was an ability for us to have incredibly open and frank exchanges of views without jeopardising our love for one another. I never felt I had to prove myself to my father in the same way that Freud and many other sons struggled to be valued by overly critical fathers. Both my parents encouraged a fierce independence of thought in their children. Open arguments were common but never lasting. Culturally, our family dynamics were not characterised either by hierarchical deference to parental authority or suffering in silence.

Peeing was also associated with two other memories from the Carlton years. On one trip to the city with Mum to buy a chamber pot, we walked past one of the cinema theatrettes that screened all-day newsreels, cartoons and short comedies by the Three Stooges or Charlie Chaplin. Outside the cinema was a life-size cardboard figure of Charlie Chaplin. About fifty metres down Swanston Street, my mother was shocked to see that I had quietly seized Charlie under my arm and was proceeding to take him home. After returning Charlie to his position outside the cinema, we bought a new chamber pot for use at night instead of going to the outside toilet. On the bus back home, the driver suddenly slammed the brakes. As the back door opened, being a four-year-old, I lost hold of the wrapped-up chamber pot, and it flew out of my hands and out of the bus. The passengers laughed to see the pot come out of its paper wrapping and bounce along the street. Fortunately, the bus driver let my embarrassed mother retrieve it before the bus recommenced its journey with a damaged but still useable night pot.

Another memorable incident from my early childhood in North Carlton occurred on a Sunday afternoon at nearby Curtain Square Park which was only several houses away from our place. As was common in many suburban parks, a local brass band would entertain park visitors and neighbouring residents. On this particular Sunday, the band was seated near the edge of the park close to the street pavement. I was standing with my parents listening to the music about twenty metres away on the opposite side of the street that bordered the park. Most of the neighbours were sitting on seats on their home verandas or standing near their front gates and listening to the band play music.

Suddenly a woman appeared with a young child and walked along the pavement bordering the park. She stopped in front of the band, lifted up her dress, pulled down her underpants and began peeing. The band kept playing but various members missed a few notes while stunned silence quickly changed into gasps of disapproval from the neighbours and onlookers. Words of shock and outrage were expressed as the Sunday peace had been defiled. Undeterred, the woman finished peeing, pulled up her undies and walked away leaving a puddle of urine as if nothing unusual had happened. Listening to the Sunday band would never be the same for the musicians, neighbours and onlookers who witnessed the extraordinary event of that day. Would they be able to relax and enjoy the music again while nervously half-expecting the 'mad-woman exhibitionist' to appear again and interrupt the routine calm in the park?

Left culture

At home, music and literature were important to my parents. Years later, I realised that a home full of books was a stark contrast with the home life of many other kids at school. Although Dad didn't earn much, he spent money on books and records whenever he could afford to over the years. My parents had a friend called Phillip Bray who also loved classical music. He told them of standing with a friend at the bar of a local pub talking about various composers, including Schubert. Partly mishearing the conversation was a bloke standing nearby who asked Phillip: "Is Schubert racing in the fourth or the fifth at Flemington?" Mum and Dad related this anecdote to remind us that the purpose of socialism was to educate and enrich workers' lives rather than celebrate existing impoverished workers' commercial culture heavily dominated by gambling and alcohol.

Family outing, 1948

Chopin was one of the first composers that stayed in my memories of Carlton. A good friend of my parents was an older Russian single man who was simply called Nicolayev and who had lived in Melbourne for many years. He loved music and literature and enjoyed sharing these pleasures with my parents. One day, Nicolayev brought us an old record player that had to be wound or cranked up rather than plugged into electric power. He also brought us a 78 RPM record of Chopin Nocturn op.9 no.2 in E flat major played by the old master Arthur Rubinstein. Genia and I would often wind up the player and listen to this music played on what eventually became a scratchy disc. For me, it was the beginning of my love of music which was especially encouraged by my father over the years.

Genia and Boris, Carlton, 1949

Unfortunately, my parent's low income prevented me from having the opportunity to learn to play a musical instrument while growing up. In the late 1960s, I was working at a squash centre in St. Kilda at night while studying at university. One of the players was a second-hand car salesman with tattoos over his arms which was rare in those days. I was listening to a classical composition on the radio, and we started a conversation about music. He asked me if I would like to learn to play the piano and, if so, that he would teach me for free. In my arrogant snobbish response based purely on his appearance,

I responded, "what would you know about classical music?" He told me that he had been trained as a concert pianist but turned away from this professional life and these days just enjoyed teaching people. "If I wanted to learn", he said, "I would need a piano and also make a commitment to practice every day." Regrettably, I neither could afford a piano nor had the time to take up such a generous offer. Very importantly, however, he did teach me another lesson, namely, not to judge people solely on their appearance.

Back in the 1940s, it was Nicolayev, as an ardent supporter of the Soviet Union, who encouraged my father to become involved with the Australia-Soviet House. He thought that as a native speaker with a clear strong voice that Dad would make a good teacher of Russian for those attending classes on language and Russian culture. My father began teaching Russian language and literature classes from the opening of Australia-Soviet House. Alongside him was another young person teaching Russian there. Nina Christesen (nee Maximoff) was also born in Russia and married Clem Christesen the long-time editor of the literary journal *Meanjin*. It was Nina Christesen who founded the Department of Russian Language and Literature at the University of Melbourne in 1946. Nina, Clem, and my father were all later subjected to ASIO surveillance and interrogation.

Very sadly, about a year after bringing us the record player, we heard the tragic news that Nicolayev had died while going home in a taxi. He went to open the window for some fresh air but mistakenly turned the door handle which suddenly opened the door. In a time before seatbelts were introduced, he fell out of the taxi onto the street and died from head injuries. We were all heartbroken when we heard about the death of dear Nicolayev, a good man and a dear friend.

Another close friend of the family was one of Mum's former boyfriends, Len Dowdle, who would also come and look after me to give her a break. After serving in the forces, he went with a group of Australian and British Communist volunteers to help rebuild war-torn Yugoslavia. This was before Communist leader Tito had split with Stalin in 1948. Ahead of returning home, Len spent a month in

Bulgaria and in October 1947, wrote a postcard that echoed the sentiments of many an Australian traveller in the era before the Internet.

> Dear Abe and Tania,
> Greetings, you so and so's. Why haven't you written? Haven't I got any friends at all back home? I've got a cramp in the hand from writing letters home and I can count the replies on one hand.

Len and others helped Frank Hardy by providing material about local Irish-Australian politics and entrenched corruption that Hardy used to research his controversial book, *Power Without Glory*. Being a gifted musician, Len would play his guitar and entertain us with folk and other traditional songs. Several years later in March 1953, the premiere of *Reedy River* opened at the New Theatre in Flinders Street. Dick Diamond wrote the text based on the shearers' strike of the 1890s and Doreen Jacobs, Helen Palmer and Chris Kempster wrote the music and additional lyrics. Our whole family went to see the production in which Len played the character 'Irish'. It became a roaring success for the New Theatre. Through numerous performances and hundreds of thousands of attendees across Australia it helped revive folk music by introducing songs that later became so well-known such as 'Click go the shears', 'The old black billy' and 'Ballad of 91'. We had a 45 RPM recording of the show which we would play for many years. In 1955, Len married Rae Hollis who danced in the chorus of *Reedy River* and other New Theatre productions. A year earlier, he published *Songs of '54: New Theatre presents songs from an Australian Musical Play* which commemorated the one-hundredth anniversary of the Eureka Stockade. It did not have the same success as *Reedy River*.

Despite a traumatic experience with Len when he left me as a three-year-old crying in his hot car for ages while he visited someone in Fitzroy, I always liked Len who was an easy-going working-class bloke. He laboured in various jobs, including kitchens and other catering jobs and during the 1970s and 1980s I used to regularly come across him in the St. Kilda neighbourhood and we always would talk about family and politics. Len and Rae never abandoned their pro-Soviet politics right through to the fall of the USSR. They were part of the rigidly loyal Moscow-line Communists who split with the majority of the Communist Party of Australia (CPA) in 1970/71. This followed the CPA's criticism of the 1968 Soviet suppression of Dubcek's reform government in Prague and led to the establishment of the Socialist Party of Australia (SPA). Following our dramatic return from the USSR in 1960, my mother had little time for Len. I also strongly disagreed with his uncritical Moscow-line politics, but it was hard to dislike him as a person.

Reedy River left an impression on me as it was the first musical I had seen as a seven-year-old. Another cast member and friend of the family was Ronnie or Ron Pinnell who played the character 'Glover'. Ron was a small man with the capacity to steal scenes in whatever role he played. He brought the house down with his comic talent. In August 1958, Ron played Edna Everage's husband, Norm, in Peter O'Shaughnessy's New Theatre production, *The Rock 'n Reel Revue*, which introduced to Melbourne theatre audiences, the characters Barry Humphries created. I was not in Melbourne to see it, but apparently, Ron upstaged Humphries in their comic *ad lib* routine and consequently Humphries dropped Norm as a speaking character in future productions. Although Humphries was later strongly associated with the political Right (for example, his long association with *Quadrant* magazine in the 1970s and 1980s), it was a sign of the times in the 1940s and 1950s that many artists upset about censorship, and the lack of opportunities in conservative Australia, gravitated to the literary, theatrical and film opportunities that were supported by the Communist Party or its front organisations.

Ron Pinnell went on to act in many plays and television productions, including the miniseries *Power Without Glory* and *The Petrov Affair*. About forty years after *Reedy River*, he came up to me at a political protest where I was speaking, and he introduced himself. Ron told me that he had been aware of me for years despite not having seen our family for decades. He remained a community activist in Richmond all his life and died in October 2021 during the Covid pandemic.

Our time in Canning Street, North Carlton was marked by the peak of Communist Party popularity and the beginning of its rapid decline. My father did not directly see the passing of the radical moment as he was far too immersed in a range of political activities. Mum also maintained her commitment to the cause despite the new climate of anti-Communism and her preoccupation with childcare and domestic labour. The passion and commitment they showed was a barometer of how much they would suffer psychologically in later years once they realised how their dream had been tarnished and defiled by the Soviets.

As young children, we were taken to the Yarra Bank to hear political speeches and also watched my father march in the May Day parade. Later, as we grew older, we would also march on May Day to the Yarra Bank, a democratic site of political expression that has long ceased to exist in its original form. Current passers-by would have no idea of the speeches, debates and fights that took place there every Sunday afternoon for decades.

Melbourne, December 1941, Abe in front row on right.

Dad was an active unionist but changed jobs over the years. Before he worked as a welder at Kent Steering and Brake Company at the top of Swanston Street in Carlton, he had a job in a textile factory in Collingwood. One evening on night shift in 1948, there was a storm with high winds which blew one of the top windows out in the factory. The pane of glass fell on him and split his head open. It was a miracle that the sharp shard did not kill him or leave him with a brain injury. Drenched in blood, he was taken to hospital where they stitched him up. The accident left a large scar on the left side which one could see running from his forehead and along his scalp that was not covered by his receding hair. Whether it was the shock of the accident or a coincidence, but his hair turned grey. He received no worker's compensation for the unsafe working conditions, typical of the times when there was no protective occupational health and safety legislation.

Not long after, another accident affected the husband of my mother's Polish girlfriend, Lil. She had married an Aboriginal man called Bob and they had moved to the Geelong region. Working with dynamite, Bob was involved in an explosion that caused severe head injuries. A metal plate was inserted and years later when Bob and Lil visited us with their children in the early 1950s, I would look in wonder at his head. The concept of a metal plate behind his forehead had to me, an air of science fiction about it. In an odd coincidence, both women who travelled from Poland together married men who suffered industrial head injuries.

From anti-Fascism to Menzies and the Cold War

The ten to thirteen years that my parents spent in Carlton – from arrival in Melbourne in 1937 and 1940 to being evicted from Canning Street at the end of 1950 – were a momentous period. They had shared political and cultural activities during the 1940s while raising two children. Dad was now forty-two and Mum was thirty. My father had lived through two world wars and two civil wars in

Russia and Palestine. My mother was traumatised by the loss of her family in Grodno and Leningrad but had created and nurtured two new children in 1943 and 1945.

By 1950, the post-war recovery in Australia was underway but there were still inadequate public services, low-incomes, and much poverty. Due to the wartime growth of Communist Party membership, the Party leaders had over-inflated views of Communist popularity and disastrously overplayed their hand in challenging the power of the Chifley Labor government. During the immediate post-war years, the Soviets promoted the 'people's front' to build the 'people's democracies'. The 'people' always featured large in the names of Communist strategies and policies, but the Party largely excluded 'the people' from decision-making. There was little or no internal democracy and Communists such as my parents dutifully followed policy changes or faced the choice of leaving the Party if they strongly disagreed with various directives. In return for public loyalty and obedience, the Party provided a unifying culture that embraced both industrial and socio-political spheres through various artistic, peace and other front organisations.

Party morale had been boosted by the defeat of fascism in 1945. However, by 1948, a concerted campaign against Communists had reduced their ability to campaign without disruption or censorship across Australia. A growing number of local councils refused to let Communist-led unions and Communist front organisations hire town halls and other public spaces for meetings. This became an issue for civil liberties campaigners such as Brian Fitzpatrick and various church leaders demanding that free speech be preserved. A case in point, reflecting the changed and very hostile political climate was the refusal of the Melbourne Town Hall in 1948 to permit a meeting for John Rodgers, director of the Australia-Soviet House to report on his tour of Eastern Europe and the USSR. Backed by church leaders, Rodgers failed to get the Supreme Court of Victoria to overrule the ban. He then proceeded to address a crowd outside the town hall with amplifiers until they were forced to move on.

My father had worked closely with Rodgers who was eager to see that Australia did not abandon its former war-time ally, the USSR. When Rodgers was away, Dad would take over the presentation of Soviet films at the Carlton Theatre. After Rodgers was refused the use of Melbourne Town Hall, he tried to spread his pro-Soviet anti-war message in other forums. The year 1949 was characterised by significant anti-Communist activity. In March 1949, pro-Communist militant leaders in the Wonthaggi Miners Federation invited Rodgers to speak to them about how unionists could support the peace movement. Rodgers attempted to address the miners, but hundreds of organised anti-Communists disrupted the meeting. In response, the Miners Federation called a stop-work meeting the following day in defence of free speech and miners' right to hear alternative political views.

Many prominent Communists were threatened with violence in other towns and cities. Rodgers' experience in Wonthaggi was followed in April 1949 by *The Herald* publishing a series of articles written by Cecil Sharpley, a prominent defector from the Communist Party, who wrote on the threat to Australia posed by the Party. The month of May then saw leading newspapers run front page stories about Ken Miller, editor of the Communist paper, *Guardian*, arrested on trumped-up charges of having carnal knowledge with an eight-year-old girl. The case against him collapsed in court as the girl changed evidence and admitted that a lady had told her to tell 'the story' to police. By this time, though the damage had been done to Miller's reputation.

In June, the Royal Commission opened to investigate Sharpley's claims about the Communist Party. Explosive scenes disrupted the courtroom as a torrent of abuse directed against Sharpley spewed out from the visitors' gallery. The court had to be cleared. Ultimately, the Commission report in April 1950 did not find that the Party was run from abroad but made other negative findings and cast an unwelcome spotlight on Communist witnesses. As a result, Communists and Communist sympathisers lost their journalist, teaching, and other jobs. Although not as extensive as McCarthyism in America, the 'Red Scare' took its toll as blacklisting affected Left political activists. At this point in time, my father was not blacklisted because the targets were mainly professionals or union and political leaders rather than unknown factory workers like my father. It is telling that even McCarthyism operated largely in class terms as most ordinary workers were not deemed worthy by governments and businesses of being pursued and banned unless they were migrants from 'enemy countries', that is, Eastern European Communist countries. This growing hostile public culture made my parents feel under siege.

From being the 'great' wartime ally, the Soviet Union was quickly depicted as the biggest threat to the 'Free World'. Cedric Ralph, the prominent Communist lawyer who defended Communist Party members at the Royal Commission and other legal proceedings, recalled that in 1945/1946 a meeting of CPA lawyers was attended by approximately 70 barristers and solicitors. By 1953, one was lucky to find 12 pro-Communist lawyers. Together with Ted Hill, a leading Communist lawyer, Ralph broke away from the CPA in 1963 and set up the highly secretive Communist Party of Australia (Marxist-Leninist). Ralph and Hill dogmatically defended Stalin including all the twists and turns in Beijing's line.

In August 2005, the worst storms in ninety years hit South Gippsland. A photo in *The Age* on August 12, showed Cedric Ralph aged 98, being rescued by stretcher in the deep snow. He had been living almost like a hermit for twenty-five years in the tiny hamlet of Balook (with a population of 13). Ralph went on to live to the age of 100 and died in Melbourne, one of the last of the old generation of Communist lawyers. While a few remnants of the CPA (M-L) continue to live on in political isolation, it has been a spent force for fifty years. Having abandoned Moscow in 1963, and then later seeing China eventually abandon Maoism after Mao's death in 1976, these surviving relics of Stalinism and Maoism remain frozen so deep in a bygone era that no rescuers can reach them, not even by an atomic ice breaker let alone by humble stretcher bearers.

Back in 1948 and 1949, both Labor and business organisations were determined to not let the Communist Party set the political and economic agenda. Labor had already encountered a major political mobilisation by business organisations and the mainstream media attacking 'socialism' and defending 'the individual' and 'free enterprise' over its 1947 bank nationalisation legislation. Chifley's legislation was deemed unconstitutional by the High Court. Now in the winter of 1949, the Chifley government used troops in the mines to break the seven-week coal strike by Communist-led miners in New South Wales. This use of troops as strike-breakers seriously divided the whole labour movement and voters. It partially helped the Menzies-led Coalition parties win the 1949 election and inaugurated twenty-three years of conservative Coalition governments under Menzies and his successors.

The contrast between Australian domestic politics and political struggles within the South and North-East Asian region could not have been greater. In China, Mao had led the Chinese Communist Party to power in October 1949 and across Asia, colonial powers had either been expelled or national liberation struggles were raging. Menzies was part of a vociferous chorus that labelled the labour movement and Communists as 'fifth column' saboteurs or 'the menace'. These 'traitorous' domestic forces would aid the external threat from Asian Communists – who were all seen in racist terms as culturally and politically homogenous – and who were now supposedly heading downwards to Australia. Following the defeat of the Chifley government in December 1949, the Menzies government famously introduced legislation in April 1950 to ban the Communist Party and to throw anyone loosely defined as a 'Communist' into concentration camps. A mere five years earlier, the allies had defeated fascists in Germany with their mass concentration camps. Now Menzies was repeating fascist practices but this time in the name of liberalism and the defence of the 'free world'.

To Communists, like my parents, this was no surprise. Menzies was far from the champion of liberty depicted by present-day admirers and apologists. After a visit to Germany as Attorney-General in 1938, Menzies was critical of the loss of some liberties in Germany. However, he also declared his admiration for aspects of the Nazi state, especially its 'harmonious' industrial relations system – a system based on banning strikes, the repression of free trade unions, and the internment of their leaders in concentration camps. In fact, Menzies' anti-labour movement views were standard for many conservative parties at the time. Following the Russian Revolution in 1917 and the threat posed by mobilised labour movements, liberals were divided between those who believed in civil liberties and freedom from censorship, and others who championed freedom for property owners rather than social rights for unionists or discriminated against minorities.

One of the primary reasons why Menzies sought the support of especially middle-class women after 1945 is that in pre-1960s Australia, women were not well represented in the paid workforce and had much lower educational qualifications and opportunities than even the small percentage of men who had finished high school and university. Hence, they tended to be more conservative politically and culturally than men. This situation has been largely reversed in recent decades and is one of the many reasons why the Liberal Party has lost much of its former support amongst women.

Menzies was never the so-called small 'l' liberal. This is a constructed myth as he was closer to authoritarian market liberals such as Ludwig von Mises who didn't mind fascists suppressing labour movements to protect business. Far too many people forget or are unaware that the lengthy 'dark ages' period of Menzies rule was characterised by the racist denial of rights for Indigenous people, the notorious White Australia immigration policy, strict censorship of what Australians could see or read, not to mention the rejection of cultural and sexual diversity.

Today, there continues to be a widespread overlap of various political and economic views supported by both fascist authoritarians and conservative parliamentary parties in many countries. Menzies regarded Communism as an alien, anti-Christian ideology that duped innocent people. He regarded the terms 'proletariat' and 'bourgeoisie' as dreadful but was ignorant of the origin of these terms that preceded communism for centuries. The historian Stuart Macintyre, in his last book, *The Party*, was scathing when describing Menzies as having "a profound ignorance of socialist history, theory and practice. Like the communists themselves, Menzies did not see that you could be a socialist and not a communist, a Marxist but not a Leninist." Instead, Menzies tarred all kinds of people with his ill-defined label 'communist' and wanted to ban and lock them up.

What Australians did not know at the time is that ASIO in conjunction with the Director of Military Intelligence expected war to break out and had prepared lists of people to be interned. Even though the referendum to ban the Communist Party had been defeated in 1951, David McKnight's analysis of formerly secret intelligence papers, *Australia's Spies and their Secrets,* revealed in 1994 the appalling secret that for the next twenty years until 1971, a new list was drawn up each year to intern between 5,000 and 11,000 'enemies'!

Insufficient attention has been paid by historians and the media to these alarming authoritarian abuses of power. Not only did these internment lists include leading Communists, trade unionists, journalists, academics, and professionals in bodies such as scientific and cultural organisations, but also the heads of all the migrant social clubs. Equally outrageous was that ASIO prepared lists of migrant men, women, and children from Communist countries in Europe and Asia – even though most were anti-Communist. Remember, many Italians and Germans were interned during the war simply because they were born in enemy countries, despite many being anti-fascist. Now, ASIO in its ignorance and obsessive authoritarianism tarred any social critic as a 'Communist' or 'subversive' and drew up new lists of 'enemies'. Fearing these lists could be revealed to the public and cause a scandal between 1950 and 1971, it was decided that only the Prime Minister, Ministers for Immigration, Defence, as well as Attorney-General, rather than the full cabinet, should decide which categories and names of people would be placed on the list of internees.

It is likely that our family may have been on one of the annual lists. My parents had already lived through the period when Menzies had banned the Communist Party in June 1940. A decade later, his proposal to establish detention camps and intern Communists was much more threatening. Tania and Abe not only held political and cultural values that were decidedly unpopular with conservatives in Australia, but moreover, were now labelled as 'subversive threats to national security'. This was the menacing climate in which they found themselves in Australia in the 1950s.

7

ST. KILDA CHILDHOOD UNDER THE SHADOW OF THE COLD WAR

Our move to St. Kilda did not mean that we broke off connections with family friends and political associations made in Carlton. My father would help organise screenings of Soviet films for the Australia-Soviet Friendship Society on Sundays at the Carlton Theatre in Faraday Street. Sometimes he would take both of us to see particular films not always suitable for children. After the journey from St. Kilda to Carlton by tram, we would arrive early at the cinema. Dad would tell us to go upstairs and sit in the front row of the balcony while he sold literature and talked to people before the film screening started. I remember that before the main film there were short propaganda films screened about how the Soviets were supposedly developing a wonderful society in both the cities and the countryside. A smooth, reassuring tone of voice in the commentary enthused about innovations in science and technology, and the progress made in constructing housing and social facilities.

Going to the screenings of Soviet films in Carlton with our father partly served another function, namely, to give Mum a break from us children. In 1951, Mum got pregnant again, but the pregnancy ended fatally in the eighth month. The still birth of a boy, whom my parents would have called Misha, was very upsetting especially as my father blamed the inadequate health care system that he claimed led to this tragic loss. It was felt as a devastating loss that probably compounded the deep losses my mother had suffered several years earlier when the Nazis murdered her family.

Nonetheless, the desire to have another child was strong and two years later, Mum was pregnant again. As it turned out, my sister Maya was born several days late on May 16, 1954, which was actually Mum's own birthday. From this day on, each year our family would celebrate their double birthdays. Between late 1951 and 1954, my mother had gone through two pregnancies and needed more rest and more support. During her second pregnancy, Genia and I helped her at home and later, after our baby sister Maya was born, we looked after her before and after school while Dad was at work. I was eight and a half years older than Maya and Genia was almost eleven years older. This age disparity and what happened to our family in the following years after 1954 meant that Maya had a dissimilar experience to me and Genia in Russia.

Although Dad had worked at Broon's Timber Yard in St. Kilda and also as a mechanic and electric welder during the early 1950s, by 1953 he got a job smoking fish. John Hadwen of St. Kilda, who was also under surveillance by ASIO for his Leftist views, ran a successful fish business in Port Melbourne. He employed Dad in 1953 to smoke fish. Later, a small goods and imported groceries outlet, Southern Food Supplies, based in East Preston, hired Dad to produce a line in smoked fish, predominantly mackerel and herrings. Dad had always wanted to practice his family's craft and smoke fish in Australia, but he never had the money or the opportunity. This was not another job but a vital part of his identity as he loved working with fish. Dad would come home late on some days as it was a delicate craft that involved looking after batches of smoked fish until they were ready. One of the owners lived close to us and would give him a lift in the morning and late afternoon by car, as their small factory/warehouse was on the other side of Melbourne. Gradually, over the next few years, Dad began to earn more, as the popularity of freshly delivered smoked fish led to increased sales. With an additional member of the family arriving in 1954, these extra earnings were a welcome relief from the stress of having to cope on a low single wage. Our living conditions were far from affluent. However, the extra income enabled us to keep our household finances above water and provide additional comforts for the family.

St. Kilda Mon Amour

Although I retained a soft spot for Carlton, it was St. Kilda that would become home and my love. The streets, buildings, and public spaces in St. Kilda continue to resonate with all kinds of happy, sad, and mundane, everyday memories. From early 1951 until the present day, I have lived in various parts of greater St. Kilda. Apart from several years living abroad, St. Kilda and nearby Elwood are still central to my sense of myself and my attachment to place. My personal memories of childhood in St. Kilda are related to how St. Kilda's place and space were connected to the larger social transformation of Melbourne as a city. These memories are also about how a happy childhood co-existed with the reality of Australian politics during the polarising politics of the Cold War.

When I walk today along spruced up foreshore promenades and rebuilt piers, I still see the old beach, wooden piers, and buildings that have been replaced. Long demolished or transformed buildings and streetscapes evoke memories of what has been lost to unregulated development. It is not just memories of the old foreshore that I remember but also how decades of ecological destruction have denuded the biodiversity that once characterised marine life in the waters of St. Kilda and Elwood. The proximity of East St. Kilda to the sea opened up new possibilities for the imagination and for physical and social activity. The architectural structure and ambience of St. Kilda were different from the single and double-storey terraced housing of Carlton. When I was growing up, there were more blocks of flats in St. Kilda and a greater diversity of styles of housing – from Victorian terraces, federation houses and 1920s and 1930s art deco apartments to ugly six-, eight- and twelve-pack, poorly made, orange coloured, brick veneer 1950s flats.

Also scattered around St. Kilda of the 1950s were large nineteenth-century mansions, a legacy of post-gold rush 'marvellous Melbourne'. St. Kilda Road was the Champs Elysée of the Southern Hemisphere lined with mansions and also old apartments from the 1920s. Today, only a few of these mansions remain on St. Kilda Road as most heritage buildings have been demolished to make way for the homogenous glass office towers that dominate the not so 'grand boulevard' of today. In the 1940s and 1950s, a number of the old mansions in St. Kilda were converted into rooming houses for single men, or sub-divided into apartments and rented to newly arrived migrants. Along with other kids in our street, we would explore these mansions and their surrounding gardens. They radiated a mysterious and magical atmosphere and were in stark contrast to our ordinary small houses.

The house that we rented at 12 Godfrey Avenue was a single fronted, Federation brick house (built around 1910) with a front room and two bedrooms off a corridor running to the back dining room and kitchen. Outside was the toilet and a laundry with a trough and a copper to boil water for washing bed sheets and clothing. The small back yard had a wooden paling fence and behind this fence was a tall wire mesh fence which was for the AJAX tennis club courts that backed onto our row of houses. During the 1950s, tennis reached its peak of popularity. When tournaments were played, we would climb the back fence to watch the matches and the spectators in the stands.

From Godfrey Avenue we could walk to the Balaclava shopping centre, which was ten minutes away in Carlisle Street, also the location of the St. Kilda town hall. Next to the town hall was our school, Brighton Road State school, which we would walk to or catch a tram to in wet weather. As to the other direction, we were two blocks to the Astor cinema and another block to the Windsor cinema for Saturday afternoon matinees. A further block or two would take us to the Empire cinema in Prahran. Going to 'the pictures' was a central part of social life, and we could get to these cinemas even quicker by taking a shortcut through nearby Alma Road Park.

Unlike Canning Street in Carlton, Godfrey Avenue was a small, quiet street with little through traffic. The horse-drawn milk, bread, ice, and other deliveries were easy to live with and the occasional passing car only briefly interrupted our games in the middle of the street. This was an urban environment playground relatively free of cars. It would soon disappear for generations of children growing up in the 1960s and subsequent decades as car-clogged streets destroyed the peaceful and relative safety of streets.

We soon made friends with kids in the other neighbouring houses and converted the street into a playground for various games or just sitting and talking about our favourite radio serials (which we all followed weekly), plus local gossip, and other topics. Like other children of our generation, we would play and talk until our mothers would call us to come in for dinner. I was called in twice because I was a poor eater. My mother would often cook me a barley and vegetable soup after school between 4.30 and 5 p.m. to 'build me up'. I hated eating it and she would cajole me by saying "just another five spoonful and you can go out and play for another hour before dinner."

Our small street also made it ideal for annual events such as Guy Fawkes night when the neighbours would build a bonfire in the street or for Christmas day when we would come out to show one another our new presents. Genia and I would be given small, token presents compared to other working-class families who seemed to lavish their children with expensive gifts such as a new bicycle or doll's house. Ironically, for parents who did not believe in commercial Christmas presents, my father played Santa Claus in 1951 at one of the local garages where he worked as a welder. Genia and I attended the Christmas party for all the workers and their families as Dad arrived on a big truck with a sack of goodies for all the kids. He winked at me as he asked all the kids whether they had been good during the year.

As to believing in Father Christmas, on March 3, 1956, Constable V. K. Fowler of Brighton Police Station reported to ASIO that:

Abraham Frenkel, recorded Communist, his wife and family are reputed (sic) locally that they are selling their house at 12 Godfrey Avenue, St. Kilda and are going to Russia in a few weeks.

Whilst at that address, the Frenkel children have been telling other children in the street that there is no God, no Father Christmas, no fairies and that Russia is the best place to live.

We children were also now regarded as subversives undermining sacred beliefs. As to selling 'our house', if only this false report had been true. Instead, it had been a struggle for Dad to earn enough to pay the rent and not be evicted as had happened in Canning Street, North Carlton.

Our neighbours in Godfrey Avenue were predominantly Anglo-Celtic Australians although the occupants of the nearby flats in Chapel Street and other parts of St. Kilda were full of migrants from European countries. Sociologically, Godfrey Avenue was a mixture of factory workers and new white-collar workers in the expanding service sector. There were also self-employed people such as a photographer, a bookie, and Craigie's father across the street, who was a small builder. Despite these new social strata, East St. Kilda, Balaclava, and other parts of St. Kilda, especially those areas with factories and light industry, had large numbers of low-income people living in inferior quality rental accommodation. St. Kilda continues to have a large transient and welfare-dependent population.

Next to us on the other side of our shared party wall that divided two single-fronted houses were our friends Lawrence and Terry Burns. Their mother worked to support the family as their father was at home recovering from a severe injury. Lawrence had always wanted to be a train driver and after leaving school he realised his dream. On the other side of our house were the Kerr family. The parents and adult daughter Heather would ritually dress up every Saturday in their best attire and go to the races. They were the quintessential, conservative white-collar family whose status and respectability had recently been shaken by their relative, John, a twenty-four-year-old

Scotch College-educated celebrity radio announcer, who was accused of strangling Beth Wilson on Albert Park beach in December 1949. The highly publicised court proceedings beginning in 1950 required three trials before a unanimous jury convicted Kerr and he was sentenced to death in 1951. This sentence was commuted to twenty years jail at Pentridge of which he served fourteen years and became an Australian debating champion.

Further down the street were the Gagens, a large working-class Catholic family. Their father had a small fishing boat moored in the Elwood Canal along with other boats. Every week, weather permitting, he would fish in the bay and bring home a large catch of flathead, snapper, gummy sharks, and other fish. These would then be cleaned and put in their additional icebox for eating during the week. A few years after arriving in Godfrey Avenue, Rory Gagen took me to the Elwood Canal, and we waded through the water in between the small boats while the tide was out. The Canal was full of eels and other fish, even at low tide, a sign of how much sea life was once swimming in these waters seventy years ago.

My sister Genia had a friend from school called Beverley Treloar who lived in nearby Raglan Street. Her place was double-fronted with a driveway that led to a large back yard with chickens and a vegetable garden. It seemed like a giant house compared to most of the small, single-fronted houses in our street. Her relatives lived on a farm in Gippsland and one day we joined Beverley and her parents on an all-day drive to visit this farm. It was the first time I had been out of Melbourne and on a farm to see cows, milking sheds, and a brief glimpse of the size of Australia's enormous bush and country terrain.

From East St. Kilda, a bus used to travel to the beach and finish at the St. Kilda Esplanade. At the time, many beachgoers would not arrive in their bathers, but would come dressed and go to the change rooms or to the enclosed sea baths to get into their costumes. The St. Kilda beach change rooms with showers were in a building that was later closed and is currently occupied by Donovan's seafood restaurant. When I was six years old, Genia and her friend Beverley took me on the bus to the beach. They were eight years old, and Genia asked the attendant if she could take her little brother into the Ladies. The ticket seller said yes and out of modesty, Genia and Beverley then went to get changed in another part of the change rooms leaving me on my own. I was surrounded by dozens of females of various ages and shapes. All were either naked or semi-naked and in some stage of undressing or dressing after showering. In my fear-induced delusion, I thought that they might all be looking at me as the only male other than the presence of one male baby. Consequently, I performed such a quick change that I put my bathers on inside out. Later in the day, instead of having a shower after our swim and relaxing on the beach, I avoided the repeated trauma of the female change room. I put my shorts on over my wet bathers while waiting for Genia and Beverley to shower and change.

Today, as diners sit and eat their expensive seafood at Donovans on the foreshore, I can still see the old change rooms where my emerging manhood was once so shrivelled from fright. The contrast between the private restaurant on the foreshore of today and the former public changeroom which was there to make ordinary people's swim at the beach more comfortable, couldn't be more marked.

How an expanding Melbourne destroyed old St. Kilda

When we consider size, distance, and area, it is quite common for adults to return to their former homes and other places only to find that what as children they thought were large rooms or houses were, in reality, much smaller. Because my parents never had a car, our experience of Melbourne was largely confined to walking and public transport in inner suburbs and the city. Alma Road was a long road that began in St. Kilda and ended about three miles near the corners of Dandenong and Glenferrie Roads, Malvern. Being adventurous, with a few of the kids from Godfrey Avenue we once walked what seemed like an incredible distance to the end of Alma Road. At the corner where Alma Road ended, was an old white wooden road sign that stated 6.4 miles to Oakleigh. To us at the time, Oakleigh appeared to be the outer boundary where Melbourne became the bush. Today, Oakleigh is only a middle-band suburb or almost an inner suburb given the scale of greater Melbourne.

Even more incredible was the day trip that I made with a group of children while attending a summer holiday programme at the beginning of 1952. Along with an adult organiser, we departed from St. Kilda by train to visit the wildlife sanctuary in Ferntree Gully which was regarded as outside Melbourne. The train trip took over one and a half hours through distant suburbs and bushland to the small Ferntree Gully Station. During the next twenty years, much of the bush land and rain forest would be cut down to make way for suburbia. The Bolte government from 1955 to 1972, failed to adequately protect the lungs of Melbourne and permitted intense urban development, first from Box Hill to Ringwood, and then to Ferntree Gully and Belgrave. This would transform bushland, market gardens and rolling hills into a sea of what from a distance looked like near-identical, suburbs.

Who could have imagined that Melbourne would grow to an absurd size covering a massive 10,000 square kilometres or approximately 100 by 100 kilometres! This is not a coherent or liveable city. Instead, it is a hotch-potch of relatively recent suburbs and infinitely expanding new suburbs whose names most people have not heard of and will not visit during their lifetimes. One can now travel quicker by train from Paris to Lyon or Frankfurt to Cologne than to travel from one side of Melbourne to the other. Seventy years ago, the trip we made to Ferntree Gully was the last glimpse of a fast-disappearing Melbourne and its bushland surrounds.

It is often overlooked that inner suburbs like St. Kilda became prime victims of short-sighted outer suburban property development and poor regulatory planning. Few current residents of St. Kilda would remember the old High Street that ran from St. Kilda Junction to the St. Kilda town hall. The Junction was destroyed to make way for two six to eight-lane divided highways. One extension linked the city via St. Kilda Road and Queens Road to Dandenong Road and an additional sixty or more kilometres of highway to outer suburbs that were formerly countryside. The other funnelled traffic along extra laneways from the city all the way to Frankston and beyond. This link between St. Kilda Junction and Nepean Highway required the criminal act of demolishing one-half of the entire length of old High Street up until St. Kilda town hall with all its Victorian and other old buildings.

Similarly, the old electric open tram (that looked more like a cable tram) which began at St. Kilda Station and wound its way through St. Kilda and Elwood streets to Middle Brighton was removed at the end of the 1950s. At school we travelled to the Middle Brighton baths on this old tram to get our Herald swimming certificates. I barely completed the required twenty-five yards distance, a sign that swimming was not for me. However, the ride on the open-air electric tram – which opened in 1906 – was wonderful and all the kids from school loved it. What a tourist attraction it would have made today. Instead, a bus replaced the cable tram and for decades the roads have become little more than sewers channelling tens of thousands of cars and trucks, daily. These wide roads traverse St. Kilda on all sides – from the foreshore to the East and north – as they cut great swathes through old St. Kilda with their pollution and traffic jams.

Since 1945, all governments across Australia enthusiastically embraced the road and property-industrial complex. When one looks back over the past eight decades at how cities in Australia evolved, with minimal or no consideration of how road development would destroy community life, we have to ask whether people would have given the green light to such disastrous urban consequences had they known in the 1940s what cities would look like in the 2020s. In 2021, there were 20.1 million registered motor vehicles in Australia for a population of only 25.7 million people (including millions too young or too old to drive). For decades, advocates of scaled city planning, heritage preservation, and adequate public transport, have been treated like heretics. Australian capital cities, including Melbourne, are environmentally unsustainable in their present forms.

Back in the early 1950s, only a minority of households in Godfrey Avenue had cars but they were clearly becoming a desirable object by the mid-1950s. One of the most memorable moments of my childhood in East St. Kilda was related to the purchase of a new car by Dame Purple. She lived in one of the blocks of flats which backed onto Phillips Street at the end of Godfrey Avenue. I don't remember why we called her Dame Purple. Perhaps it had something to do with the colour of her hat. Anyway, we didn't know the real names of Dame Purple and her friend. These two single women in their late forties were quiet, church-attending locals who did nothing to warrant the awful treatment that we unleashed upon them whenever they walked along our street. We simply reflected the prejudices against so-called 'old maids'.

Children are well known to be very cruel and thoughtless, especially when as a group they decide to bully or harass someone. I can honestly say that I did not initiate the pestering and name-calling but do plead guilty to an incident where I rolled a tennis ball under the feet of these women as they walked by. Dame Purple chased us and because I was barefooted, I received my comeuppance. As I ran away, a large splinter embedded itself under the nail of the big toe on my right foot. Dad tried to extract it with a needle and tweezers but failed after much crying on my part. He then took me to the nearby doctor in Chapel Street. Dr. Eagle White was, by coincidence, the same doctor who, much to my mother's embarrassment, lanced a boil on her leg near her inner groin area when they both attended a Young Communist League camp in 1939. Now it was my turn to suffer for harassing two innocent women. Doctor White eventually extracted the splinter and as an added bonus gave me a large and painful anti-Tetanus injection in the bottom.

A year later at the beginning of 1956, Dame Purple was nearly killed by our childish pranks. Road workers were repairing Phillips Street (at the corner of Godfrey Avenue) and had dug up one side of the street. They blocked the side under repair with a sign instructing drivers to use the asphalt-covered side, given that the other side was not fit to drive over because of its very rubbery or wobbly clay and mud. After the workers had departed in the late afternoon, I was playing with the local kids, and we were jumping on the bouncy clay side which was like a yellow/brown Pana cotta. Suddenly, we noticed Dame Purple slowly driving home in her new Holden car. Two of the kids quickly removed the sign and called on us to link arms blocking the good side of the road thereby hoping that she would be forced to drive on the side that had been dug up.

We could see through the front car window that she was visibly annoyed and motioned with her arm for us to move away. However, we defiantly stood our ground and not wishing to run us over, she was forced to steer her car onto this rough stretch of yellow and brown clay. All of us thought that nothing serious would occur apart from her car getting dirty tyres. How wrong we were. No sooner had she entered, than her car wheels became stuck, and the car began to sink. Fortunately, she just managed to open her door and quickly stepped out to see why her new car had not only stalled but was sinking. Another minute or two and she would have been trapped as the car would have sunk to the point just above the bottom of her door line thus preventing her from opening the door. In the next ten to fifteen minutes, her car kept sinking with the unwanted assistance of a few ten-year-old boys (I was not amongst them) who collectively sat on various parts of her car and bounced away thus making it sink at a faster rate. To everyone's astonishment, the car quickly disappeared so that only its roof was slightly visible. Had she remained in her car, she would have probably suffocated after a period of time buried underground without oxygen.

While Dame Purple was very distressed and alarmed at both her near-death experience, and the loss of her car, most of us looked on sheepishly but also in sheer amazement. We had seen Tarzan and Jungle Jim manage to extricate themselves at the last moment after stepping into quicksand. But the nervous excitement of watching our heroes defy death in Saturday afternoon serials at the pictures paled by comparison with what we had just witnessed. Never in our wildest dreams had we imagined that at the end of Godfrey Avenue we had something bigger than quicksand that could swallow not only Tarzan but a whole car!

Emergency workers were called, and they worked away all evening to finally extract the car by 11 p.m. from its clay/mud prison. The whole neighbourhood gathered to see this laborious process with excavators, bright lights and a giant semi-trailer that eventually hauled the undamaged car out of the bog. With a good wash and clean it was restored to its former condition.

I'm sure that all the kids in the street never forgot the day when Phillips Street ate the car, and we nearly killed Dame Purple. They would also remember the day when their parents could not get them to eat their dinner or go to bed until they saw her car raised from the dead.

The resurrection of Dame Purple's car symbolised a new indestructible monster far more dangerous than monster dinosaurs or the creature from the black lagoon that we feared from Saturday matinees. Cars swallowed the Melbourne of my childhood. No car would ever sink again in an ever-expanding city where thousands of open areas and unpaved roads and streets would be replaced by an ocean of asphalt and concrete. During the following decades, millions of cars on the roads would result in tens of thousands killed and hundreds of thousands injured. Blindly, and perhaps ironically, both Liberal and Labor governments would unleash decades of environmental destruction while marking vehicle number plates with propaganda such as 'Victoria – Garden State'.

An early 1950s education

I often pass Brighton Road State school where I attended classes from 1951 to May 1956. Although I had mostly happy experiences at school, as children, we were in no position to compare our conditions with other schools both in Australia and overseas. What I do remember is that we lacked a proper gymnasium and had to travel by tram to Elwood primary to attend their gym. The other notable deficiencies were the lack of a good school library and the inability of students to learn musical instruments apart from the recorder. As to class sizes and teachers, in the 1950s, public schools were, and continue to suffer from scandalous underfunding. Every class was characterised by the familiar regimented rows of wooden desks with two kids to a desk. Also, most of the teachers were male compared to an overwhelming majority of female teachers in present-day primary schools. Prior to 1956, this was partly due to female teachers having to resign their permanent jobs once they married.

Brighton Road State school had pronounced levels of poverty that reflected the class structure of St. Kilda. In some classes I remember that there were pupils who had hardly any change of clothes, no lunch boxes and smelled due to poor hygiene and parental neglect. It also had a large population of children from European migrant families. The cliché of the migrant wanting to make good in their adopted country was certainly visible. Nevertheless, statistics tell a different story. In fact, a significant minority of non-English speaking migrant children, especially from Southern Europe, dropped out of primary and secondary schools because of language difficulties, the poor level of education attained by their parents and the need to do paid work to support their low-income family. In the 1950s, it was usual for most kids to leave school at fourteen or fifteen and get a job or an apprenticeship. Those young people who had the ambition to stay on a bit longer often went no further than year ten or perhaps year eleven. To avoid factory work, please their parents, or aim for financial security, many studied for secure white-collar jobs in banks, insurance companies or the public service.

Prior to the 1970s, there was also little of the current group pressure on families for their children to complete high school, and get good entry scores for university or post-secondary credentials. In 1966, the year that I started university, only 18.8% of all Australian males and 12.7% of all females in the 20 to 24 age group had completed high school! Even more revealing was that a tiny 3.8% of males and 1.2% of females in the 25 to 29 age group had university qualifications.

By the time the Whitlam government was elected in 1972, Australia had languished for years next to Turkey at the bottom of the OECD group of advanced capitalist countries in terms of expenditure on education and the quality of schools and universities. Little wonder that Australia lacked a vibrant publishing and arts scene, had extremely low investment in scientific research and was characterised by a population where more than 85 percent had not even finished high school! It is easy to forget how uneducated and parochial most Australians were prior to the 1970s. So much for the myth that Menzies and the Coalition governments promoted and adequately funded education for most Australians. Fifty years later, despite a massive increase in formal educational credentials, little has changed in regard to the profound anti-intellectualism and disregard for public support of the arts and sciences.

Against a background of low value placed by Australian policy makers on education, I found school easy and mostly enjoyable. I did not have to struggle like some of the other children. Woodwork was also something I always looked forward to each week. In grade four, my teacher was Mr. Galbally who belonged to the larger Galbally clan of lawyers and other professions. At parent-teacher night, Mr. Galbally asked my mother if I had expressed any interest in what I might possibly like to do after finishing school. Mum answered that I would like to become a carpenter. "Oh no, Boris is too intelligent to be a carpenter and should aim for higher things." In reply, Mum asserted that if her boy wanted to be a carpenter then that was perfectly fine by her, as long as he was happy.

While my parents introduced us to a world of literature, music, and politics, they never pushed us to become lawyers, doctors, or carpenters, or anything else. Instead, they believed that each of us should be well educated but select a vocation or interest that particularly excited or stimulated our talents rather than choose something for its social status or income-earning capacity. Twenty years later, I met my old teacher, Mr. Galbally, who had recently retired as a principal. He was the father of friend and fellow Monash University student Maryellen Galbally who at that time was married to Alastair Davidson. Alastair was a colleague and also a friend in the Politics Department at Monash University who had also taught me in previous years. "You see", Mr. Galbally exclaimed upon greeting me, "I knew you were not cut out to be a carpenter."

The other significant characteristic of our primary school in the 1950s was the use of corporal punishment. It was not just in schools where corporal punishment was dished out daily. There was a profound lack of respect for children's bodies, feelings and needs. Take, for instance, dental care. Each year or so, our school had a visit from a dentist who checked and referred children for further dental work to the School Dental Service in St. Kilda Road. This was a good and necessary service. However, the dental service offered to low-income people, still remains, after seventy years, appallingly underfunded.

Following a brief dental check at school, Mum took Genia to the Dental Service for a full check and clean when she was eight years old. After Genia returned to the waiting room, Mum was horrified and broke into tears after seeing that about ten of Genia's perfectly healthy canines and molars (which still had one to three years before they naturally fell out) had been extracted. The dentist and student dentist blasély dismissed the horror at the violation of Genia's teeth and said that these early teeth would have fallen out anyway, so why not remove them all and make way for new teeth. No consultation with child or parent and no respect for a person's body.

This was the era right up to the 1970s when authoritarian dentists knew best. It was not unusual for many working-class teenagers and young adults to have all their teeth removed. 'Better to get it over with as soon as possible' was the common refrain. There was a logic to the madness. After all, having two sets of false teeth would avoid painful and expensive trips to the dentist for the rest of one's life, and false teeth looked good compared with crooked and missing teeth or a mouth full of dark mercury-based fillings.

My visit to the Dental Service was equally memorable. I had a filling put in by a local dentist when I was seven. An abscess had formed, swelling up one side of my mouth. Mum could not afford another visit to the same dentist, so, she wrapped a scarf around my swollen cheek and head in a bow and took me to the School Dental Service. My mother persuaded me that everything would be fine, as they wouldn't take the tooth out but simply wanted to examine my mouth. She also tried to assure me that I wouldn't suffer what Genia had been through on her earlier visit. When I finally entered the dentist's surgery in the late afternoon, I could see that he was frazzled and had probably had a difficult day. He sat me down in the dental chair while I explained that my mother had said that there was no need to take my tooth out. Instead, he wound the chair up high so I couldn't get off easily, slapped me across the face and told me that he would determine what had to be done. With the help of a nurse, he gave me a local anaesthetic injection and proceeded to pull out my tooth while I was crying and screaming.

If dentists were a law unto themselves, children also had little or no say in schools. Educationally, rote learning, or an endless repetition of arithmetic tables and exercises in spelling and writing were inculcated. A great deal of time was also wasted on colouring in maps of various parts of Victoria or repeating historical dates and so forth. Apart from the arithmetic tables, it was little surprise that one forgot most of this narrow repetitive 'education' after leaving school. There was little discussion of topics and virtually no opportunity for critical thinking where children could approach their lessons in a variety of ways or through group projects. On the contrary, hierarchy, control and routine were paramount. Every Friday, in most of my grade classes, an exam was held. The results of the weekly exam would determine seating arrangements. Those with the highest results would occupy the back desks and those with lower scores would progressively be seated closer to the front where the teacher was sitting. Front-row seating was no reward.

In grade 5, 'Mr. Wilson' (not his real name) was our teacher. He was in his late fifties, had white hair and smoke-stained fingers, and wore his three-piece suit with vest every day. In warm weather he would take off his jacket and roll up his shirt sleeves. 'Mr. Wilson' was a poor teacher who relied on physical enforcement and authoritarian measures. He should not have been employed in schools. Unfortunately, it was the era of many unqualified or poorly educated teachers. Most schools had at least one or two so-called 'teachers' like 'Mr. Wilson'. Some schools probably had several.

Those sitting close to him would invariably get a rap on the knuckles from his pre-metric, yard-long wooden ruler as he reached over and smacked anybody not paying attention to him. Boys and girls would be subdivided into separate parts of the classroom. He would patrol the aisles and occasionally thump a child in the upper arm or shoulder. Fear prevailed as he would almost push them off their desk seat if they gave an incorrect answer or if he was just in a bad mood. I managed to avoid any physical punishment from him as my weekly test results were either the highest or the second highest next to Michael Rayman's test results. We shared the back desk and moved from side to side according to our weekly results. Years later, I ran into Michael at Monash University where, I recall, he was finishing an engineering degree.

At the end of 1955, I came dux of grade 5 and as a prize 'Mr. Wilson' awarded me a copy of Captain W. E. Johns' *Biggles in Australia* that had been published earlier in the year. The cover jacket blurb said it all:

> What is Erich von Stahlein doing in Australia, doing research work on marine life with a harmless group of scientists?
>
> Once again Biggles and his Air Police find peril, adventure, and final success in foiling a Communist plot.

The reference to a 'communist plot' may have been typical of dominant Cold War stories of the day. However, following the Petrov Affair and Royal Commission on Espionage that had just concluded, it was too close to home. When I showed my parents the Biggles book, they were pleased that I had done so well but my father was furious with the teacher's choice of book. "What kind of terrible education goes on in this school", he roared, "when they give out imperialist anti-Communist propaganda to children." Mum had great difficulty persuading him not to go to the headmaster and complain about the Biggles book.

My father's low regard for our school was further compounded in the new school year in early 1956. I was now in grade 6 and in the school yard one of the boys was selling risqué postcards for five pence each. This was well before the development of the multi-billion-dollar porn industry. I remember that one card entitled 'Donkey Serenade' showed a drawing of a Spanish scene of a cart and donkey. A woman was resting on the rear end of the donkey and faced the cart with her skirt up and legs spread out. The driver of the cart was standing on the step of the cart with his trousers around his ankles. His partly visible erect penis was inserted by mistake, not into the woman's vagina, but lower down into the donkey's arsehole. There was an expression of pained surprise on the donkey's face! I was too young to understand that this comical card was not just about sex. The porn artist was probably a philosopher or psychoanalyst illustrating that if most people had only followed their dreams and aimed a bit higher, their lives would have been more fulfilled and they wouldn't have ended up, consciously or unconsciously, in the wrong hole or place.

Anyway, these cards and other soft-porn scenes were circulating around the school yard. Like several boys, I purchased a couple and put them in my school bag and forgot about them. A few days later, Mum found them in my bag as she was getting my lunch box. While my parents told me off for having such rubbish, Dad went the next day to see the headmaster and to complain about why the school was permitting pornography to be readily circulating throughout the school. Boris now became the 'fall guy' for the 'porn racket'. I remained silent and the seller was not caught or punished and none of the other boys were found out. My reward was to receive the special strap from the headmaster which was indeed quite painful. To top it off, I'm sure that the confiscated cards now circulated amongst the teachers who probably had a good laugh at my expense.

ST. KILDA CHILDHOOD UNDER THE SHADOW OF THE COLD WAR

The last years of a happy childhood

Earlier, I mentioned how particular streets and places continue to resonate with memories of experiences that took place in various years. One such place was where Chapel Street met Carlisle Street close to our school. In 1954, we were all lined up along this intersection to await Queen Elizabeth and the Duke of Edinburgh as they were to drive by from St. Kilda town hall. We had spent all this time practising with our periscopes so that we would supposedly be able to see the royal party and not be blocked by people in front of us. The long wait and the milling crowd took their toll on many kids as we grew tired and impatient. It was all anti-climactic. Despite being more excited about using our periscopes than seeing the Queen, by the time we got the signal that she was about to pass by, most of us did not have sufficient time to manoeuvre our periscopes into position before she was gone.

On the opposite corner of these two streets was where I was introduced to the world of newspapers. In Carlisle Street there was a newsagency run by a man that the kids called 'Rooker the rooker'. At the end of 1955, Mum and Dad allowed me to become a newspaper boy on Fridays and Saturdays so I could earn some pocket money. I sold newspapers for several months from late 1955 until the end of April in 1956. 'Rooker the rooker' sub-divided the paper boys by allocating them distinct locations to sell newspapers and magazines. I was given the spot at the Carlisle Street tram stop. I had a pile of *Herald's* under my arm and also a few magazines and the pink *Sporting Globe* on Saturdays.

Instead of shouting 'get your *Herald*', the boys told me to shout 'Eenya *Herald*' or something like 'Eenya, Eenyer *Herald*'. "What does it mean?" I asked the other boys. But they didn't know and said that they were merely repeating what an earlier generation of boys had shouted. I would sell newspapers from approximately 4.30 to 6.30 in the evening and then walk home for dinner. Four years later in 1960, after returning from the Soviet Union, I would start my first job in the sub-editors' office of the *Herald and Weekly Times*. But that is a story to be continued later on.

Between arriving in St. Kilda at the beginning of 1951 and departing in May 1956, my childhood blossomed but also began to show signs of ending or at least transitioning to a less innocent phase. Our neighbourhood began changing as did the lives of the children around me. By 1955, some of the kids in our street had either turned twelve or almost fourteen while others were ten or younger. Even though we still saw one another in the street, the older ones had moved on from Brighton Road State school to attend middle and senior schools. Genia went to Caulfield Central School where she became life-long best friends with Sandra Goldbloom (later, Sandra Zurbo), the daughter of Sam Goldbloom, prominent, pro-Moscow peace activist. The sheer physicality of older kids going in different directions and governed by different school timetables, longer distances to travel, and new friends at a variety of schools meant that the old bonds forged through play and shared experiences in Godfrey Avenue were slowly but surely loosening and dissolving.

Socially and culturally, the Windsor and Astor picture theatres were important venues during our childhood. At the time, most of us preferred the Windsor which was later sold for the construction of a block of apartments. Seating at Saturday matinees had a distinct cultural structure. The first four rows were occupied by under ten-year-olds eager to participate in the weekly competition for prizes. After the serials and cartoons had been screened, the manager would come out onto the stage and ask questions. The person with the correct answer would get a prize of chocolates, free tickets, or something else. The next block of rows of seats were usually taken by one or both parents who chaperoned their younger kids. Finally, the back rows of the stalls were for teenagers more interested in kissing and petting than in watching the films screened.

All my life, films have been particularly important to me. Instead of popular blockbuster films such as *Peter Pan*, *Long John Silver*, or *Davy Crockett: King of the Wild Frontier,* I remember having a sense that a new era had begun in 1955 with the film *Blackboard Jungle* featuring Bill Haley and his Comets singing *Rock Around the Clock*. We were all very curious about this film as it was not only the first rock and roll soundtrack to a film but was also described by conservatives as 'explosive', 'immoral' and a depiction of the threat posed by gangs and sexually promiscuous young adults threatening the education system and society.

In early 1956, there was also much exciting talk at school about this innovative technology called television that would soon be coming to Australia. We were taken by our teachers to the St. Kilda town hall next door so that we could see how television worked. A mobile television van made it possible for students to be filmed in a make-shift studio as we appeared on nearby sets watched by other students. While we loved testing how television worked, most of us were oblivious to how this technology would eventually lead to the closure of many of the picture theatres across Melbourne and Australia that had been synonymous with our generation of children and that of our parents. Of approximately ten cinemas in St. Kilda and nearby suburbs, only the Astor and the Classic in Elsternwick continue to show films today.

As to the under-twelves, we still had much of the old St. Kilda left to explore outside the cinema. In the summer of 1955/56, I would hang out with some of the kids as we walked around St. Kilda discovering new streets and large old houses. Children's safety was less anxiety-driven compared to today. We were given much more latitude to do our own things. One Sunday afternoon, we walked all the way to St. Kilda pier. The old wooden pier still existed and was much fuller of life compared with the current concrete and metal pier that people walk along today. Along one side of the wooden pier were a few staircases leading to lower-level landing platforms that ferries could use or fishing boats full of anglers could embark or disembark from on their all-day fishing trips. Not only were many people using rods to catch snapper, flathead, sting rays and a range of other seasonal fish, but people observing the current shallow waters today would find it incredible to know that Greek and Italian fishermen used nets cast off the lower landing platforms (with sprinklings of bread and potatoes) to haul up nets full of fish.

At the end of the pier was the old Kerby kiosk which burnt down in 2003 and was rebuilt to match the original building. Next to the kiosk was an old cargo ship that was moored to the pier by an anchor and a big rope. Inside the water-filled hull of the ship were performing seals that one could see after buying a ticket. One of our group, Craigie, thought he would be smart and get on board without buying a ticket. Hanging from the heavy knotted rope with his two hands and his legs crossed over, Craigie slowly edged his way to the ship like a commando secretly boarding the enemy vessel. Suddenly, when he was only halfway across, a worker on the boat brought out a large hose and began hosing him down with a powerful torrent of water. We thought Craigie would fall into the sea, but he managed to crawl back to the pier completely soaked. None of us saw the seals that day.

Shortly after this incident, a rock-based breakwater was erected for the November 1956 Olympic Games sailing competition. The depth of the water was much deeper before 1956 due to the absence of this lengthy breakwater that had been lobbied for by the Royal St. Kilda Yacht Club (which became the Royal Melbourne Yacht Squadron in 1961) to protect yachts moored in the waters near the pier. The further extension of the breakwater in the 1970s helped change the marine ecology of West St. Kilda as tide flows were disrupted and priority was given to boats instead of to the environment. Despite a penguin colony using the breakwater as a new home, the shallow waters from the kiosk to the beach were inhospitable for medium to larger sized fish.

Instead of deeper water, the whole West St. Kilda foreshore developed a large sandbank in the 1960s and 1970s. The Cowdery Street drain outlet that had originally extended into deep water in the 1920s, was now left in shallow waters. A familiar experience confronted travellers on the train from the city to St. Kilda. As the train departed Middle Park station, a minute later passengers smelt the stench emanating from the drain as it wafted all the way from the foreshore to the train tracks. The impact of the breakwater was also felt in the other direction closer to Luna Park. Brookes Jetty, where in the 1950s swimmers dived off the deep end and fishermen caught large snapper and small gummy sharks, was now reduced to shallow water no deeper than waist level. The same was true of the stretch of beach and water (long since removed) between St. Kilda pier and the old sea baths (which later became the South Pacific gym and pool centre). Even in the 1960s, one could still swim in this area alongside the occasionally visiting dolphins.

During the winter, the old wooden pier would be covered with glistening fish scales near the light posts on the pier. This was a sign of the abundance of fish caught the night before as schools of fish swam in the dark towards the lights. Also, many people, especially Italians and Greeks, would scrape off buckets full of muscles from the underwater posts of the pier and take them home for a meal. Health authorities later warned against this practice because of the widespread presence of mercury and other toxins in Port Phillip Bay.

Back in the 1940s and 1950s, St. Kilda foreshore continued its history as a key entertainment zone for Melbournians. It was a hybrid cross between Brighton, England and Coney Island, New York. In addition to the pier with its boat rides and performing seals, there were the sea baths, the beautiful merry-go-round and penny arcade, and the steam train with carriages that children could ride on behind the Palais Theatre. On either side of the Palais was the large ballroom, the Palais de Danse and Luna Park. I would work in all three venues in the early 1960s. On St. Kilda Esplanade were St. Moritz Ice Ring which we loved attending, Earls Court nightclub, and a jazz club opposite Luna Park that later became the site for a MacDonalds cafe. Apart from the Palais Theatre and Luna Park, all the other venues and features were later demolished or closed. The foreshore that we saw in the 1950s would never be the same. As we prepared to leave St. Kilda in May 1956, it was not just the erosion of an environment associated with my childhood, but the unregulated destruction of St. Kilda's character and well-attended amenities that people from across Melbourne were able to enjoy at the time.

NO COUNTRY FOR IDEALISTS
Cold War in St. Kilda

The St. Kilda that I loved as a child also co-existed with a parallel reality dominated by the shadow of the Cold War. Directly opposite to where I was selling newspapers, were a row of shops. Above one of the shops lived a member of the Communist Party called Bill and his wife Elizabeth. I remember visiting them with Dad in early 1956. Bill was one of those members who could not, for a range of reasons, sell his weekly allocation of *Tribune* and *Guardian*. Instead, on his lounge room floor were piles of unsold newspapers that he probably paid for himself.

I had never been to an apartment over a shop which enabled one to look over the busy street scene below. On the way home, despite liking Bill and no longer being a member of the Party himself, my father criticised Bill as lazy, or uncommitted because he had not been able to sell sufficient copies of the *Guardian*. It never occurred to us that maybe the failure to sell newspapers was merely a small symptom of a deeper disillusionment and even a quiet desperation about life and the state of the world. It was only after we returned in 1960 from living in the Soviet Union that we learnt that Bill had committed suicide a year or two earlier.

Most political parties, social movements and religious groups attract a certain percentage of people who bring with them their own troubled psychological baggage. Sometimes this 'baggage' is momentarily lightened by the individual finding 'meaning' and 'purpose' in their depressed or anxious lives. For others, the gloss wears off or is made far worse by the particular organisation and its ideas and practices. They either exit the movement or party in search of new 'meaning' or, in extreme cases, exit life itself.

From Bill's flat, one could see across the road to the building that was later occupied by the St. Kilda Community Centre. This community organisation supports all those without adequate housing and income or suffering from a range of mental illnesses and disabilities. Before joining the management board in the early 1980s, my memory of this corner was also associated with a course assignment allocated to me in 1968. I was studying a subject called Political Sociology at Monash and we were investigating different conceptions of political power. One prominent concept was the 'reputational approach' or who people thought had power as opposed to those who actually wielded it. To test this theory, I stood for several hours on the corner of Carlisle and Chapel Streets near the St. Kilda town hall and asked people questions about local, state, and federal politics as well as who people thought ran St. Kilda. The answers given were depressing. Perhaps the public's woeful knowledge and ignorance about elementary aspects of politics had contributed to Bill's suicide a decade earlier in that he despaired about the possibility of radical change?

May Day 1955, Abraham centre in front of banner

Next to our school was Holy Trinity, an old Anglican church built around a similar time as the school. The minister, whose name I forget, was aligned with other Protestant clergy, such as Alf Dickie, in the Australian Peace Council. My father knew him from the peace movement and in late 1953 took me and Genia to an evening public film screening at the church. There were only a small number of people in the audience. We saw a Charlie Chaplin short and an old 1930s film version of Jaroslav Hasek's Czech satire, *The Good Soldier Svejk*. Apart from a few comical scenes, I found it uninteresting as I was too young to understand Hasek's anti-war critique of the Austro-Habsburg military during the First World War.

During the 1950s, the Communist Party shared many of the prudish and censorial conservative moral positions of the Christian churches on issues of sexuality and various cultural topics. Conversely, some Protestant church leaders actively promoted the peace movement and civil liberties which at the time involved cooperating with Communist-front peace movement organisations. The Korean War and the war against the French in Indochina had been going on for some time. Fear of a new world war was never far away. Over the years, my parents got to know various people in the peace movement. On one occasion, Dad took me to visit an old peace activist named Ross who was a retired physicist and the tallest man I had ever seen. He lived an eccentric life on a houseboat on the Maribyrnong River near Footscray. Seeing his houseboat was an exciting adventure to an unknown part of town. Decades later, I would see the houseboats in Amsterdam but in Melbourne during the early 1950s, going aboard a houseboat was indeed an exotic experience.

My father's other connections with religious people were not so positive. Every Sunday, the Salvation Army would send out committed officers to suburban streets. They would normally set up their van or small truck with music and leaflets as they spread the word of the Lord to neighbours and passers-by. One Sunday, they parked right outside our house and began delivering their sermon. Dad soon emerged and began arguing with the Salvation Army officer. It was like the Yarra Bank or Hyde Park Speaker's corner. A small crowd of interested neighbours and onlookers gathered around him as he and the officer disputed a number of theological and secular points. The following week, a letter arrived from the Salvation Army. It was addressed to

Major Abraham Frankel of the Salvation Army, 12 Godfrey Avenue, and invited the 'major' to attend a function at the Salvation Army. My father was not amused and tried to figure out whether it was a real invitation, or whether someone had played a prank on him. Mum thought it was hilarious that he had risen to the rank of major so quickly, especially as he had to debate the Salvation Army officer's interpretation of the bible and persuade the audience while the tambourines were struck and shaken.

A more profound and deeply influential connection between religion and politics was also happening without our knowledge. Nearby Alma Road Park was one of the favourite hangouts for the Godfrey Avenue kids. Not only would we regularly play games there, but it was also a site for secret activities, such as experimenting with smoking. While we were engaged in our secret activities, we were unaware that a clandestine operation and series of meetings had also been occurring right next to our furtive gatherings in the park. Christian Brothers had its college bordering Alma Road Park. On those Saturdays when we were not at the Windsor or Astor seeing films, we would occasionally watch the priests coach the football or cricket teams on the park oval.

Little did we know at the time that B.A. 'Bob' Santamaria from the Catholic Social Studies Movement had been meeting between the late 1940s and mid-1950s at various Christian Brothers Colleges in inner suburbs such as North Melbourne or St. Kilda with other 'Groupers', a faction of Right-wing Catholics that controlled the Victorian Labor Party. This group was denounced by Labor leader, Herbert Vere Evatt, in October 1954 as a dangerous faction and expelled at the Australian Labor Party (ALP) Conference in Hobart in 1955.

At a private dinner at University House, University of Melbourne, around 1977, the historian Manning Clark told a small group of us about the famous debate in March 1937 when a packed meeting of over one thousand students in the old Public Lecture theatre debated the motion: 'The Spanish government is the ruin of Spain'. It was the Spanish Republican government that was fighting a civil war against fascist rebels led by General Franco. The debate was held in the same month that Nazi planes began bombing towns in the Basque area, the most well-known being Guernica in April 1937, famously immortalised by Picasso. As these atrocities were being committed, my mother departed Grodno on her long trip to Melbourne.

At the University of Melbourne debate, Santamaria led the case for the affirmative but lost the debate to the majority of anti-fascist students. In the chaos that ensued, including fights with Communists, Santamaria, and a large group of supporters of Franco from the Campion Society chanted 'Long live Christ the King' as they departed. As is now well known, Santamaria went from being a defender of Mussolini and Franco, to working for Archbishop Mannix in Catholic Action which treated Communists and the Labor Left as the main enemy to be fought during the next sixty years. With Mannix's help, Santamaria gained exemption from military service from Catholic Labor Minister Arthur Calwell. However, a few years later, Calwell would become an enemy of Santamaria and the Movement. In return, during the 1960s, Santamaria would make it impossible for Calwell to defeat the Liberals in 1961, 1963 and 1966, by directing the preferences of DLP voters away from the ALP.

What was unbeknown to the Australian public, or even to most ALP members, is that Santamaria and secretary of the National Civic Council, Norm Lauritz, had top-level secret discussions in 1965 with Leader and Deputy ALP leader in the Senate, respectively, Nick McKenna and Pat Kennelly. They met for six weeks at a newsagent's house in Yarraville with the aim of reintegrating the DLP back into the ALP. The ALP Senators agreed to this proposal if the party leaders accepted it. Deputy leader Gough Whitlam was in favour but, unsurprisingly, as leader of the ALP, Calwell vetoed the process.

A talented organiser and persuasive public speaker, Santamaria became one of the most influential political figures in Australia in the period between the 1950s and 1980s. He was not parochial but tailored his politics to the global rivalry between communism and capitalism. Santamaria's persistent challenge was ensuring that Christians politically and socially defended their traditional faith against the grand sweep of the Enlightenment, liberalism, and cultural modernity.

A photo of my father from the 1940s in Carlton shows him lying on a bed settee reading a book. Above him are shelves of books and sitting on top of the shelves is a famous stylised picture of Lenin in declamatory mode as if he is moving forward alongside the Red flag. In the early 1950s when he was a student at Oxford, and before he became the arch-conservative media baron, Rupert Murdoch, also admired Lenin and kept a bust of him on his mantel. The other arch-conservative, Bob Santamaria, was never Left-wing in his youth but he did keep a portrait of Lenin on his mantlepiece at home. He also believed, like the Hungarian Leninist, Georg Lukacs, of the 1920s – whose work Santamaria had probably not read – that 'organisation is the mediation of theory and practice'.

Young Communist Abe beneath picture of Lenin, Carlton, 1943

In an interview with Robin Hughes in April 1997, Santamaria said that "ideas without organisation don't get you very far ..."

What do you do about it? What ... Lenin asked the question in 1902: what is to be done? That's always the critical question. So, in the

Rural Movement, if you wanted to spread those ideas about which we've spoken, you had to go physically into country districts. You had to organise what we used to call NCRM Branches, rural groups and so on. And gradually you simply built up the organisation.

By learning from the tactics and practices of the Communist Party, the Catholic Social Studies Movement evolved into a powerful organisation until it encountered opposition from bishops in New South Wales and then from the Vatican. This forced Santamaria in 1957 to formally create the National Civic Council (NCC) as an organisation independent of Church authority while continuing to use its facilities and resources. Like the Communists, the NCC set up various front organisations on social, defence and cultural issues. Much later, Santamaria explained:

> I thought to myself at the time, there's no better way of knowing how to fight the Communists than to have a look at the constitution of the Communist Party and I suddenly saw the way. In other words, we would mould our constitution on the model of theirs so that if they believed in training cadres, we believed in training cadres. If they believed in forming union cells, we'd form union cells. And if they believed that you needed central direction, we'd have central direction.

In other words, Santamaria developed an anti-communist strategy via educational groups and industrial labour movement 'groups' to spread the message and struggle for hegemony in leading political, social, and economic organisations. This may seem paradoxical today when trade unions are so weak. In the early 1950s, however, control over the union movement would, Santamaria argued, lead not only to control over the ALP but also to control over federal and state governments should Labor succeed at elections. At its peak, the Movement had approximately 6,000 activists working three or four nights a week to spread the word and campaign against the Left.

This was an incredible feat from a dedicated army. None of the major political parties or the Communist Party could mobilise so many people on a weekly basis for so much concerted political effort for years on end. Notably, his newspaper *News Weekly* mirrored the style of the Communist paper *Tribune*.

The fact that Bishop Carroll from Sydney and other senior Catholic figures actively opposed the Church being used to control the ALP, meant the Labor Party did not split as badly in New South Wales as in Victoria and Queensland. Hence, the Catholic Right remained in control of NSW and thereby also of the Federal ALP. What appeared to be a victory over Santamaria in the 1950s, proved to be a long-term disaster for the centre and the Left and became a large stone hanging around the ALP's neck in subsequent decades. Others argue that a clean-out of the Catholic Right would have made it impossible for Labor to win nationally. Perhaps. Nonetheless, the NSW ALP branch continues to prevent desperately needed reform in Australia and has been involved in decades of corruption and conservative policies.

After 1954, Menzies and subsequent Liberal leaders owed much of their electoral success to Santamaria. Little surprise that John Howard and a cavalcade of conservative political leaders visited Santamaria on his deathbed in 1998. Since the 1980s, when Prime Minister Bob Hawke supported the re-admission of former DLP/Santamaria 'grouper' unions, the ALP has consolidated its present-day Right-wing positions on key policies. There is no longer any real threat from the Socialist Left faction which, apart from a few exceptions, has itself largely embraced similar policies to the Right of the ALP.

Ultimately, Santamaria's legacy proved to be mixed. Hawke and Keating initiated the neoliberal marketisation of Australia in the 1980s. This put Labor to the Right of Santamaria on economic policies because he was opposed to the privatisation of public sector utilities and favoured the regulation of finance, tariff protection and other anti-free market policies to protect local industry and male employment as the bastions of the traditional patriarchal family. Santamaria's anti-neoliberalism was not a sign that he had moved to the Left. Rather, it was perfectly consistent with his unchanged Catholic traditional views from the 1930s.

Like Christian Democrats in Europe, Santamaria supported rural co-operatives, small business, and non-Communist unions at the same time as endorsing policies that kept capitalist corporate interests in their dominant position. Hence, his policies were completely contradictory. He was, for instance, consistently hawkish in support of American foreign and military policy but was utterly silent concerning the fact that you could not have the American alliance without supporting the military-industrial complex based on the most powerful of capitalist multinational corporations. This defence of corporate power nullified any chance of Santamaria's ideal economy based on small business and co-operatives ever being realised so long as the military-industrial complex remained the backbone that propped up global corporate capitalist power.

Santamaria could not cope with post-Communist Left critiques of contemporary capitalism. In his newspaper column in the *Weekend Australian*, he lumped me in with what he called 'nihilists' because of my criticism of conservative social policies. The reality was that Australia had changed so much, especially socially, economically, and culturally that Santamaria and his worldview became irrelevant. Well before his death in 1998, B.A. Santamaria had become a political zombie, one of the walking dead who had lost most of his former power.

Importantly, no longer, do those remnants of the Old Right that are still visible in the public sphere, share an interest in the labour movement like Santamaria. While they were his anti-Communist political allies in the period from the 1940s to the 1970s, in the past five decades they have depended on the mining industry and corporate capital to fund their think tanks and other anti-environmental, anti-Indigenous and anti-egalitarian ventures. Tellingly, during the 1950s, Santamaria wanted the labour movement to reject Moscow but adhere to Rome. Yet, many non-Catholics favoured neither Moscow nor Rome. By the 1980s, most Australians, including an overwhelming majority of Catholics, rejected Rome and supported the liberalisation of censorship laws, the right to abortion, the introduction of no-fault divorce, and decriminalisation of same-sex relationships – all the things that Santamaria called 'nihilism'. Church attendance continued to plummet and the Catholic Social Movement and its successor the NCC, like the Communist Party, after decades of struggle, became irrelevant in contemporary Australian society.

Seventy years earlier, however, both the Right and the Left would have regarded all these eventual historical developments as either unimaginable or utterly absurd. Cold War political polarisation was so rigid that there were few places to avoid it. As we innocently played in Alma Road Park in the 1950s, the anti-Communist storm clouds would soon burst, and our family would be caught in the deluge and flood that was to follow.

8

'PETROV THE RAT'

I REMEMBER VLADIMIR PETROV AS THE 'NICE MAN' WHO gave me a box of chocolates on one of his visits to our home in 1952. While I saw him eating and drinking with my parents and other guests, like Dad and Mum, I had little knowledge, that this lazy drunkard would become ASIO's prized catch who would supposedly reveal all the dastardly secret deeds going on in Australia. Apart from those familiar with Petrov, most Australians were unaware of Petrov the badly behaved alcoholic. Four years later, this was to become public knowledge.

In November 1956, ex-Soviet intelligence operatives, Vladimir and Evdokia Petrov, fearing KGB agents arriving for the Olympic Games, were temporarily moved by ASIO from their Bentleigh Melbourne address to Surfers Paradise. On November 27th, the Petrovs were having another loud argument in their safe house in Surfers Paradise. Evdokia would never forgive Vladimir for disappearing and then defecting in April 1954 while she was left alone in danger for more than two weeks at the Soviet Embassy. According to Harry Blutstein's account in 'Drunk and Disorderly: Vladimir Petrov's Queensland Escapade' (reprinted in *Quadrant*, February 2018), Vladimir stormed out of the place without his ASIO minders hearing that he had left. After drinking heavily at the local pub, Vladimir headed home but tried to gate-crash a nearby party. Refusing to leave, Petrov then got into a wild fight with the owner, army Sergeant Bill Thompson and two neighbours who sat on him until the Southport police came. All bloodied and bruised from the fight as well as minus his trousers, the police arrived, charged him with being drunk and disorderly, and threw him into a cell for a night before releasing him on bail the following morning. Despite calling himself 'Jack Olsen', police and journalists easily recognised him, and he eventually admitted that he was Petrov. He did not appear in court to answer the charges made against him.

In what Blutstein called a grovelling letter to Robert Menzies, ASIO Director-General, Charles Spry, wrote:

> My dear Mr Prime Minister. No doubt you have seen in the newspapers a report to the effect that a person, who gave his name as V. PETROV, was charged with drunkenness in the Southport police court on 28 November 1956. I regret to say that the person concerned was our Vladimir PETROV.

Spry also told Menzies that the Petrovs were 'psychopathic' but avoided taking blame for the debacle. On the same day, he also wrote to Vladimir a 'no nonsense' letter which stated:

> I personally am fast reaching the end of my tolerance and sympathy for your predicament. You have received a great deal from our country: safety, protection, subsistence, and many kindnesses. Any further acts such as this will utterly destroy my little remaining patience.

Following Spry's letter, there were no further public reports of drunk and disorderly conduct as Petrov feared that if ASIO were to cut off their support that had already cost taxpayers 'a great deal', he could risk being found and killed by the KGB. On the other hand, for Spry and ASIO, the effort poured into maintaining Petrov's public credibility by hiding his alcoholism, had been seriously undermined.

Exactly two years before the fiasco in Surfers Paradise, on the evening of November 29, 1954, two ASIO officers came to our home in Godfrey Avenue, East St. Kilda, to interview my father in relation to Vladimir Petrov and the Royal Commission on Espionage. One was Ernest Redford, and the other officer's name remains redacted on this formerly secret, but now released ASIO file. Petrov had visited our home three times as did a couple of other Soviet Embassy officials in previous years, so my parents were not surprised by a visit from ASIO.

Petrov in context

Few people born in recent decades, realise the enormity of 'the Petrov Affair' and how its legacy loomed in Australian politics between the 1950s and the 1970s. Whether on the Left or the Right, it was unusual to have a neutral position on the highly polarising consequences of the defection on April 3, 1954, of Soviet intelligence agent, Vladimir Petrov, Third Secretary of the Soviet Embassy in Canberra. Petrov was secretly paid five thousand pounds (the equivalent of twelve to fifteen years of average male wages in 1954) by ASIO and the Australian government in exchange for Soviet classified documents and information about a Soviet spy ring in Australia. This payment was not disclosed during the 1954 election. On the evening of April 13, the final sitting day of parliament before the federal election on May 29, Prime Minister Menzies dramatically announced Petrov's defection and the establishment of a Royal Commission on Espionage. On April 19, Soviet security police dragged Petrov's wife, Evdokia, one shoe missing, to the plane at Mascot Airport in front of about one thousand screaming protestors (largely anti-Communist East European migrants) trying to prevent her departure. Later, at Darwin Airport, Australian officers overpowered the armed Soviet 'escorts' and prevented her from boarding a flight to Moscow.

What divided political opinion and historians is whether Robert Menzies had, together with ASIO, deliberately contrived the timing of Petrov's defection in order to win the 1954 election. The conservative media had long depicted Labor leader Herbert Evatt as 'soft on

Communism' ever since his leading role in defeating Menzies' 1951 referendum to ban the Communist Party. Polls before the 1951 referendum showed up to 82 percent of voters in favour but by the time of the vote, Evatt and many others had helped change public opinion by whittling support down to only 49.4 percent.

As to the Royal Commission, the fact that it opened on May 17th in the midst of the 1954 election campaign indicates political contrivance given it could have been postponed for a further two weeks until the election was over. Although Menzies and Evatt did not raise Petrov's defection as a central issue in the election, opening the Royal Commission twelve days before the election would have harmed the ALP's electoral campaign given that conservative media depicted Labor as weak on protecting Australia from Communism. The Coalition won the 1954 election with a reduced majority, but the Royal Commission ran for ten months into 1955 investigating the character and extent of Soviet espionage in Australia. During its public hearings, the Petrov Affair also raised unavoidable questions about the judgement and role of Evatt who believed that Menzies and ASIO had conspired to damage both himself, members of his staff and the ALP.

Prior to Petrov's defection, Evatt had agreed to B.A. Santamaria's and the Labor Right's policy demands. The ALP ran in 1954 on what was described by those on the Left as 'the most Right-wing platform ever'. Labor had been ahead in the opinion polls, but the Queen had just concluded her extraordinarily successful long tour which would have boosted Menzies' electoral standing. His public display of devotion to the Crown was well-known. Questions remain about the role played by both the Petrov Affair, and the Royal Commission on Espionage (where Evatt's staff were investigated) in the subsequent ALP loss and 'the Split' within Labor in late 1954 and early 1955. Without the Petrov Affair and its repercussions, would 'the Split' have occurred that kept the Labor Party out of government until 1972?

When Ernest Redford and his unnamed colleague from ASIO came to our home in late November 1954, the timing was peculiar.

The Royal Commission had already issued an interim report in October. Prior to its release, Redford had lived with the Petrovs during the Royal Commission and had interrogated them concerning all the information they had about individuals that they had contact with across Australia. Later, Redford related in a report and interviews the terrible unhappiness of Evdokia whose wailing at night and tantrums during the day drove Redford mad. She was more intelligent and stronger than Vladimir but was more difficult than Vladimir who drank and argued with her.

In a scathing 'Top Secret' report to Ron Richards, ASIO Deputy Director General (Operations) entitled 'Conduct and Problems of a Safe House', ASIO officers (including Redford) outlined the difficulties they faced in the immediate period following the defection of the Petrovs in April 1954. Vladimir was described as "a lazy man, unwilling to revert to any form of manual or mental labour. He envisaged his future as having no menial tasks, plenty of money, a reasonable home, and his time spent in indulging in hunting and fishing; his favourite sports." The report declared that his alcoholism knew no bounds and caused great embarrassment, including running down the street in his underpants looking for women. "Drinking is an obsession with him, and now controls his existence ... The effect of drunkenness can well be described as a paranoic state. His right eye becomes stary, his left half closed, but the general appearance is that of a madman. In such a state, he is incapable of reason or logic, and he becomes aggressive, ever ready to air his grievances. His voice assumes bellowing proportions, his language filthy. At times he becomes physically aggressive, but this is usually directed against his wife."

A summary analysis of Evdokia was equally damning. She was characterised as attractive on first meeting, but was "shrewd, cold, calculating, vain and selfish, a woman who appeals for sympathy yet gives little in return." ASIO agents clearly had no love of the Petrovs and were fed up with their constant arguments and failure to fully co-operate. They had a strong dislike of their mercenary attitudes, including a list of claims drawn up by Petrova that they should be paid over £20,000 as compensation for their personal losses. The Petrovs also made ungrateful criticisms of their accommodation and menu, despite all the things ASIO had done for them. While the official report used polite language, in plain Aussie masculinist terms of the day one could imagine ASIO men privately calling Vladimir 'a pathetic no-hoper' and Evdokia 'a cold, manipulative bitch'.

Ernest Redford standing behind Vladimir and Evdokia Petrov and ASIO's Ron Richards.

During their time in the safe house at Pittwater, on August 31, 1954, ASIO headquarters in Sydney sent Redford and the other Interrogation Officers a point form summary on 'Abraham Frenkel' together with questions that should be put to both Vladimir and Evdokia Petrov concerning their intelligence and personal knowledge of my father's political activity and meetings with other Soviet Embassy officials. Point 3 stated:

> He probably met PETROV for the first time at his home at 12 Godfrey Ave., East St. Kilda when he gave a farewell party for Nikolai Vansiliovich YALINICHEFF, on 5th July 1952.

FRENKEL has recently declared that he would like to testify at the Royal Commission that PETROV has been intoxicated in his company on several occasions. At YALINICHEFF'S party he says that PETROV and ANTON CHERVINSKI came to blows over a personal dispute.

To clarify, when Petrov visited our home for a party to farewell young Soviet seaman, Nikolai Yalinicheff (also spelt Ialynychev), it was because Petrov himself processed Yalinicheff for his return to the Soviet Union. This was unusual because another Embassy official, Gordeev, usually handled all people wishing to be repatriated. Yalinicheff had jumped ship in Alexandria, Egypt, in January 1950, and had made his own way to Australia. Sheila Fitzpatrick, a scholar of the Russian communities in Australia, argues that Soviet intelligence was probably recovering one of their agents that they had launched two and a half years earlier in Alexandria, hence Petrov's involvement in processing his return. Yet, following his defection and debriefing by ASIO's Ernest Redford on September 29, 1954, Petrov contradicted Fitzpatrick's claim that Soviet intelligence were recovering one of their men. Instead, Petrov asserted that Yalinicheff "definitely did not carry out any assignments in Australia on behalf of the Soviet Union and his repatriation was in my opinion genuine. Yalincheff approached the Soviet Embassy for repatriation to the Soviet Union on the advice of Frenkel with whom he was on friendly terms."

Whatever Yalinichev's real status as a displaced person or Soviet agent, my father and other guests at his farewell party were certainly not aware of it and merely treated him as someone wishing to return home. Interestingly, Petrov also told ASIO on January 11, 1955, about the other guests at our home to farewell Yalinicheff in July 1952. These included three Russians who feared giving Petrov their surnames, and a Malay student at the University of Melbourne, Subramanian Ratnavel, whom Petrov wanted to recruit for the MVD. In a further interview with ASIO on September 7, 1955, about the party for Yalinicheff, Petrov stated that Anton Chervinski (with whom he got into a physical fight at our home) sold tickets for Russian films at the Carlton Theatre but was anti-Soviet. According to Petrov, Chervinski criticised Yalinicheff and said: "Why are you going back, you will be killed."

On the instructions concerning which points ASIO officers should ask the Petrovs about my father, a central question remains unanswered. Did my father actually contact the Royal Commission about testifying, or did an ASIO informant report that Dad had told other Russians in Melbourne that if called, he intended to testify? As ASIO had not yet interviewed my father or asked Petrov about Frenkel, how else did they know that Petrov and Chervinski had come to blows at our home other than through one of their undercover informants?

On September 29, 1954, Petrova stated that she had never met Frenkel but recalled his name in connection with a passport application to re-enter the USSR. She also knew nothing about my father's meeting with Soviet attaché Janis Edvardovich Plaitkais other than overhearing a conversation between Plaitkais and her husband at the Embassy mentioning that Plaitkais was in contact with Frenkel.

As to Vladimir Petrov's answer to ASIO's interrogators concerning my father, there is an interesting side story of historical coincidences. In 1984, the Hawke government opened the Petrov and Royal Commission files to the public. During the next two to three years, Robert Manne began researching his book *The Petrov Affair* (published in 1987). More than fifteen years later, over dinner, he told me that he remembered my father's file from his research. My father stood out in his memory because he was the only person in Australia who was not intimidated by ASIO. Other Communists and people on the Left feared the publicity and negative consequences of being called to appear before the Royal Commission. They would politely offer ASIO investigators cups of tea, while my father, by contrast, told them to get their dirty feet off my sister's bed.

Robert Manne was also approached by journalist, Sam Lipski, to assist in the writing of a mini-series of the same name. Lipski produced the television series together with Bob Weiss whom I knew as a fellow student in Politics at Monash University during the late

1960s. In another coincidence, my sister Maya, lived at that time in a block of flats in St. Kilda. The flat below her was rented by the actor, Alex Menglet, who played Vladimir Petrov in the two-part television series screened on Channel 9 in 1987. One day during the television production, Alex, whom she knew, brought Maya an ASIO file about Dad which was part of the released files that the film producers were using to write the script.

In the document dated September 29, 1954, the same day as Evdokia's answer to ASIO about my father, Vladimir Petrov stated:

> FRENKEL was considered a useful person by the Soviet Embassy, for the purpose of establishing contacts amongst displaced persons, but he was not considered for MVD work.

Here we had it from the horse's mouth. The assessment by even a lazy intelligence officer such as Petrov was that anybody who knew my father would have quickly recognised that he was too honest, too outspoken in his opinions and lacking discretion to become someone engaged in deception, a condition required for ongoing espionage and subterfuge.

Given Petrov's declaration that my father was not suitable for espionage work, why then did ASIO officers come to interrogate him two months later at the end of November on behalf of the Royal Commission on Espionage? It was clear that 'espionage' was merely an excuse to investigate his contact with Soviet Embassy officials, his involvement with the Australia-Soviet Friendship Society, Russian emigres, and the Communist Party of Australia. All were considered by ASIO as a threat to Australia's security and regarded as illegitimate subversive organisations or groups of individuals. The so-called defenders of the 'Free World', had a very narrow concept of democracy and civil liberty.

Former Communist and editor of *Tribune*, David McKnight, points out in his 1994 book, *Australia's Spies and Their Secrets*, that ASIO saw little distinction between espionage and subversion. They only saw the

Communist Party in narrow terms as an operational arm of Soviet intelligence – in the period from the 1920s to the 1960s – because of the CPA's former rigid adherence to Soviet Marxism. ASIO refused to recognise that the CPA was also very much an Australian radical group which "drew from the wellsprings of native Australian radicalism: trade unionism, the Irish-English conflict, egalitarianism, republicanism and intellectual dissent." Unsurprisingly, Menzies and ASIO also regarded church leaders and other members of the peace movement as pro-Soviet subversives rather than people genuinely worried about the outbreak of another world war. They opposed rights for Aborigines and worried about Communist attempts to unionise Indigenous workers who were treated appallingly by their pastoral owners.

From its origins in 1949, ASIO and its conservative supporters were ideologically blind and organisationally unable to recognise that ninety-nine percent of members of the Communist Party of Australia were not Soviet subversives but rather wished to change Australian society to make it more equal and democratic. ASIO was also unable to distinguish between the varieties of socialism in non-Communist parties and movements (such as the ALP and later the 1960s New Left) and why the latter was opposed to the Soviet Stalinist model. Stereotypes about Communists, Jews (anti-Semitism), or xenophobia towards those with an accent or those who spoke languages they didn't understand, prevailed.

ASIO versus Frenkel

It is no surprise that Robert Manne remembered ASIO's interrogation of my father on November 29, 1954. Judging by the ten-page report signed a few days later by Ernest Oliver Redford on December 3, it was clear that they had probably encountered few others like him. The following is an abridged version of Redford's account minus some details which I will come to shortly. I believe that large parts of the transcript of this recorded interview are important to read as they reveal both my father's foolish assertiveness and combativeness as well as the assumption by ASIO that Dad was a 'subversive Communist'. Redford's report begins:

> I am an officer of the Australian Security Intelligence Organisation. At 6 p.m. on Monday, 29th November, 1954, in company with Mr. X of the Victorian Office of A.S.I.O. I went to No.12 Godfrey Avenue, East St. Kilda, where I saw a male person.
> I said to this person, "Is your name Abraham FRENKEL?"
> He replied, "That is me – what do you want?"
> I said, "We are officers of the Commonwealth Attorney General's Department, and we wish to see you concerning matters now under enquiry by the Royal Commission on Espionage."
> He replied, "Oh, that is the Petrov case."
> I said, "Yes, it is in connection with that. Do you know Petrov?"
> He replied, "Yes, the drunkard – I do know him."
> Mr. X then said to FRENKEL, "Did you know any other members of the Soviet Embassy with whom you made any contact?"
> He replied, "Yes, I know a lot."
> Mr. X said, "Who was the first member of the Soviet Embassy with whom you made contact?"
> He replied, "VLASSOV."
> Mr. X then said, "What was the reason for your first contact with VLASSOV?"
> He replied, "I am a Soviet citizen. I have been here 15 years. I had my passport prolonged by the Soviet Embassy. It was in connection with citizenship only."
> I said, "You are still a Soviet citizen?"
> He replied, "Yes, and proud of it."
> I said, "Have you ever applied for naturalisation as an Australian citizen?"
> He replied, "No, I haven't. I intend to return to Russia."
> I said, "Why have you not applied for naturalisation?"
> He replied, "Well, if an Australian went to America and wanted

to live there for 15 years, it would not be necessary for him to change his nationality and I think the same should apply to me."

I said, "That is a matter which concerns yourself."

Mr. X said, "Did you ever meet VLASSOV personally?"

FRENKEL replied, "No, I never met him personally. I received correspondence from him but that had been opened like all my correspondence. It was even opened with PETROV and SADOVNIKOV."

Redford and Mr. X then proceed to ask Dad questions about various Soviet Embassy staff such as Lifanov, Makarov and Sadovnikov. My father replied that his contact was only related to his passport renewal and annual application for a re-entry visa. He also said that Makarov and Sadovnikov came to his place at 317 Canning Street North Carlton sometime in the late 1940s and met Nicolayev, who was now dead. Dad said the three of them discussed literature.

By this time, it is clear that my father is becoming progressively annoyed with the tone of ASIO's questioning.

FRENKEL then said, "Why do you want to know all these questions. Do you think everyone is a bloody spy? Is that what this gentleman, if you can call a bastard a gentleman, told you?"

I said, "You will realise, Mr. FRENKEL, that we are here to ask you questions, not to enter into any discussion with you concerning PETROV."

Following a few more questions about Makarov and Sadovnikov, Mr. X then asked:

"After SADOVNIKOV, who was the member of the Soviet Embassy with whom you had contact?"

He replied, "PETROV, the rat. He is a traitor to his own country and a traitor to this country too."

I said, "Did you regard him as a traitor to this country and to his own country during your association with him?"

He replied, "That is different." "He came to my home. We extended him hospitality. He abused this country; now he has abused his own and got £5000 for it."

I said, "How many times did you meet PETROV?"

He replied, "About three. I contacted him each year about my passport."

Mr. X, "How did you first make contact?"

He said, "I wrote to him about my passport."

I said, "Did PETROV ever visit you at home?"

He replied, "Yes, the bastard, he sat at that table and got drunk."

I said, "How did PETROV come to visit you on the first occasion at your home?"

He replied, "A boy we knew, Nicolai YALINICHEFF, who had run away from a Russian ship was being repatriated to the Soviet Union and he rang me as we were giving him a party and asked me if he could bring a friend. He would not tell me the name of the friend but when they arrived, he introduced me to Mihailovitch PETROV, the person who has now sold his country."

COMMENT: *Yalinicheff must have called Dad at work, as we could not afford a telephone at home.*

I said, "Were there any other persons present at that party?"

He replied, "Yes, two New Australian friends – one played a mandolin. They were friends of Nicolai: I do not know their names. We had a lot to drink. Petrov got drunk."

I said, "Who supplied the liquor for the party?"

He replied, "We all supplied it."

I said, "Was anyone else drunk?"

He replied, "We all had plenty."

Redford then asks how many times Petrov visited in 1952. My mother enters the room with a reminder that Petrov came the next day for another drinking session and one more time with someone

'PETROV THE RAT'

who drove him, but the person did not come in. The report continues:

> FRENKEL then said, "So you reckon I may be called to tell what I know about this traitor?"
>
> I said, "That will be a matter for the Royal Commission to decide."
>
> He said, "I never could believe that a Russian patriot would turn a traitor like PETROV did, and like Dr. Evatt said he did. He is a bloody man as a Russian and I hate him. He is a traitor to Russia and to Australia too."
>
> I said, "When did the visits of PETROV to your home take place."
>
> He said, "In 1952 I think."
>
> FRENKEL said, "Excuse me, will you tell the Commission all I have said to you about PETROV?"
>
> I replied, "The Royal Commission will be fully advised as to our interview with you."
>
> He said, "In that case I will be careful from now on."
>
> Mr. X then said, "Did you ever see PETROV at all at the Soviet Embassy in Canberra?"
>
> He replied, "No."
>
> Mr. X, "Did you do anything for PETROV?"
>
> He replied, "No."
>
> Mr. X, "Did PETROV ask you to do anything for him?"
>
> He replied, "No, but I asked him for literature and did not get any."

COMMENT: *Dad was always keen to read Russian books.*

Both Redford and Mr. X now turned to questions about attaché Janis Plaitkais and how Dad met Plaitkais through a friend called Galanin.

> Mr. X said, "Who is GALANIN?"
>
> FRENKEL replied, "GALANIN is one of the New Australians like myself who could not get £5,000. He is a young chap – a mechanic, I think."

COMMENT: *My father's sarcastic remarks were due to £5,000 being an enormous amount compared with the annual wage of £300 to £400 for the vast majority of male workers and £140 to £200 for females. With the money Petrov received from ASIO, he bought a house in the modest Melbourne suburb of Bentleigh which in 1954–55 would have cost between £3,000 and £4,000 pounds. Today, similar houses in Bentleigh cost between $1.2 and $1.7 million.*

Following further questions about Plaitkais, Dad told ASIO that he had met him on two or three occasions, in June 1953. He said that he accompanied Plaitkais to a Greek restaurant in the city, then a Soviet film and to visit somebody in Fitzroy that Dad did not know. Dad then took him back to his hotel. On the second occasion, Plaitkais came to his home and brought Dad some Russian records. They also went to the cinema and around the beach before visiting someone in Brighton that my father did not know.

> Mr. X, "Do you know what PLAITKAIS had to see this person about?"
> He replied, "No."
> Mr. X, "Did you go in with PLAITKAIS while he visited this person?"
> FRENKEL replied, "No. I went to a hotel for a while, and then went to a shop and bought some sweets."
> Mr. X, "You have no idea then what PLAITKAIS saw this person about?"
> FRENKEL replied, "No, I have no idea, He never told me."
> I said, "Why are you so friendly with PLAITKAIS?"
> He replied, "He was one of my own nationality and I am entitled to be friendly with him."

COMMENT: *Actually, Plaitkais was Latvian rather than Russian, but what Dad meant here was that he was a fellow Soviet citizen.*

'PETROV THE RAT'

Redford and Mr. X then asked why my father had dealings at the same time with both Petrov and Plaitkais if it was only about passport matters.

He replied, "PETROV told me that PLAITKAIS was his right-hand man and I could deal with him at any time."
I said, "What did you think when PETROV told you that?"
He replied, "That PLAITKAIS was his assistant."
I said, "Assistant in what capacity?"
He replied, "In the Embassy. In repatriation."
I said, "Anything else?"
He said, "No, no."
I said, "Were you aware that PETROV and PLAITKAIS were M.V.D. personnel?"
He replied, "No, I was not."

ASIO proceeded to ask whether he knew Gordeev and Pavlov from the Embassy, but my father did not. He was also asked whether he volunteered to assist members of the Embassy in any way in regard to persons with whom they wished to make contact and whether he worked for the Embassy in the repatriation of Soviet citizens. My father said no to all these questions. Redford then asked:

"Do you take any special interest in the repatriation of Soviet Citizens from Australia?"
He replied, "of all the New Australians in the Russian community I know, the majority want to return to Russia."

COMMENT: *Dad was deluded in either hoping or imagining that the majority of ex-Soviet displaced persons would return. The simple truth was that hardly anybody apart from a handful of people shared his intention of returning.*

After answering questions about men called Bronski and Ostrowski who either returned to the USSR or intended to return, Redford asked,

"Have you ever applied for repatriation to the Soviet Union?"
He replied, "Yes, I have."
I said, "Was your application granted?"
He replied, "No or I wouldn't be here now."
I said, "Do you know of any reason why your application was not granted?"
He replied, "It is like this. When you have been away from Russia for a long time it is very difficult to get back. It is easy for New Australians though."
I said, "Why are you and your family so anxious to return to the Soviet Union?"
He replied, "I am a man of culture. This country lacks culture and I would like to bring my children up in the atmosphere of culture."
I said, "Are you a member of the Communist Party of Australia?"
He replied, "I am not."

COMMENT: *Regarding Communist Party membership, my father was telling the truth. When he received his Soviet passport in 1947, the CPA Carlton branch told him that he could no longer remain a member of the Party. They could not afford to have Soviet citizens compromising the independent standing of the Party, especially following media and political accusations of so-called Soviet-controlled 'Communist subversion'. However, the following answers make it clear where Dad's sympathies lay.*

I said, "Do you support the Communist Party?"
He replied, "Well, if it means better education, more schools, better employment, then I do. I do not support this Capitalist Government and this man, Menzies, who is like PETROV."

(Note, ASIO transcribe Menzies' name in lower case unlike all the foreign names in upper case.)

I said, "Do you attend meetings of the Communist Party?"

He replied, "I go to the Yarra Bank and anywhere I can learn anything of interest to me."

I said, "Do you consider yourself a loyal citizen of Australia?"

FRENKEL'S wife, interjecting, said, "That is not a fair question."

FRENKEL said, "Do you know what you mean by that question?"

I said, "I am fully aware of what I meant when I asked the question, which I will repeat." Question repeated.

COMMENT: *Redford ignored the fact that my father had already told him that he holds a Soviet passport and is not formally a citizen of Australia, so the loyalty question is blatantly politically prejudiced. In short, Redford's questions follow the organisational political culture of ASIO that assumes that Communists and Russians are either actual or potential traitors and engaged in subversion.*

FRENKEL replies: "I obey the law. If I see a blind man I will help him across the street, but if you mean I should be asked to fight to kill my brothers I would refuse. You could throw me into a concentration camp. I would still refuse."

I said, "You are still evading my question. Are you embarrassed?"

He replied, "No, but it is unfair."

Mr. Ernest said, "What would be your attitude if, for example, a state of emergency existed?"

He replied, "Well, if it means war between Russia and Australia, I would not take up arms against Russia."

COMMENT: *It is clear that Redford followed the 1940s and 1950s McCarthyite line of questioning, namely: "Have you ever been, or are you still a member of the Communist Party?" The major difference is that in Australia there was an openly authoritarian political culture devoid of any protection offered by a Bill of Rights as in the US. Those summoned to appear before the House Committee on UnAmerican Activities could plead the 5th Amendment that gave people the right to not self-incriminate themselves and remain silent. In Australia, Redford tried to bully my father into admitting that he was 'disloyal', hence, his follow-up response:*

"You are still evading my question. Are you embarrassed?"

Upon hearing my father's declaration that he would not fight in war, Redford states:

"The Interview then concluded. As we were leaving the premises FRENKEL said, "Well, when do I get called to tell what I know about this traitor? Is he happy with his £5,000?"
I said, "Your appearance before the Royal Commission is a matter which will be decided by the appropriate authorities. As to your enquiry regarding the present welfare of PETROV, I do not think it is of any concern to you, but what does concern you is your past association with him and other members of the Soviet Embassy."

Readers of this interrogation of my father may not be fully aware of the tense and hostile atmosphere under which it was conducted. Very importantly, shortly after Redford and Mr. X arrived, they began asking questions in our front room where there was a table and chairs and also a bed where my sister Genia slept. One of the officers rested his shoe on the bed and my father, already feeling annoyed by the tone of questioning, told him to get his 'microbial' or dirty foot off his child's bed. It was all downhill after that.

In these head-to-head exchanges, ASIO described my father as arrogant. Perhaps in their experience of interrogating others, they were used to more compliance or deference. My father, however, made his resentment of ASIO's assumption that he was engaged in spying or subversion because he met Soviet Embassy officials, extremely clear. He was a proud man and clear about his moral compass. Crucially, there is certainly *no* evidence in the transcript that he had: *"violently condemned Australia, its government, and its social and educational system (to officers of A.S.I.O. acting on behalf of the Royal Commission on Espionage)."*

Unfortunately, the claim of 'violent condemnation' was repeated several times between 1954 and 1963 in secret reports about my father. Once entered into a report, it remained as an unquestionable 'truth' for others to repeat. There is a clear distinction between criticism of Australia and violent condemnation. This highly exaggerated description undoubtedly affected my father's reputation in the eyes of federal government ministers and ASIO when they were considering his fate after 1956.

My father was a complex mixture of boastfulness and honesty, always fearlessly declaring what he thought. With hindsight, this bravado was extremely foolish. It would be an understatement to say that his responses to questions were not well received by ASIO. Also, Dad 'big noted' himself in claiming that he knew a lot of people from the Soviet Embassy. In fact, he did not know any of them well. Instead, his contact was limited to either correspondence with consular officials or only one, two or three brief visits from Makarov, Sadovnikov, Petrov and Plaitkais when they made their rare trips to Melbourne between 1946 and 1954. Sadly, his pride, his chutzpah and lack of caution would later cost him dearly.

As to the Royal Commission, a week after ASIO's visit, Ernest Redford wrote on December 7, 1954, to Ron Richards, Deputy Director-General (Operations) in Sydney. He stated:

> Attached is a copy of our interview with FRENKEL. FRENKEL reacted to the interview in an arrogant manner, and it will be noted that he is extremely hostile towards PETROV. He denied membership of the Communist Party of Australia, and from his demeanour it appeared to us that he would welcome the opportunity of being called as a witness before the Royal Commission on Espionage.

Yet, my father was never called to appear before the Royal Commission. ASIO probably judged that he would simply emphasise Petrov's alcoholism and thereby help discredit Petrov and his key function for ASIO in the eyes of the public. Crucially, my father had no access to powerful people or to important government files and was therefore useless as a source for uncovering any so-called spy ring.

It is indicative of the narrow focus of the Royal Commission that anti-Communist White Russians were also not called to appear, even though they were eager to testify about Soviet espionage in Australia. Either ASIO was correct in its assessment that they would have been unreliable witnesses, or the Royal Commission displayed a lack of deep concern about a possible Soviet spy ring amongst ex-Soviet migrant communities. Perhaps Evatt was justified in seeing the Commission as a witch-hunt against himself and his staffers as this became a central feature of the public hearings at the expense of probing Soviet activities elsewhere.

Curiously, on the one hand, ASIO were extremely interested in questioning my father about his contact with Petrov and other Soviet officials concerning repatriation activities. Yet, on the other hand, ASIO both mistrusted displaced persons and were not as actively involved in East European migrant community affairs as were the CIA and their counterparts in West Germany. ASIO had notoriously inadequate 'foreign' language skills and hostility to 'enemy aliens' regardless of the fact that most were anti-Communist. This was combined with the controversial issue of immigration in Australia during the 1950s, an extremely sensitive topic. This sensitivity would impact my parents, before departing Melbourne in 1956.

Misguided and ever-costly legacy

Our family lived through these tumultuous events and perceived them from inside the political circus. Reading through the newspaper accounts of Petrov and Menzies in the 1950s, and the books and articles written in subsequent decades, it is noticeable how the treatment of the 'Petrov Affair' lost its sharpness over time. Part of the reason is that both Soviet and Australian archives were eventually opened to get a fuller picture of people who were accused of being involved in espionage. Historical perceptions also changed once Menzies had departed the scene, the hatred generated by 'the Split' within the ALP gradually faded and Eastern European Communism collapsed.

In recent years it has been possible to document more fully the jaundiced and destructive interference of ASIO in domestic politics. For most of its history, ASIO's energy was almost wholly deployed against the Communist and non-Communist Left rather than against fascists and other Right-wing extremists. Such was the one-sided perspective of ASIO, that the ALP was very hostile to it and regarded ASIO as a mere tool of Liberal governments since the 'Petrov Affair'. It is important to be reminded that at the 1971 ALP Party conference, a proposal to abolish ASIO was only defeated by *one* vote. Shadow Attorney-General, Senator Lionel Murphy opposed the abolition of ASIO because it would not look good in the coming election. Yet, only two years later in March 1973, Murphy, the new Attorney-General in the Whitlam government, ordered Commonwealth police to raid ASIO's office. He feared ASIO were failing to disclose full and accurate information about far-Right Croatian terrorists who might endanger the life of the Yugoslav Prime Minister, Dzemal Bijedic, who was due to visit Australia. Murphy's raid on ASIO in March 1973 did not cause Petrov to have a severe stroke in 1974 as hyperbolically claimed by Right-wing columnist Gerard Henderson.

In their analyses of ASIO's rigidly hostile and blinkered lumping together of anti-Stalinist New Left radicals in the 1960s and 1970s as 'communist subversives', historians Stuart Macintyre, Phillip Deery, and others pointed to the long history of ASIO's deliberate anti-democratic tendencies. Although ASIO has been forced in recent years to pay more attention to the upsurge in Right-wing extremism, the long history of ASIO disproportionately focussing on the Left, environmentalists, and other social movements, continues today. It is indicative of the blinkered and prejudiced view of intelligence organisations which are still shaped by a Right-wing political culture deeply opposed to domestic social, economic, and environmental reforms. On a simple cost-benefit analysis, the billions spent on ASIO have not only been a gross waste of public money but constitute an enduring threat to Australian democracy.

Most anti-Communist defenders of ASIO would argue that Australia was merely one regional setting in a global struggle against the attempted Communist destruction of parliamentary democracies, free religious worship, and competitive markets. ASIO may have made mistakes, but their surveillance of people such as Frankel was fully justifiable given my father's association with Soviet Embassy officials and his promotion of Communism. There was no middle ground, anti-Communists argued, in the life and death struggle against totalitarianism.

Hence, the significance of Petrov and the Royal Commission is also not fully comprehensible without understanding the experiences of a generation of people who had lived through the Great Depression, the Second World War, and the emerging tensions of Cold War hostility. As the decade of the 1950s began, there were hot wars in Korea, Vietnam, and other parts of the Indo-Pacific region. These struggles were all simplistically and erroneously reduced to mere episodes in the global conflict between the 'Free World' and 'totalitarian Communism' by ASIO, the Liberal Party and mainstream media.

In fact, as we know, the Communist governments in China, Vietnam and North Korea, as also other national independence movements in Africa and Asia, had their own agendas that would become apparent later in the 1960s and onwards. During the war against the Japanese, Mao's Communist Party had good relations with its American allies, but these were broken after 1946 with the rise of McCarthyite, anti-Communist witch-hunts in the US State Department. It was not until Gough Whitlam's visit in 1971, followed by Richard Nixon's official visit in 1972, that Western relations with China began to thaw.

Decades of massive destruction and loss of life proved to have also been an unnecessary catastrophe in Vietnam. Rather than being part of a uniform global Communist system controlled by Moscow, Vietnam, despite having a repressive regime, followed its own nationalist agenda after defeating America in 1975. It took the Sino-Soviet split in the period between the late 1950s and early 1960s, followed years later in the 1980s and 1990s by the development of capitalism in China, Vietnam, Laos, and Mongolia, to shatter the powerful old 'domino theory' of monolithic 'totalitarian Communism' capturing one country after another on its downward path to Australia. By the late 1980s, ASIO's earlier rationale of stopping anyone called a 'Communist subversive' looked decidedly shaky with America doing business with China and the USSR heading towards disintegration.

While the rhetoric has changed in recent years, the old Cold War image of Communist China as Australia's greatest security threat remains firmly entrenched in the minds of a powerful segment of foreign, military and intelligence policymakers. These distorted policies only survive by ignoring climate breakdown as the greatest threat to Australia and the world. Crucially, the historical tensions and specific politics and cultures of communist countries have always been more preoccupied with their own development rather than forming an alliance to invade or control Australia. On February 21, 2023, former prime minister, Paul Keating, castigated commentator Greg Sheridan (who was deeply influenced by Bob Santamaria's Movement). Keating wrote in *The Australian* about the army of 'little Americans' that populate the media, military services, and intelligence agencies.

> The historian Manning Clark used to refer to people like Menzies, Stanley Bruce and Casey as Austral-Britons. People whose ambivalence as to their identity and allegiances compromised their commitment to Australia.

Australia now has another class of such people in its public life – Austral-Americans – people who don't know which side of the national fence they are on or should be on.

People skewered by their own ambivalence.

During the 1950s and 1960s, the group of Non-Aligned Nations, especially in Asia and Africa, attempted to follow independent policies separate from Moscow or Washington. There were many within and outside the ALP who believed that Australia should also pursue an independent foreign policy. Before becoming leader of the ALP after Ben Chifley's death in 1951, Evatt had played a prominent role in the early years of the United Nations, helping to draft the UN's Universal Declaration of Human Rights, and presiding as President of the General Assembly in 1948 and 1949. He became emblematic to many Australians of the need to prevent the erosion of civil liberties, as well as the need to establish peaceful co-operative relations with our neighbours and not just our allies.

If Evatt appealed to those who believed in the new United Nations, ASIO relied heavily on sharing intelligence information with British and American allies. Santamaria's 'groupers' within the labour movement shared ASIO's view that Communists and those Left elements within the ALP and Australian society who endorsed Evatt's perspective were potential or actual subversives. Unsurprisingly, ASIO therefore made attempts to recruit Right-wing Catholics and other conservatives. Yet, in contrast to his high-profile advocacy of civil rights and the UN, the public was unaware that Evatt was far from the principled paragon of virtue in his manoeuvring within the ALP. He shored up his leadership between 1951 and 1955 by courting the Right and the Left on separate occasions and in different years when it best suited him. Evatt's courting of Santamaria and the ALP Right prior to the 1954 election was a case of trying to win power at any cost rather than adhering to principled beliefs. Despite his political manoeuvrings, Evatt did himself in over the Petrov defection.

Timing is not everything

Robert Manne's 1987 book, *The Petrov Affair: Politics and Espionage*, remains the most detailed account of the day-to-day, week-to-week unfolding of Petrov's intention to defect from as early as 1952 to April 3rd, 1954. Manne had access to ASIO and had several detailed conversations with retired Director-General Sir Charles Spry. He is effective in debunking Evatt's and the Left's claim that Menzies and ASIO hatched a plot to time Petrov's defection just before the 1954 election. While Manne shows that Petrov's volatility and long-drawn-out on-again, off-again defection during 1953 and early 1954 made such a conspiracy exceedingly difficult to carry out, especially by reference to the chronology of events, in my view, he insufficiently questions the informal manoeuvrings between ASIO and Menzies or between ASIO and Menzies' staff.

There are still those who claim that Menzies knew much more about Petrov than he let on in 1954. It stretches credibility to believe that given the importance of the matter, that Menzies or one of his Prime Ministerial staff did not ask ASIO well before April 3, 1954, what the name was of the possible defector, and what was the nature of the significant information that he had to offer. However, this does not mean that there was a well-organised conspiracy to snatch victory from Labor, but neither does it mean that the precise dates of Petrov's defection nullify the fact that Menzies knew very well that he would most likely be the main beneficiary of the Petrov Affair. It was the electoral system that ultimately aided Menzies and denied Labor victory.

Manne is accurate in his account that Petrov's defection did not feature prominently in the 1954 election or prevent Labor from winning a majority of the votes but not a majority of seats. However, this is only part of the story. His account notes Menzies' opportunism in using Petrov's defection and the role of the Right-wing media and Coalition politicians in beating the anti-Communist drum. Yet, there were thousands of pages in the thirty-six MI5 files on the Petrov case that were released by the National Archives UK decades after Manne wrote *The Petrov Affair*. Manne did not have access to these records that included Spry's fear, before the 1954 election, that Evatt would sack him should Labor win the election. Spry therefore supported Menzies who argued that the Petrov revelations about Evatt meant that, in Menzies' words, "everything must be done in the national as distinct from political party interest to prevent Evatt becoming prime minister." This was hardly a neutral and conventional approach to party politics. It nonetheless remains unclear whether Menzies' and Spry's fear of Evatt becoming Prime Minister amounted to anything more sinister than their deeply held anti-democratic opinions.

In 1986, when Robert Manne finished drafting his book, he was a Cold War liberal closely aligned with the anti-Communist Right. As American Samuel Moyn argues, "Cold War liberalism was a catastrophe – for liberalism." This was a view of the world that justifiably emphasised all the horrors of Communism but unjustifiably and often conveniently closed its eyes to authoritarian abuses within the 'Free World'. Many anti-Communist liberals and conservatives tolerated attacks on the civil liberties of both Communists and non-Communists as if they were simply 'tools of the Soviets.' In Australia, such views meant that all was permissible by ASIO as the 'good guys', supposedly defending democracy.

Robert Manne has significantly changed his political views in the past twenty-five years and no longer would be identified with the Right. In 2004, a second edition of *The Petrov Affair* was published. Surprisingly, apart from minor changes, such as the deletion of endnotes and a considerable amount of detail on Soviet intelligence in Australia and abroad, Manne reaffirmed in this new edition that "[T]he historical interpretation is, however, unchanged." His account therefore remains written very much from the perspective of some of his key sources, namely Spry and ASIO. It remains largely uncritical of Menzies and glaringly bereft of any criticism of ASIO's political culture, its organisational operations, its definition of 'subversives', or its targeting and scandalous annual list, through the 1950s and up until the early 1970s, of thousands of domestic 'enemies' that would be rounded up and interned in any so-called 'emergency'.

I am not suggesting that Spry, Richards, Redford and others were corrupt. Rather, they dutifully and diligently operated within a Cold War paranoid organisational culture that treated a range of legitimate critics of Australian politics and society as potential or actual traitors or subversives rather than legitimate defenders of social rights, greater democracy, and civil liberties. Nor am I denying the existence of a tiny number of 'true believers' in the pre-1960s Communist Party who could have been persuaded possibly to work for the Soviets in espionage, even though the Royal Commission found that no one revealed anything consequential in the 1950s.

Today, with hindsight, we can reject both sides in the Cold War propaganda wars. It was not a simple struggle between good and evil as it was so portrayed at the time. Crucially, both historical records and reports on current practices show that regardless of political regime, the likelihood of any secret police force or intelligence organisation anywhere in the world *not* abusing its powers was and still is extremely rare. The *only* difference between particular national policing and security forces is *the extent* of their abuses and corruption.

It is not just that leading powers have deployed undercover operations to assassinate and torture. Security agencies across the world have a long history of acting as agent provocateurs in propaganda wars. They have triggered violence at peaceful protests or even carried out atrocities, air crashes, and violent attacks in order to make these look like the acts of political opponents – all with the aim of discrediting particular governments or movements in the eyes of public opinion. Some countries try to minimise abuses by police and security forces. So far, despite inquiries into police corruption, Australian governments have failed abysmally to reform, adequately monitor and hold intelligence organisations accountable to the public, despite the Hope Commission in the 1970s.

In 1987, Manne's anti-Communist sympathies meant that he lauded Spry and ASIO uncritically. He cited James Angleton, the CIA's master of counterintelligence from 1954 to 1974, who claimed that information gained from Petrov's defection was one of the most valuable ever. It is true that the Petrovs provided further insight into how Soviet security agencies worked and gave the CIA (via ASIO) the names of many undercover agents or contacts working for the Soviets in Western countries. However, the problem is that Petrov's information was likely to have been inflated, due to his need to cover up his laziness and boost his 'importance' to his new masters. His confirmation of the veracity of Venona, the code-cracking system used by American counterintelligence against the Soviets, failed to disclose to ASIO that the Soviets had long been aware since 1947 that their codes had been broken.

Similarly, Angleton's credibility also proved to be incredibly questionable for quite separate reasons. In his youth, Angleton was editor of the Yale modernist poetry journal, *Furioso*, and established contact with Ezra Pound, T. S. Elliot, and other leading poets whom he continued to visit on CIA missions abroad. Elliot coined the phrase, "a wilderness of mirrors" and Angleton used it and Modernist poetry, as a counterintelligence tool to decipher the ambiguity of words, disinformation, and deceptive strategies. Robert Manne, like so many other Cold War warriors of the day, was silent about Angleton's abuse of power when writing in 1987, despite the fact that Angleton was publicly disgraced and sacked by the CIA in December 1974. The *New York Times* revealed Angleton's continual violation of the CIA charter which forbade domestic operations within the US. Instead, he illegally ordered the mass surveillance of the domestic civil rights movement, anti-war movement, black activists, and other dissidents. These were all the same activities that ASIO was 'legally' permitted to do on a lesser scale but with impunity in Australia.

James Angleton was so paranoid that he also falsely accused Australian Prime Minister, Gough Whitlam, Canadian Prime Ministers, Lester Pearson and Pierre Trudeau, British Prime Minister Harold Wilson, West German Chancellor Willy Brandt, Swedish Prime Minister Olaf Palme and even Henry Kissinger – who many would see as a Right-wing war criminal – of aiding the Soviet Union or being

Soviet agents! Despite Angleton being sacked in 1974, CIA Director, William Colby, secretly rehired him in 1975 at his old salary to continue his earlier paranoid practices. He was also awarded the CIA's Distinguished Intelligence Medal in 1975!

Following Senator Frank Church's American Senate 1975 Committee inquiry into intelligence agencies, the 1976 final report revealed the global scale of abuses and espionage conducted by America that either dwarfed Soviet espionage or at the very least rivalled the latter. Apart from the assassinations, attempted assassinations, and numerous interferences in national affairs across the world, the CIA mobilised hundreds of businesspeople, academics, journalists, trade union leaders, clergy and public servants and politicians to spy for them. Australia was no exception. There should be no doubt that the Soviets actively tried to recruit local Australian-born people or migrants into their network. But in reality, they would have dearly loved to have had a tiny fraction of the many prominent people who worked and continue to work for American intelligence and government agencies. The Royal Commission on Espionage in 1954 was, of course, not interested in uncovering Australian spies and agents working for American and British intelligence.

We have never had an open investigation in Australia such as the Church Committee. The nearest we have had is the Whitlam government's commissioning of the Hope conservative investigation of ASIO which did not challenge ASIO's undemocratic role and interference in Australian society. Nevertheless, even much of Hope's report – which he undemocratically agreed to keep secret for at least thirty years – contained scathing criticisms of ASIO's 'shambolic' record keeping and the need for it to be more professional and accountable. In fact, the KGB's most successful spy in Australia was ASIO's own head of operations in Sydney, Ian George Peacock, who offered his service to the Soviets and revealed numerous Australian and US intelligence secrets between 1977 and 1983.

Despite its hearings, the 1954 Royal Commission's final report in September 1955 recommended no prosecution of six people accused of passing on low-level information to the Soviets (rather than vital military or other security intelligence), and only revealed a few possible or actual spies back in the period 1943 to 1948. Petrov's and Menzies' claim of an active spy ring in 1954 (like the Cambridge spies Burgess and Maclean) proved to be hollow. However, the consequences of Evatt's appearance at the Royal Commission on behalf of his staff members who had written documents that Petrov handed over to ASIO, was disastrous. When Evatt attacked the Report of the Royal Commission in October 1955, he foolishly and naively announced in parliament that he had written to Soviet Foreign Minister Molotov to ask whether the documents under dispute were genuine. Molotov replied that they were fabrications. Upon hearing Evatt, the parliamentary chamber broke into roars of laughter. Evatt's credibility was thus destroyed. Menzies seized the opportunity and called a snap election in December 1955. With the help of the bitterness caused by 'the Split', the Coalition won a decisive victory on the preferences coming from the expelled Anti-Communist Labor Right. The simultaneous Petrov Affair and civil war within the ALP during 1954 and 1955 left the ALP in a grievously wounded state.

Winners and losers

Apart from Menzies and senior ASIO personnel, the Petrov Affair did not end well for a number of participants. Evatt's last years as leader of the ALP were a failure until he retired ill in 1960. The Petrovs assumed false names and lived quietly in Bentleigh. An interview with them in *The Australian* but conducted much earlier than the published date of August 27, 1979, revealed that they did not like their new life in Australia. Mr. Petrov said: "I am very unhappy. We have nothing. No friends, no future." Mrs. Petrov added: "I wish I was dead. Nobody could dream of our misery." Vladimir suffered a series of strokes in 1974 and spent the remaining seventeen years of his life in a nursing home until he died in 1991 aged eighty-four. Evdokia was reunited with her sister (who came to Australia in 1990) and died eleven years after Vladimir in 2002.

As for my father, within a few months of Menzies' victory over the ALP in December 1955, his focus moved away from life in Australia. The first half of 1956 would begin excitedly as he planned our transition to the 'Communist society of the future'. Unbeknown to him, the second half of the year would usher in years of pain and suffering.

Paradoxically, the Petrovs lived long, isolated, and miserable lives to the ages of eighty-four and eighty-seven. My father was less isolated than the Petrovs but would die much younger at the age of sixty, his health damaged by his experiences in Russia and arguably by ASIO's negative reports about him to Immigration Minister Alexander Downer and Prime Minister Menzies.

There is no Olympic gold medal in the race to see who is the most miserable and unfulfilled. The Petrovs swapped Russia for Australia. A higher standard of living and protection from Soviet terror and bureaucracy did not bring them happiness. My father swapped Australia for Russia which did not bring him, or our family any happiness. The classless society or a higher form of 'socialist culture' to replace capitalist consumerism that he was looking for was not to be found in his prematurely shortened life.

9

DEPARTING FOR PARADISE

IT WILL BE RECALLED THAT BEFORE MY FATHER CAME TO Australia in 1938, he had wanted to return to Russia from Palestine in the 1930s but could not do so because he was both denied a visa by Soviet authorities and his sister could not afford to sponsor him. What troubled me when I read the released secret files about him, was that in 1945, he had applied for a Soviet passport which was granted but not issued until 1947 by the Soviet Embassy in New Zealand. From this point on until 1955, he applied annually to the Soviet Embassy in Canberra for a re-entry visa to the USSR. He was always rejected.

The disturbing aspect of this revelation is not that it was a surprise that my father wanted to return to the Soviet Union, but that he was so persistent in his desire to leave Australia, especially to return to a war-ravaged country. This was the worst possible time to take Genia as a toddler and me as a new baby between 1945 and 1947. I am not sure that my mother was ever fully aware of these annual visa applications during the second half of the 1940s. Even more disturbing is the realisation that my father both did and did not want to live in Australia. He lived an almost schizophrenic, unsettled existence as a loving and caring husband and father trying to ensure that his family were able to thrive in Australia, and yet at the same time, like a religious fanatic, yearned to fulfil his Soviet ideals and return home to help the motherland.

The clash between Dad's emotional, ethical, and political life can partly be understood in terms of the distinction between 'particular' and 'universal altruism' made by the philosopher G. W. F. Hegel. My father's ethical idealism propelled both his 'particular altruism' manifested in the care for his family, and also his 'universal altruism' or support for the Soviet state. In contrast to the defence of the capitalist class by the government in Australia, he uncritically accepted Communist political propaganda that the Soviet state was altruistic and cared for all members of the Soviet Union's so-called classless society. If only this phantasy had been true.

Others, such as my mother's relatives in Melbourne, saw Dad as a dogmatic and selfish narcissist who put his desire to return to the USSR ahead of the needs of his family. This was particularly true from 1951 onwards after they heard about his intention to return to the Soviet Union. For my mother, his desire to return to Russia was particularly distressing and unsettling. Between 1951 and 1954 they had simultaneously gone through two loving pregnancies and yet his stubborn and blind political desire outweighed his responsibility to his newborn daughter or respect for his wife's pleading that she did not want to leave Australia. In his defence, my father always said that his longing to return to the USSR was not selfish or pursued for his benefit alone. Rather, he foolishly but sincerely believed that we would all be the beneficiaries of leaving capitalist Australia and moving to live in a truly socialist society. He particularly believed that instead of the inferior quality of education in Australian schools, we would all receive an education of the highest standards there. My father's emotional commitment to an idealised USSR overwhelmed and clouded his intellectual judgement.

Apart from his voluntary work at the Australia-Soviet Friendship Society, he was actively involved in helping former residents of the USSR now living in Melbourne, to return home to the places where they were born. So ardent was he in his desire to return to the USSR, it was hardly surprising that his enthusiasm motivated his actions in helping others to return home. Through meeting ex-Soviet emigres at

Australia-Soviet Friendship functions and film nights at the Carlton Theatre, he set about assisting several of them to return home. These people from Russia and Soviet republics such as Latvia and Estonia were a motley bunch of lonely and disturbed characters. They had mainly arrived as displaced persons after the war. A few were only in their early twenties when they were taken as prisoners of war or fled with Hitler's armies as they retreated from the Soviet Union. Some had probably done terrible deeds for the Nazis who employed local Russians, Latvians, Estonians, Ukrainians, and others to slaughter fellow men, women, and children. Mum felt particularly uncomfortable with some of them being in our house, especially after hearing their stories and yet still grieving for her own exterminated family. The borderline between being forced to kill others and volunteering to murder and oppress communities was far from clear in the case of a certain number of these Soviet post-war arrivals in Australia.

Strangely, Dad was like a Christian turning the other cheek. He condemned their wartime acts but forgave them in a paternalistic manner. Largely isolated in far-away Melbourne, these lost and damaged characters wanted to return home to their families and hoped they would not be punished by Soviet authorities. They were indeed lucky they did not return to the USSR during the Stalin era. Many homecoming prisoners of war were mistrusted and sent to the Gulag by suspicious authorities who accused them of desertion and cooperating with the Nazis.

Back in far-away Melbourne, most of the single ex-Soviet men had extremely poor English or lacked knowledge of how to fill in applications for visas, organise tickets and so forth. Consequently, they approached my father for help. He was extremely happy to assist in their repatriation to the Soviet Union because he naively and dogmatically believed that life would be more enriching for them back home rather than remaining isolated in capitalist Australia. There was a certain degree of truth in my father's logic that these lonely men would perhaps be better off returning home. At least they would be able to speak their native language, reunite with their families and be part of a shared culture, despite a repressive regime and a much lower standard of living that my father in his delusions about the Soviet Union prior to mid-1956, never acknowledged. Whether they would simply swap their unhappy lonely drinking in Melbourne or Sydney for widespread alcoholism in the USSR was an unknown and potentially unhappy fate that one could not be sure awaited some or all of them.

Apart from several of these migrants visiting our home when Dad had a party to farewell a couple of them before their ship departed, I distinctly remember my father visiting an Estonian who wanted to return home in early 1956. This man lived in Chaucer Street St. Kilda close to Luna Park. We made a brief visit where passport and travel issues were discussed for about fifteen minutes. The reason I remember the brief visit is not for what was discussed but for what happened afterwards on the way home. As we walked to catch the tram, we passed a portrait artist sitting outside Luna Park. He asked Dad whether he wanted his portrait drawn. Surprisingly, Dad agreed. The artist then sketched a profile of Dad's large head sitting atop a short body and legs with a giant penis protruding from his pants. The sketch was entitled 'More hair on the other side'. My father was outraged at what he labelled a 'pornographic' insult. He refused to pay him unless he deleted the penis. The street artist then rubbed out the penis and substituted a table with legs. In later years, whenever I looked at the censored version of this portrait, I invariably laughed as I always saw the original satirical version.

Perhaps the street artist sketched Dad as a 'dickhead' or else recognised something in my father's personality that he could mock. Whatever the reason for his mischievous drawing, it was the opposite of what ASIO saw in my father. Crucially, from ASIO's Cold War perspective, these annual visa applications to the Soviet Embassy in Canberra and the repatriation help he extended to others, made him a subject of surveillance. The fact that he came into contact with various staff in the Embassy, including the notorious Vladimir Petrov, as discussed in the previous chapter, only blackened him further in the spy-obsessed culture of ASIO.

A secret file in the National Archives dated October 18, 1954, from the Regional Director of ASIO Victoria to both ASIO headquarters and the Deputy Director of Operations at the Royal Commission on Espionage, details a telephone message concerning Abraham Frenkel. It states that:

> There is a group of which the top man is Abraham FRENKEL, who is working for the U.S.S.R. Embassy.
>
> VASSILIEFF was also in charge of a group, and VASSILIEFF worked for FRENKEL. Contact between FRENKEL and VASSILIEFF has now stopped.
>
> Boris BRONSKY was head of another group comprising sub-sources CHERVINSKY, OSTROWSKI, STRATONOWITSCH.
>
> FRENKEL is alleged to be in contact with the U.S.S.R Embassy in New Zealand.

Anyone reading this message from an unidentified ASIO informant could easily gain the impression that my father was Mr. Big in charge of subversive groups working for the Soviets. No corroborating evidence is provided other than approximate dates and places which were later obtained by ASIO through questioning my father. The answers given concerned when and where he had met with Soviet officials such as Makarov and Sadovnikov at 317 Canning Street North Carlton, or Petrov and Plaitkais at Godfrey Avenue or in the city. Far from running any subversive groups, these visits by Embassy cultural attaches were principally related to Australia-Soviet Friendship events as well as my father's desire to obtain a visa to return to Russia.

During the 1940s and 1950s, it is crucial to understand that ASIO and its predecessor the Commonwealth Investigative Branch were essentially semi-amateur counter-espionage officials recruited from the military and police forces. These recruits were poorly educated and had few if any linguistic skills, especially in Slavic languages. For targeted individuals like my father, ASIO was forced to rely heavily for their information on a range of dubious informants from anti-Communist immigrant communities: namely, individuals with their own personal agendas and axes to grind. ASIO officers were usually unable to verify the quality of the information provided because they could not speak Russian or other languages and were mostly culturally and linguistically ignorant of divisions within migrant communities. Unsurprisingly, ASIO files included all kinds of nonsense based on rumours or malicious statements, inaccuracies, and ideological prejudices. Either through understaffing, incompetence, or the wilful embrace of conspiratorial fantasies, ASIO failed to verify these accounts. Consequently, these inaccuracies and prejudicial assessments remained in an individual's files for a lifetime, and in the case of my father, for over 50 years after his death.

The whole contentious and largely fabricated issue of Russians being repatriated *en masse* from Australia, came to a head, especially following the Petrov Affair in 1954/1955. By the time we set sail from Melbourne in May 1956, my father's departing remarks to journalists and the way his comments were edited and represented, would coincide with exaggerated media-fed stories from ASIO about a conspiracy involving coercion by Soviet agents forcing 'migrants from the Iron Curtain countries to return home'. There is also no doubt, whatsoever, that the Soviets had intelligence agents like the Petrovs and their predecessors and successors who were collecting information and making connections with potentially useful locals who could be groomed for espionage. However, my father was not one of them. As discussed in the previous chapter, even Vladimir Petrov could see that he was not suitable for intelligence work.

Essentially, Abraham Frankel was a naïve and gullible pawn in a larger Cold War drama played by actors representing Soviet power and Western governments and intelligence agencies such as ASIO. For all his delusions and over-confident behaviour, he was no spy or subversive agent working for the Soviet Union. He neither received payment for his assistance to those who wanted to return to the USSR nor ever sought payment from the Soviet Embassy. Instead, he enthusiastically championed the Soviet Union and believed that Russians like himself should go and live there. Unlike ASIO, Dad did not see helping several isolated people return home as 'subversive activity'. This characterisation by intelligence officers was in fact the last thing on his mind despite it being blown out of all proportion by ASIO and echoed by senior Ministers in the Menzies Coalition government.

My father also did not fully understand why the Soviet Embassy continually refused his annual application for a re-entry visa. He did not grasp that the consular officials in the Embassy whom he contacted seeking entry visas on behalf of others in Melbourne, almost certainly regarded my father as a useful idiot. Rather than allowing him to return to Russia, he was more valuable to the Embassy as someone who could help with the repatriation of several ex-Soviets from Australia. Little did my father realise that his active role in helping estranged émigrés and displaced persons would take such a heavy toll on him and on our family in subsequent years.

Misunderstanding the Soviet repatriation strategy

In the 1950s, Australia was still quite isolated from the main economic, political, and cultural centres of power. There was far less awareness of the world amongst both many government officials and ordinary citizens that decisions made in foreign capitals would affect the Australian population sometimes with a delay of several months or a year or two. It seemed like we got our news by camel. This lack of awareness of policy changes made in other countries dramatically affected our family.

After applying on an annual basis for a re-entry visa and being regularly rejected by the Soviets, my father's disappointment – which in fact had been his, and our good luck – suddenly changed at the end of 1955. What determined the Soviets issuing a re-entry visa to my father was the new Soviet campaign of repatriation commenced in 1955, a campaign which especially flourished until 1959. In far-off

Australia, both my parents and ASIO did not grasp the hidden intent of this new Soviet strategy. Instead, they basically took at face value the Soviet public calls for all ex-Soviets to return home. Had my father been as central as the ASIO files suggested, he would have been aware of the real purpose of this key Soviet policy change and strategy.

According to Benjamin Tromly in his 2019 book, *Cold War Exiles and the CIA: Plotting to Free Russia*, the Kremlin launched a massive psychological warfare campaign to convince Soviet exiles to return home. This campaign centred on West Germany as a deliberate counter to CIA-sponsored anti-Communist organisations. West Berlin and Munich in particular, were hotbeds of Russian and East European émigré intrigue and tension. The Soviets adopted a two-pronged strategy regarding Soviet exiles in Germany. The 'bad cop' approach was represented by Soviet premier Nikolai Bulganin who, prior to West German Chancellor Konrad Adenauer's visit to Moscow in 1955, demanded that all Soviet citizens in Germany be returned to the USSR. Bulganin's demand was later rejected as it contravened the official status of many émigrés who were refugees. Nonetheless, this demand created panic within the ex-Soviet communities who feared that they might be forcibly repatriated to the USSR.

The 'good cop' strategy was also evident in 1955 when the Supreme Soviet passed a decree on "the Amnesty of Soviet Citizens who collaborated with the occupiers during the Great Patriotic War of 1941–1945." In welcoming exiles who returned to the USSR, West Germany became the front line of the battle for the 'hearts and minds' of the diverse factions within the displaced persons and émigré communities. These new Soviet strategies also reverberated amongst East European migrant communities in less important countries such as Australia. The Amnesty decree did not apply to my father as he had left Russia in 1921 and had not fought in the Second World War. Nevertheless, he became both a beneficiary and a victim of a Soviet Cold War strategy that was primarily focused on Western Europe. He certainly did not understand or know anything about the new strategy deployed by Soviet intelligence, naively viewing the repatriation campaign as an altruistic and generous offer extended to Russians abroad. Not only did the Soviets now grant my father a re-entry visa, but they also paid the fares for returning Russians and their families. This was indeed a double bonus as the cost of fares for the five of us and shipping assorted items of our household furniture would have been prohibitively expensive.

Rather than being an anti-Communist deceived by the repatriation campaign, Dad was a Soviet enthusiast and fanatic who couldn't believe his good fortune in being repatriated. Finally, after waiting all these years, the fact that the Soviets paid for our fares only seemed to confirm his long-held faith in the Soviet Union as the 'society of the future'. By contrast, ASIO, like most Western intelligence agencies and governments, were equally duped by the repatriation campaign and sought to implement countermeasures to prevent Russians and East Europeans from returning *en masse*. What was the background to the new Soviet strategy that ensnared my father and our family? Tromly shows how émigré organisations misled intelligence agencies about their activities, and spies on both sides of the Iron Curtain carried out devious psychological operations against each other. Within the various factions of the Russian, Latvian, Estonian, Ukrainian, Polish, Czech and Hungarian communities in Australia, similar mutual denunciations, duplicitous acts of subterfuge and deliberate misleading of ASIO also occurred. If the Soviets, the CIA, and German intelligence were often 'taken for a ride', ASIO certainly lacked the resources and experience to identify this. They were like babes in the woods when trying to distinguish between the truth and disinformation.

From its headquarters in East Berlin, the new Committee for Return to the Homeland, a Soviet intelligence front headed by former prisoner of war, major-general N. F. Mikhailov, waged a sophisticated psychological warfare campaign to destabilise and divide ex-Soviet communities globally, but particularly in Germany and Western Europe. Contrary to ASIO's and the Menzies government's assumptions, the KGB did *not* aim for or even believe that large numbers of ex-Soviet displaced persons and émigrés would return to the USSR.

Soviet intelligence knew extremely well that the vast majority within these communities were anti-Communist and would not succumb to seductive propaganda campaigns. Yet even anti-Communists were fooled and caught off guard. A poster from Struggle for the Liberation of the Peoples of Russia – an anti-Communist Vlasovite group which had fought alongside the Nazis – was ineffective against the Soviet strategy. It showed Russians returning to the Soviet Union as a giant concentration camp under the caption *My vernulis' domoi!* ("We have returned home!") which also spelled out the acronym for the Soviet Ministry of Internal Affairs (MVD).

Such crude anti-Communist propaganda appealed to the converted but was useless against the Committee for Return to the Homeland's strategy because the Soviets were not aiming for mass repatriation. Instead, as Tromly argues, the Soviet campaign wanted to create even more distrust within émigré communities by convincing just a small number of anti-Communists or fence-sitters to become pro-Soviet. If war broke out in Europe, the Soviets were concerned to weaken Russian émigré communities that might aid the West.

Prior to the accelerated new 'repatriation' campaign in 1955, ASIO shared with diverse sections of the political spectrum within Australia both a hostility towards and suspicion of East European émigré and displaced persons communities as well as a profound ignorance of their cultural and political differences. Within the labour movement, Communists and Left Labor supporters were often suspicious of displaced persons from Eastern Europe as being either anti-union or former pro-Nazis. Part of the reason for this suspicion was that many displaced persons in European camps learned how to lie to ensure their survival. They emphasised their anti-Communism to officials determining whether they would be sent to America or Australia rather than sent back home. By the late 1940s, Cold War hostilities meant that in many instances, displaced persons who were former Nazi or Nazi collaborators were looked upon more favourably by Western authorities than Communist or Communist sympathisers.

On the opposite side of the political fence, Jack Lang, ex-Labor Premier of New South Wales, and leader of Right-wing Lang Labor, (who was also a mentor to Paul Keating), led a vociferous campaign against Russians coming from China and Europe. Like many other anti-Communists, Lang regarded Russian migrants as 'communist subversives' ignoring the fact that the majority of migrants from Eastern Europe and China were strongly anti-Soviet. This bigoted hostility to anti-Communist ex-Soviets was equivalent to the widespread anti-Semitic opposition in the US (during the late 1930s and early 1940s) to letting Jewish refugees into the country on the flimsy excuse that the Nazis might have blackmailed them to become spies for Hitler!

It is also important to remember that in the 1950s, immigration was an extremely sensitive issue for the government. The need to bring in large numbers of migrants from diverse backgrounds to help develop the economy was far from universally welcomed by Australian-born citizens. Dislike of 'whinging Poms' and Left-wing 'Pommie shop stewards' stirring up trouble in workplaces, or fear of so-called 'Communist subversives' upsetting migrant communities, were familiar stories that featured regularly in the Australian media. The uptight, English-influenced cultural complaints about 'wogs' and their smelly, garlic-infused food were also pervasive in the 1950s. In recent years, a similar 'siege mentality' fuelled Brexit. This mindset was vividly captured in comedy sketches by Catherine Tate showing two Little Englanders disgusted with any foreign food and repeatedly calling Europeans 'the dirty bastards.'

Most ASIO officers were politically narrow-minded at best and culturally ignorant at worst. They subscribed to the conservative notion of Australia that required migrants to abandon their culture and assimilate to Anglo-Australian practices. Many Australians did not realise that immigration figures were misleading and imprecise because large numbers of ex-Soviets in displaced persons camps in Europe gave their identity as 'Poles' or 'stateless' so as not to be forcibly sent back to the Soviet Union. Yet, ASIO misconstrued why many displaced persons learnt to tell untruths so that they would not be sent back to the Soviet Union. This was the very opposite of ASIO's belief that because East Europeans were untrustworthy, they were therefore potential Communist subversives. From 1955/56, ASIO's suspicions and delusions were fuelled by the East Berlin-based, Committee for Return to the Homeland, but as mentioned, they misunderstood the strategy provoked by the 'repatriation' campaign. Penetrating and monitoring ex-Soviet communities and creating mistrust had certainly been the task assigned to Soviet intelligence agents. Yet, despite the Soviet's best efforts and ASIO's prejudices against émigré communities, it is no surprise that of the more than twenty to twenty-eight thousand Russian, Ukrainian, and Baltic migrants in Australia by 1954, the vast majority had no desire whatsoever, to return to the USSR.

Much later, on October 20, 1960, Ernest Redford from ASIO once again appeared on the scene and this time conducted a long interview with my mother about her experiences in Russia and in Melbourne before we departed in 1956. When asked why Soviet agents Petrov and Plaitkais visited them at home and whether they tried to influence my father to return to Russia, Mum answered that they also visited others and did try to influence my father. Redford next enquired as to what were some of the reasons that Petrov and Plaitkais advanced for returning home. My mother replied:

> They stressed that education is free, that everything else is free, that the future is there, that things are wonderful and that here it is nothing like that. Every Russian should be back in his homeland and they used to tell us of the wonderful things there. Petrov also talked about the big forests and hunting and fishing.

Redford then asked whether Dad was happy in Australia before he was so influenced and at what stage he became restive. Mum answered that when she first met Dad, he was happy, but things changed after "the New Australians came here, when lots of Russians came from Germany. There were many and they told him they did not like it here and he believed them."

Question: "Do you know whether members of the Soviet Embassy used your husband to spread repatriation propaganda?"

Answer: "I do not know what they used him for. They used to get together and start talking."

Question: "Where did they hold their meetings?"

Answer: "The Carlton Theatre, they showed films there, all propaganda, which influenced them and after seeing these films and hearing the language they used to get together and talk."

Even in 1960, Redford and ASIO were still working with the old, flawed assumption that the Soviets were subverting Australian immigration policies by trying to get Russians and East Europeans to return home *en masse*. They paid far less attention to how intelligence agencies tried to monitor and divide émigrés.

Media 'red scare' and misreporting

Four years earlier, on May 7, 1956, the day that we sailed from Melbourne, as well as in the following days and weeks, Australian newspapers were full of stories about migrants being forced to return home by 'Iron Curtain' agents. For example, *The Argus* (a leading paper in Melbourne at the time) ran an ASIO-planted story on May 7, under the headline: ARE REDS AT WORK ON OUR MIGRANTS (no question mark). The article began with the announcement that "the Commonwealth Security Service (sic) is investigating a possible Communist organisation in Australia which forces migrants to return to Russia and Iron Curtain countries." It went on to proclaim that:

> If the Security Service reports that they have left as a result of Communist pressure, the Government will consider launching a propaganda campaign to dissuade migrants from leaving. It will also consider passing special legislation to prevent Communist organisations and individuals from putting pressure on migrants.

The Government fears the present trickle of Russian migrants out of the country may swell to a torrent.

This was precisely the effect that the Soviet-controlled Committee in East Berlin wanted Western intelligence agencies, governments, and émigré communities to believe.

On the same day, *The Age* reported from Sydney that according to Herman Laas, an Estonian migrant, the Russians have begun a worldwide move to bring migrants from Iron Curtain countries back home. As I mentioned before, the news from Europe was belatedly relayed here. Laas said that 'burglars' had broken into an Estonian newspaper office in Germany and stole the subscription list. Soon after, thousands of Estonians in Australia received letters urging them to go home.

It was unfortunate that my father stepped right into the middle of the ASIO and media campaign about a torrent of 'Iron Curtain migrants' returning home. Some newspaper reporters boarded the *Orcades* in search of supposedly dozens of Russians returning home, but couldn't find them (see article by Barney Porter, 'They must be invisible', *The Argus*, May 7, 1956). This campaign about 'Iron Curtain migrants' being coerced to return, meant that our departure on May 7, was front page news in the Melbourne *Herald*. Under the headline RUSSIANS GO HOME – WITH SMILES as well as a photo of all of us (except Genia), the article quoted my father as saying, "Conditions are much better in Europe now. After the Olympic Games they will go home in their thousands. Not only Russians but all New Australians."

The mood of the article then changed to a sinister tone with the sub-heading 'Keep Silent'. According to the report,

> neighbours would not answer any questions about the departure of the Frankel family. One said: "Don't be silly. Do you want me to finish with a bullet in my back?"
>
> Neighbours who lined Godfrey Avenue as the family drove off in two taxis were strangely silent in answer to Frankel's last shouted "Farewell friends."

Frankel got into the front seat of the first cab beside a burly, grey-suited man.

It was as if the *Herald* wanted to paint a picture of terrified neighbours being intimidated into silence by the KGB. The term 'burly' is often used to describe police. The so-called 'burly, grey-suited man' was the taxi driver and not, as implied, some Soviet official escorting us to Port Melbourne. In fact, there were no Soviet Embassy officials in Australia since diplomatic relations were broken in 1954. Also, my father occupied the only seat in the front that was next to the taxi driver.

Following this Cold War caricature and beat-up, the article then reverted to a friendlier tone and quoted Dad as saying:

> I say good luck to Australia. I have grown to love Australia since I came here. Anyhow that doesn't matter. What really matters is that I have a mother in the Soviet Union. She is my flesh and blood, and I must rejoin her.
>
> I have enjoyed reading Shakespeare and Byron and Henry Lawson while I was here in Australia. I wanted to take back Lawson to Russia with me, but I could not get a copy of his works in any bookshop. You would not find that in Russia.
>
> At the ship the family was greeted by Russian and Australian friends. They all looked very happy and often laughed heartily. There were bunches of flowers in the cabins and toys for the children.

Finally, the article finishes with a report on other Russians who also intended to leave but would not give their names.

The following day, on May 8, both *The Sun* and *The Argus* featured a large photo of all of us (except Genia who had her photo inserted separately below us), as we posed on the *Orcades* waving goodbye. *The Sun* repeated the misreporting of *The Herald* in stating that my father was returning to see his mother who in fact was living in Israel, not his sister who was in the USSR. If Dad was not misreported, perhaps he unconsciously regarded his older sister as a 'mother figure' or was he thinking about his motherland? It is curious then that the newspapers reported him as saying that he was returning to the 'fatherland' when this term is associated with countries such as Germany and it is difficult to imagine him using it. In Russia, it is always 'Mother Russia' (mat' Rossiya) or rodinya (birthplace).

The Argus, May 8, 1956.

The large headline in The Argus proclaimed: I WASN'T FORCED – I'M HOMESICK with a sub-heading 'Russian returns after 18 years' that partly countered ASIO and special branch propaganda about East Europeans being forced to return.

> I'm homesick – yes, that's the word. I've been away from Russia for 18 years and I want to go home." Mr. Abraham Frankl (sic) told an *Argus* reporter this yesterday as he prepared to sail from Melbourne. "If you were 14,000 miles away from your home and had been away for 18 years, wouldn't you want to go back?" he said. No one had brought any pressure on him to return. He had been away from the "fatherland" for a long time, and he particularly wanted to see relatives of his who were still in Russia. He claimed that Russians in other countries were also going home.

At this point, my father uttered a few sentences that would seal his fate in the eyes of the Menzies government and ASIO. In addition to his words published in the *Herald*, *The Argus* reported:

> "There are about 780 Russians in other countries leaving Buenos Aires in the Argentine for Odessa." He said. "And I know there is another ship leaving Chile with many Russians on it." ... Conditions were now much better in Europe. Not only Russians but all New Australians would feel the "pull" of their homelands", he said.

However, the article went on to cite security officers who said that:

> thousands of propaganda sheets, printed in various languages, had been distributed in Victoria asking New Australians to 'come back home'. They said the main theme of the Russian propaganda sheets was that mothers, fathers, and relatives of migrants in Australia wanted them to return to Iron Curtain countries as conditions were now much better than they were in past years. They had not yet been able to establish whether any organisations in Melbourne were in league with Russia in the 'come back home' move.

Given the political sensitivity of the immigration issue, Dad's comments were greeted with profound hostility by all those who alarmingly assumed incorrectly that thousands of migrants might return home. It also confirmed in ASIO's mind that Dad was a 'subversive' as they continued searching for a mythical 'Communist ring' supposedly trying to either force or persuade émigrés to return home. Actually, my father had no knowledge about hundreds of Russians in Argentina and Chile returning home as he was foolishly, as it turned out, repeating some Soviet propaganda that he had read. Perhaps it also reflected an unease he may have felt. He wanted so desperately to believe that he had made the right decision to return by publicly claiming that many other Russians would also join us. It was a grossly exaggerated hope without any substantive foundation.

A month earlier on April 8, 1956, my father introduced three Soviet Olympic officials to the audience at the Carlton Theatre. ASIO reported that they received a 'tremendous ovation' from the audience. Buoyed by their reception, Dad is reported by ASIO to have sought a large hall to entertain Soviet athletes when they arrived later in the year. The Hungarian revolt instead produced real tension between Soviet and Hungarian athletes, especially in water polo, but we were not in Melbourne to see this conflict. The Olympics was still six months away and, in the weeks leading up to our departure, my father was deluded in thinking that thousands of Russians would return home simply because three Olympic officials received such an enthusiastic reception from Russian emigres.

On the same day that we departed, Harold Holt, Minister for Immigration, stood up in Parliament to respond to the media focus on the supposed mass return of migrants, including my father's comments (without mentioning his name). He effectively dismissed ASIO's planted stories about 'Reds' forcing a mass return of people as rubbish. He also said that it was nonsense to believe my father's repeat of Soviet propaganda that soon thousands of 'New Australians' would also return home. Rather, Holt informed parliament that only 41 out of 21,000 Russians and those from Soviet satellite countries had returned in the year 1955/1956 for a range of reasons. Four days later, he told the first Victorian migrant congress that only two percent of Europeans had returned and only six percent of British migrants had. Even though the numbers were small, British migrants were three times more unhappy with Australia than Europeans. Holt also warned migrants from Eastern Europe who were considering returning home that they would find it difficult to re-enter Australia should they change their minds after they returned to Iron Curtain countries.

Why was Harold Holt one of the few sober and sane voices discrediting the beat-up generated by ASIO-planted stories in the media? One reason is that despite also being a Right-wing Cold War warrior, Holt was competing with R. G. Casey and other senior Liberals in the race to succeed Menzies should rumours prove to be true that Menzies intended to retire in 1958. He could not afford to be seen to be mishandling a vital portfolio such as Immigration if his critics were warning that tens of thousands of migrants were going to return home.

Despite Holt's intervention, he failed to curb ASIO's and the media's preoccupation with a 'Communist ring'. A few weeks later on May 30, 1956, *The Argus* ran an article "TELL US OF RED THREATS" police plead'. It reported: 'Police last night appealed to all migrants: "Tell us if Communists are putting pressure on you to return home. We will protect you." The article then stated that 'Special Branch detectives were investigating reports of a "Communist ring" using "stand-over" methods to get Czechoslovakian migrants to return home. One Czech told detectives that the "ring" consisted of a Czech and a Russian intimidating him." In capital letters, the article absurdly proclaimed, "THE PAIR INDICATES THE RING KNOWS THE ADDRESSES OF NEARLY ALL IRON CURTAIN MIGRANTS IN AUSTRALIA." It is one thing to steal the subscription addresses of readers of an Estonian magazine in Germany and Australia. However, it is quite another thing to publish falsehoods about a 'Communist ring' knowing nearly all the addresses of tens of thousands of migrants from Eastern Europe! This would have involved a herculean intelligence operation well beyond the capacity of ASIO in pre-Internet days, let alone a handful of so-called Soviet and East European intelligence agents and their informers.

While there were some émigrés from Eastern Europe who undoubtedly had pressure placed upon them to return, there was no evidence of a mass Soviet campaign to coerce migrants to return. Instead, the Committee for Return to the Homeland used *non-coercive* propaganda methods in order to divide émigré communities. Given the climate of fear generated by the media, ASIO, and the special branch of state police forces, the timing of my father's comments on the *Orcades* proved to be more than unfortunate. He inadvertently added weight to all those who had their own agendas concerning the Soviet repatriation campaign.

As I would learn many years later, the common image of government or 'the state' as a monolithic power with a consistent voice is largely untrue. No government acts like an individual subject, as even dictatorships have to see their orders implemented by others within the different branches of government. Files in the Australian National Archives would reveal the conflicting opinions between cabinet ministers, government departments and agencies such as ASIO over how they treated not only our family but also others. While security agencies within Australia and the USSR were quite powerful, they also had to compete with bureaucrats and advisers in other government departments. Victims often got caught between the respective ambitions, prejudices and institutional power plays exercised by particular officers and ministers.

Not always smooth sailing

As we sailed away from Melbourne, my mother, Genia, and I had very mixed emotions about leaving our home and friends. As mentioned in an earlier chapter, Mum did not want to leave. She reluctantly agreed to join Dad only to prevent breaking up the family as my father was so determined to pursue his dream. I was excited by the trip but also particularly upset about having to part with my dog Peter, a golden Labrador, who was a much-loved member of the household. On many nights he would sleep alongside me in bed. I cried when we had to give Peter away a few days before departing Melbourne. Fortunately, we found a loving home for him. Fast forward to an incredible forty years later when I received surprising news about Peter's new owners in November 1996. It transpired that Belinda Probert and John Murphy from RMIT University were doing research on working-class families in the Western suburbs. They came across Ray and Pat Ashton from Maidstone in Maribyrnong council who told them how they came to Godfrey Avenue with their kids to foster Peter before we left for Russia. Pat Ashton gave Belinda and John their telephone number and as I knew both Belinda and John, they passed the Ashton's number on to me.

I contacted the Ashtons and heard how Peter became a beloved pet for their five children until he died of old age. I told Pat Ashton about some of our experiences and what happened to our family. Later, she penned a very warm letter to me in November 1996 and included post cards and letters that my mother had apparently written to them from various stops on the voyage to London in 1956 and also letters from Kerch in later years. Pat wrote:

> Your mother wrote as though we were close friends, but we only met the once, when we, my husband and three children, went to your house to be 'vetted' before we could be entrusted with the treasure of the family your dog 'Peter', well loved by the family I know that.
>
> I'm sorry part of one letter is missing, I haven't a clue what happened to it. It's a 'miracle' really to have anything after forty years and five children who would rummage through my treasures occasionally.
>
> This to me is like a fairy story with a happy ending.

Back in May 1956, our sorrow at leaving our friends and familiar life was mixed with the anticipation and adventure of being on an ocean liner that would visit exotic cities and countries. Maya was barely two and was secure with her loving family around. My father was enthusiastic but also anxious that he had made the right decision. In the months before we left, my parents had made lists of what to take with us and what to leave behind. Key items were packed in a freight container and shipped separately to our personal suitcases and hand luggage. These items of furniture and household goods were packed and dispatched a couple of days before we boarded the *Orcades*. They would take months to arrive at our new address in the USSR. Apart from taking clothing that would not fit into our suitcases, and knowing that we would encounter cold winters, Dad bought all members of our family warm jackets and coats lined with sheep's wool. Little did he know that some of these items would later be sold to buy food to help us survive.

The Soviet repatriation Committee had paid for our tickets which my father then arranged through Thomas Cook Travel. On board the ship, we three children shared an inside cabin with our mother while Dad was in another cabin which he shared with another returning Russian called Ivan Goncharov (not Gantivan as named in an ASIO file) and his female de facto spouse Alexandra Rokitianski. Prior to 1954, Goncharov had been regarded by ASIO to be the nominal leader of the Cossacks in Melbourne and had been anti-Soviet until his recent pro-Soviet turn. Goncharov and his spouse would drink a lot and after a week or so, he called my father a dirty Jew and threatened to kill him. So, the atmosphere in his cabin was far from comradely.

From Melbourne, our first stop was Port Adelaide and then Fremantle. At both ports, reporters came on board seeking interviews, but none were given. We picked up the local papers from the previous day and read about our departure which was also featured in the Adelaide newspapers. Several days later we briefly went offshore in Fremantle. I was struck by the number of local Aborigines sitting on the grass in a nearby park and drinking. They appeared to be much darker than the occasional local Aborigines in Melbourne and were also much more visible than in St. Kilda and nearby suburbs. This was an Australia that looked both unfamiliar and disturbing as Indigenous people were neglected but visibly so and distinctly marginalised compared to their relative invisibility in largely white Melbourne.

In contrast to present-day giant tour ships with thousands of passengers, the *Orcades* was relatively small at only 28,000 tons. Nevertheless, for its day, it was reasonably large and was one of the popular passenger ships travelling to the UK via the Suez Canal. While First Class was closed to us commoners in steerage or lower deck tourist class, there were ample decks, lounges, dining rooms and entertainment facilities to engage us for the almost four week trip to London.

I loved the ocean and the sea air, the sight of whales, dolphins and flying fish, the sharks trailing the ship and various seagulls and petrels. Upon leaving Fremantle for Colombo in what was then called Ceylon, we headed straight into a massive storm with giant seas. For the next three days, the lower decks were closed as the waves could have easily washed people overboard. Without stabilisers, the *Orcades* was tossed around like a little toy boat. What initially looked like a scene from a Buster Keaton or Charlie Chaplin film with dishes sliding from one end of the dining table to the other end and waiters barely able to keep their balance or falling over as the ship was tossed up and down, soon turned into a near disaster. Such was the level of the storm, that all the pieces of furniture in the lounge rooms were assembled in large piles and tied down with ropes. Elderly passengers had their arms and legs broken from falling over, and most passengers were sick in their cabins and did not come to the dining room.

All of our family were seasick except me. In the dining room where I ate with a minority of other passengers, brackets were fitted to all the tables so that the dishes would not fly off and smash. Instead of sleeping in the cabins with the nauseating smell of people being sick, the ship provided camping beds on the upper deck where I slept with others during the warm evenings. It was a wonderful experience sleeping in the fresh air as the ship tipped from one extreme of facing the sea to the other extreme of facing the sky. Once the *Orcades* had passed through a few days of turbulent ocean with giant waves, we encountered the calm tropical islands dotting the coastline near Indonesia and then some of the many tiny islands between what is now the Maldives and Ceylon. The traditional festivities of crossing the Equator were great fun.

Despite arriving in Colombo in what was supposed to be a cooler period than summer, the temperature was still extremely hot. Going ashore was my first taste of a foreign country and the realisation of how privileged we were. Colombo still had all the characteristics of a British colony even though it had gained formal independence eight years earlier in 1948. My memory of the city was dominated by the many beggars and pervasive extreme poverty. I also remember the zoo with its giant snakes and tigers. Here we watched performing elephants as they mounted each other's backs in a congo-line while the lead elephant with trainer blew a mouth organ and they danced around.

The abusive treatment of animals was characteristic of the times, yet we were completely enchanted by these giant creatures.

From Colombo we headed for Aden (now in Yemen) near the Red Sea. It was another poverty-stricken colonial outpost presided over by a British military garrison in a hot and dusty part of the world. Aden was the port that strategically guarded the entrance to the Suez Canal. It was also the point where the Gully Gully man with his dancing cobra and magical tricks boarded the ship to entertain the passengers. As we slowly cruised towards Port Said in Egypt, the Gully Gully man wove his magic by planting a seed and amazing us as it grew into a large plant. He approached my father and asked for his watch which he then proceeded to smash into pieces – much to his alarm – and then threw the pieces overboard. After the performance he returned the watch to him in its original state.

Travelling along the Canal was a slow journey with desert on either side. Several months later, the UK, France and Israel would attack Egypt in an attempt to gain control of Suez following Nasser's nationalisation of the British/French company. The US and USSR would force the three attacking countries into a humiliating backdown and defeat. Upon reaching Port Said, the *Orcades* did not dock but was instead met by a flotilla of small boats with various wares and souvenirs to sell. Ropes were thrown to passengers on the decks and goods were placed in baskets which were hauled up to be inspected and paid for by customers.

We were now in the Mediterranean and headed for Naples via the Strait of Messina. In the dark we could see the eruption of red lava from the volcano on Stromboli. Arriving in Naples, we were taken on a tour of the city and then onto Pompeii. In 1956, Naples was tougher and poorer than in recent decades. Mum was initially denied entry because they thought she was a local Italian. Many years later I would revisit the vibrant and chaotic city of Naples, and also the remarkable archaeological site of Pompeii. Like Colombo, Aden, the Suez Canal and Port Said, the opportunity to see an ancient city and the modern slums of Naples left an indelible impression on me. Staying in Melbourne at Brighton Road primary school would not ever have competed in terms of educative and formative experiences. This was also true of our next stops in Marseilles and then Gibraltar where we gained brief glimpses of French and part-Spanish life, as Gibraltar was still heavily shaped by British military occupation and culture.

Pompeii, May 1956.

From Gibraltar we exited the Mediterranean and sailed through the Bay of Biscay bordering Spain and France on the way to the English Channel. The small rolling waves got to me compared with the giant waves in the Indian Ocean. I was seasick for the first time. Soon we would reach Tilbury docks which were the home port closest to London. I did not want to leave the *Orcades* and all the fun and games, fancy dress parties, quiz nights, entertainment, and sitting looking at the ocean or sleeping on the various decks in the fresh sea air. It was a city on the sea and provided release and respite but there was no preparation for what was to come.

More misreporting from London

Disembarking from the *Orcades* was anti-climactic. Our family together with the other Russian couple were supposed to have been met by someone from the Soviet Embassy and taken to our London hotel. Nobody came. After hours of waiting on board the *Orcades* and phone calls made by the ship's purser to the Embassy at around 11p.m., we were eventually picked up hours later and taken late at night to our hotel in Kensington where we arrived about 4 a.m. in the morning. This was not a favourable first impression of Soviet organisation. To add to our distress, the driver of the Soviet vehicle to London whispered to my mother that she was a mug for returning to the Soviet Union.

The three days we spent in London were taken up with tourist sight-seeing and going to the nearby Soviet Embassy to arrange final details of the trip to Leningrad. In London, the Soviet Embassy was located on an exclusive street called Kensington Palace Gardens which housed other embassies and large wealthy homes. The entrance and exit to the street were guarded, as was the Soviet Embassy. After finally entering the Embassy and having our passports and travel documents confirmed, the Soviet official told my father that they would like him to fly to East Berlin to meet the Mikhailov Committee for Return to the Homeland. They undoubtedly hoped to use him in one of their propaganda publications. However, he declined and said he did not want to be separated from his family. My father was genuinely excited about returning to Russia, but he was not interested in self-promotion or being used for propaganda purposes.

Both the Australian media and ASIO were aware of our movements in London. An Australian Associated Press reporter interviewed Mum and Dad on board the *Orcades* shortly after arrival on June 4, 1956, while we were waiting to be taken to our hotel. This was published in Australian newspapers the following day under the heading: 'Russian Found Life Dull Here'. Paradoxically, it was Mum who was most critical. According to the report,

"A Russian woman (sic) returning home after 18 years in Australia (meaning Dad rather than Mum), claimed in London today that she and her family had to wait three months for a visa to return to Russia. The Russians also complained that there was a good deal of "anti-foreigner" feeling in Australia and that life there was "very dull for Europeans."

The Russian family, middle-aged Mr. and Mrs. Abraham Frankel, arrived in the liner *Orcades* with their three children on their way to the Soviet Union.

"If this is democracy as they say it is, why can't we leave when we want to?" Mrs. Frankel said. "Some Australian papers said we were forced to leave, that letters came from Russia to persuade us. It is all lies."

Her husband remarked: "We want friendship between peoples, trade and cultural relations like the ballet and Russian circus now visiting London. We want to live in peace and understanding and not to have press attacks."

The three month wait for visas that my mother referred to in this interview had particularly annoyed my father. An ASIO report on March 16, 1956, stated that an officer at Thomas Cook & Son informed ASIO's Victoria Office that four families would soon be returning to the Soviet Union. The person from Thomas Cook also told ASIO that "Abraham Frenkel remarked that representations had been made to the Soviet delegation to the United Nations Organisation to lodge an official complaint regarding the investigations into the repatriates in this country (by ASIO) who are returning to their homeland." Dad was not going to be intimidated or go quietly. Little wonder that ASIO had little love for my father.

In the following years when ASIO repeatedly rejected the re-entry of my father back into Australia, their reports would cite the June 5th article in *The Age* as further evidence of my father's 'violent attack' on Australian institutions. In a terrible irony, it was Dad who in this article was conciliatory in his emphasis on 'peace and understanding between peoples'. My mother, on the other hand, not Russian but Byelorussian, was the one who didn't want to leave Australia, and who didn't want to say anything pro-Soviet, but was nonetheless upset by the misreporting of our case. Hence, she vented her feelings about media misreporting and about how many migrants found life in Australia dull and also discriminatory.

ASIO and the Australian media failed to understand that one didn't have to be an affluent European bourgeois to find Australia boring, anti-intellectual, and parochial in its cultural offerings. Many working-class and professionally educated European migrants were shocked by the 'cultural desert' they found in 1950s Australia and the impoverished offerings in education and the arts, especially classical music, theatre, literature and poetry readings. Little wonder that so many Australian artists and writers had to leave Australia during the arid Menzies years. Crucially, without the disproportionate involvement and patronage of 'New Australians', especially Jewish migrants, most leading arts institutions would not have developed or survived in the post-war decades.

Meanwhile, in a secret report entitled 'Abraham Frenkel' and dated June 19, 1956, ASIO noted our arrival with Goncharov and his partner at Tilbury and how we were all escorted by Soviet Embassy officials to London. It noted that the group then departed for Leningrad on the *Vyacheslav Molotov* on June 8, 1956. The memo then goes on:

> 2. A reliable and delicate source has reported that it was originally planned to separate FRENKEL from his family and send him by air to Berlin. It is not known why this plan was abandoned, but it is possible that no air passage was available at the appropriate time.
>
> 3. An independent source, also reliable, has stated that FRENKEL has been co-ordinating his activity over the repatriation of Russians to the U.S.S.R. with a Mr A. DUBOVIKOV, "Return to the Homeland", 65 Behrenstrasse, Berlin (Russian Sector). There is no conclusive evidence, however, that FRENKEL'S proposed journey to Berlin was in order to meet DUBOVIKOV.

Clearly, ASIO and their London intelligence sources in MI5 were labouring under the false impression that 'Frenkel' was a 'top man' in Australia who worked with the Committee for the Return to Homeland and that he intended to fly to Berlin soon after arriving in London. The truth is that my father did not work for this Committee and was quite surprised when the Soviet Embassy asked him to fly to Berlin. He was neither a 'subversive' undermining Australia, nor a willing tool to be used for Soviet propaganda. His main relationship with Mikhailov's Berlin Committee was as a recipient of Soviet journals and propaganda literature that were mailed to many Russians in the West. The ASIO files in the National Archives, however, do contain a letter which my father wrote to Dubovikov on March 21, 1956, or six weeks before we departed Melbourne. The handwritten letter in Russian which ASIO secretly copied but probably didn't translate, dealt with ticket arrangements at Thomas Cook Travel and also Dad's interest in various Soviet literary journals. So much for the accusation of subversive activities!

On one of our remaining days in London, we went to Leyton in East London to see the parents of Joan Brettargh and spent an enjoyable time at their home. Joan was a nurse and had come to Australia and married Reg Brettargh who worked as a printer at the *Herald and Weekly Times*. They were sympathetic to Left causes. In fact, ASIO records from April 28, 1958, show that Reg had been a 'subject of interest' since 1953 because he had signed a petition calling for a cease fire during the Korean War and also because of his membership of the Australasian Book Society in 1955. Book readers were regarded as potential subversives. Constable Geoff Welch of Camberwell Special Branch reported on July 27, 1953, that Brettargh was "an atheist with strong socialistic tendencies" but lived a quiet private life with wife Joan and two children in Hawthorn. We had become friends with Reg and Joan since the late 1940s, and before we departed Joan had asked Mum to visit her working-class parents when we arrived in London. Little did we know in London that Reg and Joan would become so supportive and generous (as I will later discuss) that they were prepared to foster us children should the Soviets not let our parents out and we had to return to Melbourne on our own.

Our stay in London was all too brief. Boarding the *Vyacheslav Molotov*, we could immediately see that it was much smaller than the *Orcades* and lacked the facilities of the bigger ship. While the food was much better than anything inside the USSR, it was an inferior quality to what we had become used to on the *Orcades*. Fortunately, the trip was only about six days with stops in Copenhagen, Stockholm, and Helsinki to break up the journey. Apart from the group of about fifty returning to the Soviet Union, the majority of passengers were tourists from the three Scandinavian countries heading on a tour of Leningrad and Moscow. Any grumbling and complaints about food or service on the ship would soon be forgotten and instead fondly remembered as we were soon to be confronted with the new reality of life and hardship in the Soviet 'paradise'.

10

'IF I COULD ONLY SWIM THE ATLANTIC OR THE PACIFIC ...'

THE POPULAR IMAGE OF 'TOTALITARIAN COMMUNISM' in Western media and literature was of a highly bureaucratised society exercising strict control over every facet of people's lives. The reality of the USSR we found upon arrival in June 1956 was more shambolic than either rigidly controlled or hyper-organised. While the Soviet population knew that rules had to be obeyed, the actual organisational principles in many institutions were sometimes vague, sometimes contradictory, or often bent to suit particular needs and interests. Institutions of law and order generally worked effectively when implemented in order to discipline and repress people. As with many other social and economic structures and organisations, there were significant contrasts between how they were supposed to function and their actual day-to-day practices.

Reading the released files about us in the National Archives, it is clear that ASIO's intelligence was based on malicious and absurd information about my father's new role in the Soviet Union. As I will later discuss, the accounts written about him were completely at odds with his real-life status and work. Given ASIO operated on the grossly distorted assumption that he was a 'Communist subversive', they assumed that upon our arrival in Leningrad that Soviet intelligence would debrief him about Australia, Vladimir Petrov, and other topics. Nothing of the sort happened.

The truth was that the Soviets neither believed that there would be a mass repatriation of Russians from abroad, nor were they equipped or well prepared to handle even the exceedingly small numbers of returnees. Disorganisation prevailed upon our arrival. We were directed to get on buses with the arriving tourist passengers from Scandinavia and transported to a hotel in the centre of the city. After waiting for hours to be checked in and desperately hungry, we were then told that a mistake had been made and were then driven back with others to a drab hostel close to where our ship had originally docked.

During the next four or five days, we just idled away the time waiting in this desolate 'reception' centre until we were given our Soviet documents and transit instructions for Baku. Instead of being 'debriefed', nobody seemed to care. Dad was not asked anything about the politics in Australia but merely why he had returned, why he was going to Baku and what kind of work he was after. When he replied that he was going to where his sister lived and that he hoped to find work as an electric welder or smoking fish, they were visibly surprised. My father was offered a more comfortable non-factory job and the official suggested he might want to live in a Russian city rather than go all the way to Azerbaijan. Dad declined the offer. Such was his misguided idealism that he told them that he just wanted to be a factory worker and not receive any special treatment.

Our stay at this hostel/processing centre was dispiriting after such a long journey. There was another woman there with a baby who cried most of the time because there was no milk. The food at the *stolovka* or canteen was barely edible. It was neither a restaurant nor café but an eating venue common to many workplaces and public places. People went there not only to eat but also to drink vodka. Later, we would get used to ignoring whatever menu was printed as most of the items were unavailable. Often there would be a choice of a couple of dishes for lunch or dinner, depending on food supplies. The meat dishes were usually tough scraps of beef or pork and daily serves of *borscht* with large slices of bread. At breakfast we opted for *kefir* or *syrnik* made from *Tvorog*, a type of cottage cheese pancake. The offering of

Greshnaya kasha or a type of gruel was healthy but inedible. We never got used to its awful taste. Fruit and vegetables were very scarce, and this was summer. Luckily, we did not arrive in winter as there would have been no fresh vegetables and we would have eaten *borscht* made from pickled cabbage or beetroot.

As part of the repatriation program, we had our rail fares paid from Leningrad to Baku plus an allowance of roubles for food and accommodation. Before departing for Moscow, we briefly visited parts of historic Leningrad and also went underground to see the metro stations which were decorated like exquisite works of art rather than the bare walls of the underground in London. At the main Leningrad railway station, we boarded a crowded train on a journey to Baku that seemed like it would take forever.

Our first stop would be Moscow where we had to get off at the *Leningradsky vokzal* (station) and change for the train to Baku that departed from the *Kazansky vokzal*. Fortunately, both stations were close to each other on *Komsomolskaya* (Young Communist) Square, so we carried our bags rather than having to get a taxi or bus across town. If the journey from Leningrad to Moscow was relatively smooth and uneventful, the changeover at the *Kazansky vokzal* would truly shock us and for the first time reveal the harsh reality of Soviet life. The processing centre in Leningrad had been drab, depressing and demoralising but we had limited contact with ordinary living conditions and hoped that things would improve once we got to Baku. What we saw and experienced at the *Kazansky vokzal* would shatter any remaining illusions. It would be our first real and stark encounter with what life was like for ordinary Soviet citizens.

The shock of the Kazansky

Upon entering the station, we were struck by the number of people sitting on every available bench seat, plus many sleeping or sprawled out all over the ground. Apart from their suitcases, many either carried sacks of potatoes, food and all kinds of possessions or rested on these as they dozed while waiting for their trains. In appearance, it was clear that they were peasants as well as urban residents from all the Soviet republics. Apart from Russians and Ukrainians, a substantial number were from the Caucuses (Georgia, Armenia, Azerbaijan) as well as from distant Soviet Asian regions. The summer heat meant the station was stiflingly hot and airless.

At first, we found nowhere to sit and stood huddled with our bags while my father went to the ticket counters to confirm our seating and sleeping berths for the long, three-day journey to Baku. After interminable waiting in the ticket queue, he came back looking stunned and incredulous. All the trains were overbooked, and the earliest available places would be a minimum of two to three days at the earliest! No wonder there were so many people slumbering on the floor or on every bench and seat in the building. Like hundreds of others who arrived hopefully expecting to board their trains, we were left confronting the 'brilliance' of Soviet command planning and organisation.

Those familiar with the over-strained long-haul Soviet railway system were not surprised and had come prepared with food for days and a habitual patience that was forged from years of suffering. Their expressions showed a resigned fatalism in the face of bureaucratic incompetence, scarcity, and corruption. As novices, we, on the other hand, felt helpless from shock. Where would we sleep for days if we couldn't even find bench space or barely any room on the ground? What would we eat? Railway officials could neither tell us when our train would arrive and depart, nor whether it was safe to leave the station in case our train arrived early. We were trapped in the *Kazansky* in case our allocated seats were given to others should we fail to board when called. Other travellers told us that rail seats in peak summer months were prioritised for military officers and administrators travelling on government business or holidays. The ability to also get a seat or berth partly depended on how much additional money in the form of bribes one was prepared to pay. Soviet trains were certainly not designed for a classless society. In addition to first- and second-class carriages in capitalist societies, the Soviets added a third class of rows of plain benches (rather than seats) for peasants and other low-income people. Imagine travelling for days on hard benches without a backrest.

Hours later, we managed to grab bench space after a group of passengers were called to board a newly arrived train. As we squeezed together surrounded by our luggage, we had to simultaneously try to sleep and yet take turns to watch that nothing was stolen. My father had managed to buy some food and drinks at a nearby kiosk, but we didn't have much of an appetite. The first day and night at the *Kazansky* would be an unforgettable shock. It was more than a sobering and dispiriting experience as we had to lay on top of one another trying to sleep in the midst of constant noise and movement. My parents could not believe their eyes as they critically commented on the organised chaos, the poverty, and the unfolding scene before us.

To add to our distress, nature eventually called, and we had to go to the toilet. For the rest of my life, and on my many travels, I would never again encounter such a filthy, disgusting public toilet to rival the one at the *Kazansky*. As I opened the toilet door, I was confronted by a large semi-circled room divided into perhaps thirty open cubicles or partitions with holes in the floor that one had to squat over. Besides each hole hung a towel. Quickly surveying the room, I could see that all the formerly white towels were now covered in shit. The walls in each cubicle were also covered in shit as people had either wiped their hands on them or flicked shit in all directions.

If toilet paper existed at the time in the Soviet Union, it was probably only available for the Party elite and for tourists in selected hotels. At the *Kazansky* and most other public toilets across the country, one had to make do with newspaper or whatever was available. I entered one of the open cubicles but was so nauseated by the sight and the smell that my former bowel movement urges completely froze. For the next three days, my bowel was in shock, and I only went to the toilet for a pee until we got onto the train. According to Genia, the women's toilet was equally appalling. While later we would use open latrines elsewhere, it was the sheer size and condition of the public toilets at the *Kazansky* that would stay in our memories. We were extremely fortunate not to come down with hepatitis or other diseases as was the case with some foreign visitors including former Trade Minister Doug Anthony in the 1970s who enjoyed much better conditions than we did in the 1950s.

On the second day at the *Kazansky*, my father kept enquiring as to whether there would be a train available but was told that it would be at least another day. Hardly having slept the night before, the prospect of another night on the bench was so distressing that Dad spurred into action. He asked various administrative people in the station whether there were any places where his children could sleep, especially two-year-old Maya. One person suggested he go to the nursery or children's room (*detskaya komnata*) which was part of the station complex. He found this facility and persuaded the sympathetic woman running the place that not only Maya but also Genia and I as well as our mother could stay there overnight. Perhaps she felt sympathy for us foreigners? Surprisingly, it was not being heavily used. Dad would sit up all night and look after the luggage. I remember the relief we felt in having beds and being able to sleep away from the noise, smells, and turmoil of the main waiting hall.

It was on the way to this nursery, that we bumped into three passengers who had also arrived on the *Vyacheslav Molotov* several days earlier. They were a Polish couple in their late fifties and their twenty-three-year-old son. The couple told us that they had lived in Canada from before the war and had a successful small business. Being quite affluent, but seduced by Soviet propaganda, they had sold their business and packed several freight containers of their possessions. Their decision to move to the USSR was driven by the belief that their son would get a first-class education in the arts and have more cultural opportunities than in Canada.

Waiting for their train to Tashkent, their former naivety and innocence were cruelly shattered by the *Kazansky* and other experiences, and they hadn't even reached their new home city. I will never forget the shellshocked expressions on their dazed faces. As we exchanged stories of the depressing, disorganised and startling things that we had already witnessed, their son uttered the immortal words that would be seared in our memories: "If I could only swim the Atlantic or the Pacific, I would start swimming immediately."

Confessing that they had made a terrible mistake, we sympathetically shared their desire of trying to get out of the country as soon as possible. Yet, how was this to be achieved if we were stuck at the *Kazansky* station with no train to anywhere? Bidding them farewell and wishing them good luck, we often wondered what had become of them and whether they had ever managed to get permission to leave the Soviet Union.

After a more restful night in the nursery surrounded by all kinds of decorations based on characters from children's stories, we rejoined Dad in the waiting hall. The third day began like the other two days with little likelihood of a train to Baku. By late afternoon, however, it was announced that our train would be arriving in a few hours and departing about 8 p.m. in the evening. We were overjoyed to hear the news that soon we would be leaving the *Kazansky* but held our breath just in case it was another false alarm.

Further blows and revelations

Fortunately, our train did arrive, and we finally departed after 8 p.m. for Baku. Officially, the train trip distance from Moscow to Baku was 1,929 kilometres and would take just over fifty-five hours. Actually, it was closer to 70 hours or almost three days due to delays in various parts of the giant country. We had long learnt that the USSR constituted one-sixth of the world's surface. The trip between Moscow and Baku was only half the distance of some of the longer journeys straddling European and Asian regions of the Soviet Union. In contrast to the train between Leningrad and Moscow, this train was awfully slow. It averaged about 48 kilometres per hour, or almost as slow as some of the interstate trains in Australia that were, and still remain terribly slow in comparison with contemporary European, Chinese, or Japanese trains.

Our four-berth compartment was a great relief after the *Kazansky* station, even though Maya had to share one berth with Mum. The two conductors in each of the carriages made tea from their samovars and served them in traditional manner in glasses held within decorative metal containers. Along the route that travelled through cities and small towns in the Russian, Ukrainian and various Caucasian republics, we observed the changing scenery of large forests, rivers, lakes, and mountains. At various stops along the way, we alighted from the train and watched the impromptu food and homeware markets on the platforms as passengers purchased food for the journey or various other items of clothing or crafts. The opportunity to buy fresh fruit and local delicacies was highly appreciated after the awful food we had eaten since arriving in Leningrad.

We also noticed that our conductors were remarkably busy, not only buying food, but also selling it to particular locals at the various stops. It was only later that we learnt that getting a job as a conductor on long-haul journeys was keenly sought after and one had to pay substantial 'key money' or *blat* for any vacant position. The opportunity to carry goods in the black market from one town or region to another was a lucrative business. It more than compensated for the low wages of railway workers.

As we would soon find out, *blat* was the informal currency or grease that would make the machinery function behind or alongside the official system. A cross between bribery and the internal black market, *blat* delivered job opportunities and access to officials, helped get an apartment, entry to a top university or a plethora of goods and services that were normally scarce. Despite official warnings and penalties, *blat* was pervasive and deeply institutionalised. It ridiculed official notions of socialist equality.

On the second day of our journey, my father began talking to a person from the neighbouring compartment who was standing in the corridor to smoke. It turned out that he was one of the millions of prisoners arbitrarily sentenced to the Gulag during the Stalin years. There are no exact figures of the number of people who went through the Gulag camps between 1919 and 1953. However, there is a growing consensus that approximately eighteen million were interned in the different prisons, forced labour colonies and other parts of the Gulag with a further six million exiled. Of these, 3,778,234 people were arrested for counter-revolutionary and state crimes, of which 786,098 were shot. The day Stalin died on March 5th, 1953, Lavrenty Beria, head of MVD before being executed, reported that there were 2,526,408 prisoners still in the Gulag system. Using more reliable figures, Sovietologist, Moshe Lewin in *The Soviet Century* (2005), calculates that when those forced into exile are added, the total in 1953 exceeded five million victims. Stalin's successors ended the terror and through amnesties to innocent victims, slowly released prisoners in waves over the following three years.

The man on the train had left a young family in Rostov-on-Don in 1939 when he was sent to one of the Gulags in freezing Siberia. Describing the horrific conditions in the labour camp, he revealed that he was granted partial freedom more than a decade later to leave the Gulag but not the local town or region. Thinking that he would never see his family again, the man married another prisoner who had also been granted restricted rights, and they started a family. The terror system known as the Gulag was not just a prison system where people died like flies. It was also an elaborate industrial economy based on mining and a range of other industries operated by various agencies including the NVKD. According to historian Karl Schlögel, *The Soviet Century: Archaeology of a Lost World* (2023), even the elephants found on Soviet home mantelpieces had a Gulag connection as *slon* (Russian for 'elephant'), was also the acronym of Solovetskii Lager Osobogo Naznacheniia (the Solovki Special Purpose Camp).

The ex-prisoner on our train was now in his early fifties and explained that he was going to see his first wife and children. Through no fault of his own, he now had two families, one that he had not seen for about seventeen years. Naturally, he was incredibly aggrieved by how the Soviet system had made a mess of his life. Like countless others, he was a living example of the havoc and irreparable damage caused by the combination of systematic and random terror of the previous decades. In Aleksandr Solzhenitsyn's words, "people were arrested for nothing and interrogated about nothing." Security police engaged in sweeping arrests of innocents just to fill designated targets set by their superiors. As he described it in the *Gulag Archipelago*:

> Arrests rolled through the streets and apartment houses like an epidemic. Just as people transmit an epidemic infection from one to another without knowing it, by such innocent means as a handshake, a breath, handing someone something, so too, they passed on the infection of inevitable arrest by a handshake, by a breath, by a chance meeting on the street.

My father returned to our compartment, shaken, and told us about the man's suffering. I could see how disturbed he was to hear this first-hand account of the terror. The penny had dropped. He had naively believed in the Soviet system all the time during the same period that the ex-prisoner next door had suffered alongside millions of others. Fortunately, we had arrived during Khrushchev's de-Stalinisation period also known as 'the Thaw'. The worst of the terror was over. People were still frightened in 1956, but they were slowly gaining courage, and some were prepared to talk about their awful experiences. During the next few years, we would hear many personal stories about Soviet life in the decades before 1956. From arriving in Leningrad enveloped in drabness and disorganisation, to witnessing the chaos at *Kazansky vokzal* and now hearing directly from a victim of the Gulag, my father's long-held devotion to the propaganda image of the 'society of the future' was collapsing at a rapid rate.

Baku, the final straw

After what seemed like an expedition halfway across the world from Leningrad, we eventually arrived in Baku, the capital of Azerbaijan on the Caspian Sea. Although people spoke Russian and there were many Russians in the streets, most people were Azeris who were a Turkic people also to be found in large numbers in neighbouring Iran and Transcaucasia. The city was a contrast between old Azeri buildings and cobbled streets located behind the few remaining sections of the traditional wall, and newer Russian and Soviet era housing and buildings from the nineteenth and twentieth centuries. Given that we had no idea when we would arrive from Moscow, our aunt, my father's sister could not meet us at the railway station. The grand station building looked as if it were from the Middle East or North Africa with its Moorish design and minarets. There were also quite a few men dressed in what looked like pyjamas but were fine suits made of striped fabrics. Some wore decorated skull caps. We had left Europe and were now in a truly foreign place that had more in common with Yemen or Port Said rather than with any Western or Eastern European city.

Hailing a taxi, we all packed in with our luggage for the short trip to the Russian part of the city where Dad's sister Nusia lived with her husband Misha and adult daughter Alla who was in her early twenties. Fortunately, they were home as we ascended the staircase to the second floor of an old building from the 1890s or early twentieth century. My father had written from Leningrad to let his sister know that we were on the way, but the three-day delay to get a train at the *Kazansky* had thrown our itinerary out of order.

When the door opened, Dad and Nusia passionately embraced. Although they had corresponded and sent photos over the decades, they had not seen one another in the flesh for thirty-five years since 1921. She was now 59 and Dad was 48. Next, we all took turns to embrace Nusia, Misha and Alla as many tears flowed and the air was full of joy and laughter. After bringing in our luggage and sitting down at a small table that could not accommodate all of us, my parents exchanged many stories with Nusia and her family about their lives, the long journey to Baku and so forth.

Following the excitement of seeing his sister and her family, what disturbed, and particularly shocked him was the small one-bedroom apartment with a tiny kitchen and bathroom that barely accommodated three adults let alone an additional family of five persons. Where would we sleep without extra beds or mattresses? How could Nusia have agreed to sponsor Dad or provide housing when she and her family were living in such a confined space that her adult daughter Alla did not even have a separate bedroom? Although a doctor, she was not affluent like most doctors in Australia during the 1950s. Instead, doctors in the Soviet Union were poorly paid and she struggled to make ends meet.

In these very cramped conditions, we all slept on the floor and one on the couch while Nusia and Misha were in their own bed. Alla went to stay at night with her fiancé Yura who lived in the old town. For the next few weeks, whatever illusions remained about the 'society of the future' soon evaporated. My father went out day after day to the local authorities to try to find separate housing for us, but none was available for at least nine to twelve months. In desperation, he even naively sent a telegram to Mikhailov's Committee for Return to Homeland in Berlin requesting help with accommodation in Baku. Unsurprisingly, they never replied.

Baku was the centre of the oil industry at the time. It had not been directly attacked during the war, but such was the massive task of reconstruction across the USSR, that there was a desperate shortage in most Soviet cities of single rooms, let alone separate apartments. The centrally planned economy was still primarily geared to heavy industry and producer goods rather than consumer goods and services. Housing was a priority, but with only eleven years having passed since the widespread destruction of the war, this had been insufficient time to provide adequate housing for a long-suffering population. Waiting lists for housing were extremely long and bribery or having connections only worked in a limited number of cases.

To add to the housing worries, we soon discovered the vicious cycle of work and housing: the allocation of housing was connected to employment but finding an ongoing job depended on having registered accommodation. The internal passport system of the USSR operated to prevent people from especially poor regional and rural areas flooding into large cities without work or accommodation. Free mobility was only possible for short visits, and everyone had to register with local authorities if they exceeded the number of days away from their registered locality. Having accommodation meant that any job obtained in an industrial plant, institute, or workplace helped you with healthcare and other social services, including a retirement pension. Peasants and members of *Kolkhozes* or collective farms were not entitled to public old-age pensions until 1964 and they continued to work more years than industrial workers before retirement. Not having a job or not being able to freely move and get a job in one's preferred city because of lack of housing were thus interdependent as were so many other aspects of Soviet daily life.

While my father did the rounds of the local bureaucracy trying to find work and housing, we explored the old and new parts of Baku. Alla took us to the old city behind the wall where her future husband lived. The narrow-cobbled streets were mysterious as they looked quite different from European and Australian urban centres. I played with a few Azeri boys as we roamed the car-free streets. The other unusual characteristic of the city was its arid, hot climate. In the summer evening, the large central park had its own beauty and was full of people having their stroll through the gardens. We were amazed to see that there was not a single blade of grass in this large garden or across this dry and hot city. I found the street scene very lively as many people were dressed in colourful robes and striped suits, although the women did not have their heads covered as in traditional Muslim societies.

After two weeks of depressing news about work and accommodation, the mood inside Nusia's small apartment changed from joy to distress and accusation. My father blamed his sister for misleading him about life in Baku and the Soviet Union. "Why did you tell me to come if you knew conditions were so terribly bad?", he asked bitterly. Nusia replied, "I couldn't write you the truth as I would have been in trouble, and you probably wouldn't have believed me anyway." This was absolutely true on both counts. It was clear that the situation in Baku was hopeless as far as getting housing. Even if Dad found a job, there was no accommodation available until at least the middle of 1957. My parents discussed the impossible situation and agreed that my father should request permission to let him move to Kerch where he was born. At first, the authorities refused this request but after more pleading by my father they reluctantly agreed to pay our fares for the long train trip that would take over two days. The official in Baku also gave us a living allowance until Dad found work in Kerch.

We therefore reluctantly left Baku after little more than three and a half weeks of setbacks and shocks about housing and work. Once again, there were no available seats or berths and we had to wait days for a booking. Dad parted with his sister on strained terms, but he couldn't blame her for the lack of housing or a job as she would have loved for her brother to remain and live in the same city. Within two years, Nusia would die of cancer and my father would return to Baku for her final days and funeral. Misha, her husband, who was a very warm and gentle man would be left as a widower after a long marriage. Their daughter Alla would later marry Yura and after two decades would be allowed to migrate to Israel with their children in the 1970s.

The Baku chapter was brief but memorable. I was given a souvenir in the form of an embroidered and embossed traditional Azeri skull cap. Mum, Genia and Maya were pleased to be leaving the overcrowded conditions of Nusia and Misha's apartment. While my father was depressed, he revived his boyhood memories of Kerch and tried to be optimistic. Dad hoped that life would be better there, but it was clear that the reality of Soviet life had already shaken him to the core of his identity and eroded most of his long-held beliefs.

As the crowded train travelled via different stops through the Caucus region and Southern Russia on its way to Crimea, we reflected on the amazing and unusual sights we had seen and on the enormous distances we had already traversed since leaving Melbourne in May. What would Kerch be like, and would it be any better than Baku, the *Kanzansky* station or Leningrad? Were we simply going from one wretched part of this giant country to another miserable town run by this bureaucratised but poorly organised and restrictive government, or would Kerch be different? It would only take a couple of days for us to find out.

11

SOVIET LIFE IN THE RAW

MUCH HAS BEEN WRITTEN ABOUT THE BLINDNESS and naivety of Western intellectuals and fellow travellers such as Sydney and Beatrice Webb, who visited the Soviet Union before the Second World War and effusively proclaimed the birth of 'Soviet Communism as a new civilisation'. Following the onset of the Cold War in 1946, however, there were hardly any tourists as Stalin discouraged foreigners from coming to the country. By 1955, the total annual number of foreign tourists from across the world was only 56,000. Apart from some Australian Communist Party officials who attended training courses, few Australians visited the USSR.

When we arrived in 1956, there were many cities and areas of the Soviet Union that were closed to foreign tourists. Yet, even in the 1970s when over four million tourists visited the Soviet Union annually, most visitors had to do so via the official tour operator *Intourist*, a Russian contraction of *'inostranii toorist'* meaning 'foreign tourist'. International visitors were strictly confined to 'showcase' cities like Moscow and Leningrad, or to several other cities and historical places determined by *Intourist*. Foreign tourists could not simply hire a car and drive all over the country or get a train or bus to any destination of their own choice. For example, in Crimea, the tourist resort town of Yalta was open to a small number of foreign tourists but provincial towns such as Kerch where we lived, were closed.

Following an exhausting rail trip in a packed train from Baku, we finally arrived in Kerch at the end of July 1956. Most of the passengers had already alighted at the various other towns well before we reached Kerch. Arriving at night, we encountered a small, isolated city with nowhere to stay except at the one and only hotel. This hotel mainly catered for Soviet administrators on official business. It was more than half-empty and additionally quite expensive. In 1956, we had no option but to stay there for two weeks until we found some form of housing. All the money they had given us as an allowance for our food and accommodation was quickly used up.

My father found it exceedingly difficult to reorientate himself in Kerch as the city suffered much destruction during the Second World War. He could recognise a few surviving historical landmarks but most of the new city was unrecognisable. Not only did the old Kerch not exist, but my father's dreams of seeing Kerch as an attractive symbol of Soviet society were equally shattered.

The following day after arrival, he had to go to the mayor's office and apply for work and housing. To simplify, the Soviet system was a complex hierarchical administrative structure of local district (*raion*) administrative bodies answerable to regional (*oblast*) authorities which in turn were subordinate to those in the capital of the fifteen Republics making up the Union of Soviet Socialist Republics (USSR). Each of the Republics, and various autonomous regions within these Republics, had their own administrative divisions and were represented in the Supreme Soviet which managed or was co-managed by the Politburo and Council of Ministers that was elected by the Central Committee of the Party in Moscow. Kerch was only a provincial town with a *Gorkom* (city party) that answered to the *Obkom* (regional party) in Simferopol in Crimea which in turn answered to the big shots in Kiev (now called Kyiv) and Moscow.

All nation states are artificial constructs and Ukraine is no exception. In 1954, two years before we arrived, Khrushchev made an arbitrary decision of transferring Crimea from the Russian Soviet Federative Socialist Republic to the Ukrainian Socialist Soviet Republic.

Between the time we arrived in 1956 and 2014 (when Vladimir Putin retook Crimea), more than 75% of the Crimean population were Russian, Tartar or others. During the same period, the population of Ukrainians in Crimea varied only slightly from a minority of 22% to 24% – hardly a predominant centre of Ukrainian life. While there has long been a distinct Ukrainian language and culture, our experience of Crimea in the late 1950s was that Ukrainians were only a small minority. Politically and personally, the transfer of administrative control of Crimea from Moscow to Kiev (Kyiv) was unfortunate for us, as most of the Ukrainian bureaucrats in Simferopol and Kiev were even more blatantly anti-Semitic than the Russians. They treated Dad and all of us with great hostility.

On reflection, it was a stupid idea to go to Kerch just because my father happened to be born there. Understandably, he was desperate to find a place that felt familiar. In 1956, every Soviet city would have been difficult for new arrivals, given the shortage of housing and the bureaucratic hoops one had to jump through. Yet, if one of the reasons we were brought to the Soviet Union was to have access to its so-called superior education and culture, Kerch would not have ranked high on his list of desirable cities. As we were to find out, Kerch and its surrounding districts were a provincial backwater with few offerings when compared to large Soviet cities. Despite being a strategic port with metallurgical industries that linked it to heavy industries in the cities along the Azov Sea, in the 1950s it was not a centre that attracted a large influx of Soviet citizens compared to those who desired to live in larger capital cities.

Before the revolution in 1917, the population of Kerch was little more than 33,000 people. While it grew substantially by the time we arrived, it was still only a town with combined industrial districts of less than 80,000 people compared to Melbourne's population of 1.5 million. Locals who wished to gain higher education credentials or succeed in the arts, sciences or technical fields invariably had to leave Kerch. It had other attractions such as its archaeological ruins, beaches, and a less severe winter climate than many other regions.

But as a centre of education and culture Kerch, did not set the world on fire. While Melbourne had its own provincial limitations, swapping Melbourne for Kerch turned out to be ludicrous and only fuelled our desire to return to Australia.

Getting work and housing was easier said than done. Almost every second day for the next two weeks of our stay in the hotel, my father was interviewed and interrogated by one official after another. Whereas in Leningrad the officials at the processing centre were positively disorganised and uninterested in returnees, each local bureaucrat in Kerch responsible for housing, employment, passport registration and other residential requirements zealously asked the same endless questions several times over. In conversational style, they wanted to know why he came back after living so long in Australia.

Like many others we met, it seemed difficult for them to fathom why foreigners would come to live in far-off Kerch. In contrast to the misinformation ASIO wrote about my father's experience during this time, nobody asked us a single question about Petrov, the CPA, the Australian government, or anything else that would be useful intelligence. One person had heard about Woomera and asked Dad what he knew, but my father replied that he had never been there as it was so far away from Melbourne and knew nothing about it other than what was reported in newspaper articles. Nearly all the questions were about personal details of our family or what work and living conditions were like in Melbourne. Actually, it was 'the local bunyip aristocracy' that could determine your fate as far as the allocation of work and housing, but these officials had little authority or responsibility for larger issues of security, repatriation or exit visas compared to their seniors in Kiev and Moscow. Importantly, they were certainly not the Soviet KGB and MVD intelligence operatives that ASIO erroneously imagined my father was supposedly being debriefed by on his return to the USSR.

The truth is that just as most in ASIO were ignorant about the USSR and uninformed about the significant cultural and political differences within migrant communities in Australia, so too, most of these local Kerch officials were thoroughly ignorant when it came to Australia. They didn't care about Australia, and most didn't know anything about Australia apart from kangaroos and that it was at the other end of the world. It was quite common for people to confuse Australia with Austria, as the concept of Australia and Australian society was so foreign that it was beyond their imagination.

If the locals were ignorant of Australia, we were equally ignorant about life in the Soviet Union. Forget about all the propaganda in glossy Soviet magazines or in the films we watched at the Carlton Theatre that my father proudly hosted. The more we encountered new things or had new experiences of life in Kerch and the district of Arshintsevo, the more we were shocked and embarrassed by how little we had known about this society and what we had to learn.

However, the harshness of life, the poverty and inequality, the corruption and abuses were unlike the squalor and poverty that we had earlier directly confronted in the transit ports of Colombo, Aden, or Naples. Instead, Soviet street scenes were often drab, but they were clean and orderly. Some beggars were visible on the streets, especially the war-maimed with one or more limbs missing. I had never seen the distressing sight of men with no legs who were a torso propped on a small wooden platform with ball-bearing wheels and begging in the street. Begging was generally condemned by the government as *parasitism* and lumped in with thieving, black marketeering, and avoidance of honest work.

In towns and cities, the streetscapes were dominated by uniform new apartment blocks mixed with old houses and apartments, plus the Palaces or Houses of Culture (*Dvorets* or *Dom Kultury*) containing a cinema, theatre, and art venue. There were also various shops, schools, and administrative offices. These generally looked neat and attractive. The combination of Soviet and Russian architecture mixed with mock ancient Doric or Roman columns helped shape parks, city squares and streets. Public spaces were usually adorned with urns and arches, war monuments, or statues of Lenin and various revolutionaries, war heroes and Russian authors such as Pushkin or Gorky.

Decoding Soviet life

It took some time living in this country to recognise that the public veneer of order and functionality disguised a quite different reality inside all these offices, shops, factories, or apartment blocks. While one could see the poverty of passengers on trains and buses or waiting in queues for milk or meat, it took a more experienced eye to decode Soviet life. It was far more complex and disquieting than the fleeting impressions gained by tourists or fellow travellers in Moscow or Leningrad. The majority of foreign and Russian academics, journalists and writers who lived in the Soviet Union or continue to write about its history and society still focus on the years of revolution, the Stalin period up until 1953 or the later decades of the decline and end of the Soviet Union. Khrushchev's period has not been ignored but still receives far less detailed analysis than what preceded or succeeded developments in the late 1950s.

We found ourselves living in a restricted zone where the blatant aspects as well as the less obvious tell-tale symptoms of scarcity, privilege, corruption, violence, and misery were more on display behind doors rather than in full public view. Apart from beggars and alcoholics, there were none of the familiar scenes of large-scale homelessness and begging that increasingly characterise street scenes in contemporary Western capitalist cities. Soviet authorities ensured that the homeless were quickly removed from public sight. The occasional drunks who fell asleep on the pavement in the warmer months were often found dead after freezing in the snow during winter.

Importantly, Soviet life, particularly after Stalin's death, was not based on the stereotypical Western image of daily terror, dire poverty, and so forth. The standard of living was much lower than for white Australians and there was widespread poverty but notably, the majority of people were not starving or desperately poor like in Asian countries during the 1950s. Instead, there were hierarchies of comfort and privilege, degrees of loyalty and patriotism. Alternate waves of happiness and grumpiness or misery were enabled by either varying levels of material possessions and signs of improvement, or regression and unpredictable shortages of goods and services.

These states of hope or disillusionment were all mediated by individual and family fortunes and opportunities in a social system that was not completely static and nor was it predictable. Rather, it selectively rewarded people within an official framework of incentives as well as permitting limited individual choices and disagreements as 'safety valves' to let off steam. This was both an official and informal method of keeping social order and control. Corruption also offered limited fluidity and mobility, but this had to be kept in check by periodic anti-corruption campaigns lest the system lose its overall legitimacy. Black markets and bribes were pervasive but were never permitted to become the main avenue to success. Instead, there were heavy penalties for those engaged in illegal activities called *ekonomicheskaya spekulyatsiya* or economic speculation, including long jail sentences, or being executed for large-scale theft and fraud.

In other words, just as the outward presentation of public life masked the reality of less obvious practices, so too, the public machinery of respect and acclamation existed alongside a subterranean set of life practices. These private forms of behaviour were driven by alternate bouts of dissatisfaction, resignation, or the desire to manipulate the system to gain either personal material benefits or increased individual recognition and status. In subsequent years, we would gradually learn about all these contradictory features of Soviet daily life.

After beginning to lose hope that we would ever be allocated any housing or work for Dad, the local officials finally found a job for my father. The unwelcome news was that it would not be in Kerch but rather in a new satellite industrial district or settlement called Arshintsevo about fifteen kilometres from the centre of Kerch. His new job would be as an electric welder in Central Mechanical Machinery (C.M.M.), a factory that repaired machinery used in iron ore mining and related processing industries. We would also be allocated a temporary room in Kamysh Burun which was the old part of Arshintsevo.

The move from the hotel room to the small room in a housing block built by German prisoners of war proved to be a further decline in our fortunes. We were now subjected to the whims of the local bureaucrats, and we were in no financial position to turn down this only room and sole job offer. The bus from Kerch to Arshintsevo passed fields and small housing settlements. Kerch was like a metropolis compared with this small industrial district. It looked somewhat like a cross between a rural hamlet and rapidly constructed housing blocks dotted with factories, shops, and a few public buildings. Some streets looked reasonably attractive in the Soviet urban design formula of neatly laid out facilities. Other sections were semi-developed with unpaved streets, and an air of temporary dwellings quickly erected to clear away the massive destruction left by the war, a little more than a decade ago. During the following few years, Arshintsevo would rapidly expand.

On the bus we were already in a dejected and chastened state. By the time we walked from the bus stop to our housing block and opened our ground-floor room with the key provided, we were almost speechless. Mum began crying and my father was unable to console her except to say that it would only be temporary. We had already slept for weeks on the floor in Baku, but at least Nusia's place was furnished. This room was as basic as it got. One small window, a wooden floor, a small stove but no tap with running water, let alone a small kitchen, toilet, or bath. We had no furniture, as it was still in transit from Melbourne. Our block was one of several two-storey blocks built around a communal area with a few park benches and a central hydrant that delivered water from a well. The local authorities felt sorry for us and provided a bucket to collect the fresh water, some cups, cutlery, a few dishes, and a basin for washing things, plus a couple of pots for cooking. They also organised for a couple of chairs and a small table, but the room was too small to accommodate any actual furniture for five persons.

For sleeping, we were given no bedding apart from a few covers and pillows. We improvised by laying down our clothing to cushion the hard floor. Fortunately, it was summer and not cold. Every day we washed our faces and bodies by pouring water from the well into the basin and also went to the public bathhouse once a week. We also had a few towels in our suitcases which seemed like a luxury.

Outside the block were barrack-style open latrines. They were painted with calcimine whitewash and looked clean. Inside was another story, just like the reality of most Soviet institutions. While these latrines were nowhere near as large or as disgusting as the toilet in the *Kazansky Vokzal*, there were no doors but short partitions dividing about eight large holes in the wooden planks that one had to squat over. This was a new experience that took all of my stamina to adjust to. The combined smell of sprayed chlorine (to prevent disease) and accumulated shit and urine made me dizzy and nearly faint from the stench. I risked the daily balancing act of holding my breath and not falling into one of the holes and drowning in the shit below. The one positive benefit of experiencing these harsh conditions is that I developed a much stronger capacity for tolerating nauseating smells. In later decades, I was usually tasked by others in various households to clean up shit or vomit by babies, adults, or pets and other such 'pleasures' winced at by less hardy or more delicate souls.

The beginning of resistance

It was in this room in Kamysh Burun that as a family we decided to devote all our energy to getting out of this 'Soviet paradise' as quickly as possible. The cumulative shocks of everything from Leningrad to Baku via the *Kazansky* had shattered my father's illusions. He was already extremely critical of life in the Soviet Union after the first few weeks. Kerch and Kamysh Burun swept away any vestiges of doubt or remaining illusions that he may have harboured since arriving in Leningrad.

He often cried and apologised profusely for bringing us to this god-forsaken hole of a place. He cursed the propaganda machine that deceived him and confessed that he was a complete and utter idiot for believing in the Soviet paradise for so many years. Although my father had been fanatical in his devotion to Soviet Communism, there were different degrees and causes of fanaticism. He was not, as Eric Hofer, the American author of *The True Believer* (1951) argued, someone in flight from a 'damaged self', that is, a person who felt worthless, guilty, or incomplete and thereby sought to lose himself by converting to a religious or political mass movement. My father, by contrast, had a healthy dose of self-love or narcissism. However, unlike narcissists, he did not lack empathy for others and did not blame everyone else for his own faults or feel in any way self-entitled.

It is certainly true that he had been single-minded in demanding that we give up our life in Melbourne in order to satisfy both his desire to return to Russia and his sincere belief that we would be the beneficiaries of living in a better society. Yet, in contrast to a selfish narcissist, he freely admitted the disastrous mistake he had made in returning to the Soviet Union. As we formulated our plans about how to leave, he was also prepared to make the ultimate sacrifice of his own welfare and forfeit his own position as the patriarchal head of the family, even if this meant that we would be able to escape this sham of a socialist society without him.

Summer was almost over. It was only a matter of a week or two before officials would come to ensure that Genia and I were enrolled in classes for the commencement of the new school year in September. We all agreed that the best tactic to adopt was for the two of us to refuse to go to school and to demand that we be allowed to return to our birthplace in Australia. We had only one trump card and that was the fact that the three of us children were born in Australia. Had we agreed to go to school, we would have become fully integrated into the system and lost this advantage. Formally we were included on our parents' Soviet passports. One obtained separate passports on turning sixteen. We decided that by refusing to attend school and refusing to become Young Pioneers we would bolster our campaign to be given exit visas. If asked, my parents would say that they tried their best but were powerless as their children simply refused to go to school.

Such was our determination to get out of the country, that our parents were prepared for me and Genia to leave for Australia on our own. At a more fundamental level, this would have been an existential calamity for the family. However, the hope was that Mum and Dad and two-year-old baby Maya could all eventually be given exit visas in future years. We were committed to the long struggle. Little did we know, when this plan was conceived in late 1956, that the Australian government would prove to be more of a problem and obstacle than just the Soviet authorities.

About ten days after arriving in Kamysh Burun, an official came to see us in regard to attending school. He didn't speak English and was not aggressive. After asking my father to translate our answers in English into Russian, as to our reasons for refusing to go to school, he shortly left to report this to other administrators. In contrast to the image of a repressive, demanding bureaucracy, when it came to our education, nobody was sent to order us to go to school. It was as if they didn't care whether we attended school or not. Perhaps these local officials had sympathy for us or were avoiding problems for themselves, fearing that forcing us to go to school would only backfire on them. Better to leave our case for others higher up the hierarchical chain of command. It would be over a year before they made another attempt to get us to attend school.

In the meantime, we stayed in this basic room for about six weeks and tried our best to make do with little bedding or anything else. Due to the poor diet and living conditions we all developed boils on our bodies. Genia's asthma worsened and her health deteriorated at the same time as we had a simple celebration of her thirteenth birthday. Finding milk, bread and other food was a daily struggle as one could never tell when any item would be delivered to the shops. Like other people, we regularly turned up to queue outside shops on the basis of rumours that bread or milk would soon arrive, only to be often disappointed and return home empty-handed.

We soon realised that our hardship was nothing unique, and that tens of millions of people lived in single rooms and suffered the daily grind of finding food in the shops. In larger cities, the crisis of accommodation produced familiar scenarios of two or three families sharing an apartment of two or three rooms with endless disputes over noise, or the use of space and cooking facilities in small kitchens and time spent in bathrooms.

Dad was also struggling to adapt to life as a Soviet worker. As a trade unionist in Australia, he was particularly shocked by the poor working conditions in the 'workers' state'. Apart from the lack of protective work clothes and the absence of elementary occupational safety conditions, he couldn't believe the extremely bad and dangerous conditions under which the workforce laboured. It was another huge shock to learn that he and the other workers had to line up after work in the dark to find out if their monthly pay had arrived or whether it would come one, two or three days late. To add to his concerns, he was initially subjected to anti-Semitic bullying from some of the workers once they saw his circumcised penis in the shower room. Fortunately, he was strong enough to fend for himself, but the anti-Semitic and more broadly racist culture – such as the treatment by Russians and Ukrainians of people from the Caucuses and Soviet Asian Republics – only compounded his disillusionment with the reality of Soviet life.

What Australian unions had struggled to achieve for workers by the mid-1950s was like paradise compared to the woeful treatment of workers in the so-called Soviet 'socialist' system. Most workers had to work a six-day week of 48 hours which was eventually reduced to 41 hours consisting of a 7-hour day and 6 hours on Saturdays. Many Soviet workers were paid by piece work, the most exploitative form of work where a worker had to drive themselves faster and faster to earn enough. This was slowly changed by the late 1950s to a combination of time worked or what a person produced during the week rather than just how many pieces of work they made.

My father was regularly amazed by the artificial massaging of pay rates and time worked to fit in with state central planning targets, the need to supplement poor wages from piece work and the unsustainable burdens of excessive overtime which led to workers leaving, or absenteeism and management worrying about declining productivity. In recent years, the Slovenian philosopher Slavoj Žižek would retell the old joke that: 'in the Soviet Union, management pretends to pay us, and we pretend to work.' If only that were true in the 1950s and 1960s. The reality was quite the opposite. Soviet working weeks were long and hard for most industrial workers. No wonder Dad heard the regular complaints from workers who were upset when local party officials ordered 'volunteer' community work (cleaning or repairing town facilities) on a number of Sundays during the year, that is, do unpaid labour on their only one day of rest. Similarly, exhausted workers were often taken after work by bus or truck to attend meetings and rallies to listen to and acclaim ideological or policy statements made from above rather than actually participate in real decision-making.

*'Volunteers' doing community labour, 1957.
Dad, 3rd from right, 2nd row.*

During the Khrushchev period, serious attempts were made to mobilise millions of workers and *Komsomols* into the official administrative and electoral system through a myriad of representative and socio-economic bodies. Outwardly, this goal of 'democratisation' and participation looked good on paper and was an attempt to show that ordinary people would be heard. While grass roots policy making did permit much more input from below compared with the Stalin period, little tolerance was shown to those who challenged major Party policy positions.

Given that there was no independent trade union movement, the official unions were toothless tigers mainly preoccupied with administering social welfare services such as organising holidays in a sanatorium, obtaining housing, or helping to look after workers' pensions and other such issues. They did not vigorously fight for better wages and conditions but occasionally spoke with other managers concerning various complaints aired by workers. Although called trade unions, they were effectively just another arm of management.

With pensions, health care, housing and other services provided by or closely tied to one's employer, loss of a job meant either great difficulty surviving or having to rely on others in employment. In 1956, Khrushchev implemented pension reforms by extending state support to dependents who had lost their breadwinner. He also introduced various categories of invalid pensions and streamlined the rate and eligibility for retirement pensions which were increased and funded by the state and not just the enterprise. Nevertheless, the 1956 reforms still left whole social categories of people either scarred by the war or neglected by the emphasis on productive workers, barely able to survive. Improvements for the disabled, sole parents, homeless children and farm workers would have to wait until the 1960s and 1970s.

We encountered a system where everyone was expected to either study or work unless they were old and retired or disabled. We were the exceptions to the rule in not going to school. This difference was exacerbated by our mother also refusing to go out, let alone engage in paid work. In the first few weeks, she would go out to try to buy food but soon became depressed with the empty shops, the queues, and our difficult living conditions in the room. Even after we moved to our apartment, her upset at leaving Australia and encountering the harsh conditions in Arshintsevo led her to decide unilaterally that she didn't want to have anything to do with the social system. Her response could be read as a form of depression and withdrawal. Yet it was also a passive-aggressive form of strike action conducted as a protest against being in Russia. Psychologically, she was conflict-averse but with a strong stubborn streak. Rather than articulate the reasons why she refused to go out, she simply stayed home and rejected all our attempts to persuade her otherwise. As I have indicated, she had also suffered considerably due to her family being murdered in the Holocaust. After several weeks of fruitless endeavours to get her to come out for a walk or get some fresh air, we let her be. Genia and I took on the role of obtaining food and negotiating the daily chores of surviving in a social system based on scarcity and corruption.

Genia, Maya, Boris and Tania, Arshintsevo, 1958.

It must have been an extremely painful experience not to leave our apartment for more than three and a half years except to go to answer questions at local administrative offices or for a trip to the British Embassy in Moscow. However, she was not in solitary confinement because we were with her at home and shared books, music, listening to the radio and domestic chores. Also, she was happy to see various neighbours or friends that my father had made who would come to visit. Nevertheless, my mother's life in the USSR was largely that of becoming an inmate in a self-made prison. Only the freedom to leave would finally liberate her from her daily suffering.

Arshintsevo – far from the big city life of Moscow

After about five weeks living in Kamysh Burun, Dad was informed of the great news that we could move into a new two-room apartment in the developing part of Arshintsevo about a kilometre from where we were staying. Unbelievably, this new apartment also had a separate small kitchen, a bathroom and toilet with hot and cold running water. It was on the first floor and also had a balcony where Mum would occasionally sit in the late evening when it was dark, especially during the months of warmer weather.

Arshintsevo 1961.

Our freight container with furniture and possessions had already arrived after being redirected from Baku to Kerch. It had been in storage as our room was too small to accommodate the table and mattresses and other household items. Now we could organise for it to be delivered to our new address, Arshintsevo, Block 9, House 15, Flat 13. This newly constructed apartment building was part of many other buildings that constituted a residential block on the rapidly expanding housing estate. The streets were not yet fully paved and would become covered in mud during the wet winter months, especially after the snow melted. Trees and garden beds were planted but would take four to five years to grow (see photo) and soften what was otherwise a stark new housing estate. Our building was almost like a shortened or flattened u-shape with a middle and two wings of apartments. It had three floors of flats with two main entrances to the staircases and a basement containing small sheds for personal storage. Each floor had four apartments and most of these had one room facing forward and one looking out the back of the building linked by a small L-shaped hallway with doors to the kitchen, bathroom, and toilet.

Behind each building were rows of outside sheds which we could look out onto and watch our neighbours who kept chickens, pigs or stored pickled food or sacks of grain. Each flat was also given a small allotment on land within walking distance of the settlement where food could be grown. The most popular food crops planted were corn and sunflowers mainly for sunflower seeds (or *semechki*). At the near end of summer, the large sunflowers would be removed from the plants, and usually an older woman or babushka would deseed them and dry the seeds in the sun on blankets or sheets. They would then be either lightly toasted or left dried and put into sacks for personal consumption or sold on the streets. A familiar sight would be women and men with one of their front teeth chipped from years of eating semechi by cracking open and dehulling the seeds. The ground next to the park benches around the housing estate would be covered in the black shells of semechki from people sitting and talking as they ate their way through pockets full, or twisted paper bags full of semechki.

Right opposite our flat was the local district party and administrative headquarters called the *Raikom*. The members of the *Raiispolkom* or Party Committee could literally see into our flat from their windows. We thought that they had possibly bugged our flat, but we never found any listening devices. At the back of our building next to the sheds of our neighbours were two garages for the senior officials' chauffeur-driven cars. Facing our front balcony was a long street with new apartment buildings. On the right-hand side of this street was the back of the Raikom which fronted onto the main street next to a square. One side of our building also faced the main square with the stop for the bus that linked Arshintsevo to Kerch. Across the square were buildings containing shops and a small park.

Further past the square next to our building was a public bathhouse which we could see from our back window. Several months after moving in, we looked out the window one evening and noticed some activity. The bottom windows of the bathhouse were frosted over so no one could look in. This did not deter a local character called Gavrik. He was in his early twenties and had part of his face and body burnt during the war. Perhaps it was his half-frightening appearance and his desperation to see a naked woman, that led him to get a ladder to climb up and peer through the window at the naked women in the bathhouse. Whatever the reason, he was soon noticed and chased away. Gavrik was one of thousands of children, teenagers and young adults who roamed around the towns and cities of the Soviet Union.

Past the bathhouse was the small football stadium and further down the street was a large coal-powered factory complex processing iron ore delivered by ship and rail from nearby mines as well as coal from Donetsk across the Azov Sea. Arshintsevo was thus a strategic industrial hub linking one of the key steel and heavy industrial sectors of the Soviet Union in the area now made famous by the war in Ukraine. The ongoing battles for Donetsk, Mariupol and other former major industry centres have left a trail of destruction in what were once thriving centres of industry development in the 1950s and 1960s.

Although Arshintsevo was characterised by heavy industry and new housing estates, it was surrounded by food crops and fields on one side and the beach and water on the other side. From our apartment building one could walk across the square and through the park until a further ten-to-fifteen-minute walk took one to the edge of the cliffs facing part of the Kerch Strait. As one descended down the cliff face via staircases, the area below was hardly an ideal summer resort. Instead, before one could reach the beach from the cliffs, it was necessary to cross rail lines and the adjacent ground which was covered in black coal and other metallic dust transported to the processing and smelting plants. During a thunderstorm in the summer of 1957, I was running to get home and fell over near the rail lines and badly grazed one of my knees. To this day I still retain a small dark mark caused by one of the metals on the ground that embedded in my open wound and could not be completely washed out before it healed.

After crossing the rail lines, one came to the beach which was relatively pleasant but quite narrow compared to Australian beaches. The sea front wound around cliffs and there was a small jetty from which boats could be launched as well as a spot to fish from. I would spend many hours over the next few years fishing at separate locations on the sea front. As I sat fishing, I would also look at the shape of the coastline and have phantasies about escaping the Soviet coastguard and border police and somehow making it to Turkey along the Black Sea.

At the giant processing factory fronting the shoreline, a large water outlet with warm water gushed into the sea. This attracted local varieties of fish, and, with luck, one could catch them here. In retrospect, the fish were probably full of toxic metals pumped into the sea. During the winter months, this was one of the few spots where the sea did not freeze over. It was indeed an amazing sight during our first winter to see the small waves frozen in place as they lapped the shore. This was as far away from an Australian beach scene at St. Kilda as one could get.

When we moved into our two-room apartment in the autumn of 1956, we were excited to unpack our books, music, and furniture to make life more comfortable. In the front room with the balcony, my parents set up our kitchen Laminex table and four folding chairs as our dining table. Their double mattress and bedding had to be moved up against a wall each morning to make room for the table. On the opposite wall we made some bookshelves to accommodate our books. Next to these we had our record player and records as well as our prized Philips radio.

In the other back bedroom, we placed two single mattresses on the floor next to one another. Genia would sleep on one side with Maya in the middle and me on the other side. Apart from our folded clothes on the floor, the room was just for sleeping as we could not afford any other furniture. In any case, it was too small to fit much into this room. We had little space in the kitchen to store our dishes, cooking utensils and cutlery. Nobody had a fridge and the space between the double-glazed windows served as a fridge. There was also a small bench top for preparing food for cooking and there was storage space in the hallway for clothing and linen. While we had no beds and other furniture, the two-small room apartment felt luxurious compared to the miserable one-room accommodation in Kamysh Burun. Week-by-week we settled into a new routine as we prepared for a campaign that, unbeknown to us at the time, would take years for us to get out of the country.

Not only were we in a restrictive country with a much lower standard of living than experienced by most white Australians, but we were also living in a new industrial settlement that contained many residents who were themselves refused permission to live in big cities. Some of our neighbours had been in prison for criminal acts as well as for political reasons. Following their release, they could only live in restricted zones rather than in Moscow, Kiev, or other major cities. The other feature of our apartment building, as with most buildings on the housing estate, is that all classes, occupations, and ranks were mixed together. There were, for instance, none of the special apartment buildings or enclaves as in Moscow that accommodated prominent party officials, senior military personnel, and leading figures in the arts. It was these spatial divisions that largely kept the working class away or out of view in the separate areas, residential buildings, or holiday dachas enjoyed by the elite.

By contrast, in Arshintsevo, local party officials, navy captains, engineers, ex-prisoners, pensioners and ordinary workers lived side by side. Class and status differences were certainly on parade, but they were manifested in a range of other practices and behaviours that I will shortly discuss. Normal life or *normal'naia zhizn* in this part of the Soviet Union was quite another world to the one that foreign academics and students, diplomatic staff, and foreign businessmen witnessed or experienced in Moscow or Leningrad. In our town, you couldn't see any tourists, or shop at special stores using foreign currency, or quietly exchange intellectual work with academics or members of the intellectual elite such as at the Union of Soviet Writers or scientific academies.

Soviet everyday life in Arshintsevo was the USSR in the raw. It was no artificial 'Potemkin village' or display for foreign visitors as in those selected parts of the USSR. Rather, it was provincial deadsville. Soviet provincialism had some similar drawbacks to life in the provinces of capitalist countries. Tellingly, in Arshintsevo one saw much more hardship and isolation than life in Moscow. We also witnessed the first years of the industrial expansion that Khrushchev's Seven Year Plan (1957–1965) promoted. Although the Plan was abandoned after five years, it eventually led to more goods and food produced, even though these outcomes were felt unevenly across the vast USSR. Arshintsevo certainly did not see the end of food shortages and there were only slight improvements in the local standard of living before 1960, judging from what we observed in the neighbourhood.

However, such was the hardship endured by most people during the previous three and a half decades, that the mere removal of the random and widespread fear of arrest, or fear of periodic famines (1920–21, 1931–33 and 1945–47), plus the cessation of war, that these improvements in life gave many people a sense of optimism. Although nuclear war was an ever-present but more abstract fear, the desire for peace held by the Soviet population was not a mere parroting of party slogans but something keenly felt by most people. Australians and Americans who had not directly experienced a world war on their territory had little idea of the extent of the genuine horror of war felt by Soviet citizens and most Soviet officials.

Of course, the desire for peace existed alongside a thriving culture of patriotism largely driven by the armed forces. Thousands of children's clubs, schools, and Komsomol organisations were sponsored by the military to bolster its image in the quest for military recruits. The military had their own academies, newspapers, a large publishing house that brought out hundreds of titles glorifying military deeds, and also ran a sub-section of the economy which not only produced military equipment but controlled vital resources needed for this massive organisation.

Apart from the Party, the Red Army was the other key institution that linked all the Republics of the USSR. Its prestige was still extremely high in the late 1950s, a legacy of its victorious struggle in the Great Patriotic War against fascism as Stalin called it. However, every family dreaded the moment when their son or sons were called up for three years military service. Neighbours in Arshintsevo knew when this frightening moment befell a family. A minimum of two or three days of drinking, eating, and singing would take place before the conscripted son was escorted by his family, accompanied by a piano accordionist and friends as they walked to the bus stop to take him to the army office to report for duty.

Conscripts would be sent hundreds or thousands of kilometres away from home, as it was the policy of the military to mix up their new recruits and post them in unfamiliar places. This was in order for the armed forces to develop loyalty to the institution rather than to their own nationality or region. Each family hoped that their son would return healthy and not suffer from bullying, injuries, or die 'accidentally' in an alcohol-fuelled and racially charged institution. Propaganda was one thing, but the reality of the tough military service conditions worried even the most patriotic of families.

The rapid industrial expansion of the Seven-Year Plan was not like the breakneck development and catastrophic loss of life in the 1930s. Still, it took its toll on human lives in the form of physical and mental injuries. The development of industry and agriculture during the late 1950s also continued a long tradition of irresponsible environmental destruction and pollution enacted by planners, management, and workers. This damage was visible in the dangerous use and disposal of chemicals and toxic materials, the violation of sensitive marine and land ecologies, and the failure to have adequate separation of residential buildings from pollution emanating from nearby heavy industrial development. Arshintsevo was an everyday example of poor undemocratic planning done in the name of the people.

Soviet industrialisation in the period after the devastation wreaked during the war years of the 1940s, had both constructive and destructive qualities. While it had similar features to earlier periods of free market capitalist industrial development, the difference was that it was driven by central planners and the benefits did not accumulate in the hands of private corporations or create the level of deep inequality seen in the West. Nevertheless, the Soviet emphasis on constant growth in production at the expense of human welfare and environmental protection was, unfortunately, the cause of much disruption and destruction, not to mention the production of newer forms of inequality.

Scarcity, hooliganism and crime

Like the 'informal sector' in low and middle-income countries, the USSR had its own unofficial market. This Soviet 'informal sector' was nowhere near as extensive as those large sectors in low-income countries that continue to employ millions of people in a lawless, precarious existence on the margins. However, given the scarcity of goods and services, 'moonlighting' or doing a second and third job was quite common. Friends and neighbours or workmates would put each other in touch with someone they knew who had household goods, food items and other items to sell, or offered electrical, plumbing, and other services.

What struck us was the ingenuity of people living with low wages and scarcity. It seemed like every second or third person stole something from their workplace, whether minor or major, and most managed not to get caught. Although utility bills were not high compared to Australia, in our building, for example, neighbours would illegally adjust the electricity meter so that they would not have to pay for the power they used. The other trick was to use the hot water flowing through the central heating radiators or panels in all apartments. By unscrewing the valve on one of the radiators, hot water would be used to fill baths for bathing or washing clothes.

Of course, such acts of theft could go terribly wrong. One evening after about a year of living in our apartment building, we heard a knock at our door. It was Zoya who lived below us with her husband who was a navy captain and their two children. He had been posted thousands of kilometres away to a ship based in Vladivostok on the Pacific Ocean and now spent most of his time away. Zoya was all flustered and red in the face. She came in and whispered to Dad so the neighbours could not hear her. After explaining that she 'borrowed' hot water from the radiator panel, she could not screw the valve back in place. Hot water was now gushing all over the floor and ruining not only her furniture but also lifting the dark red colour off the painted floorboards.

She asked Dad to quietly come down and help her reattach the valve and clean up the water which was already ankle-deep in the rooms. Zoya was in a panic because she feared being caught and her husband might not only lose his job, but worse, they could also possibly lose their apartment. The public disgrace would be too much for her status-conscious persona to bear. Dad immediately went down, took off his shoes and he and Zoya closed the valve off and spent the next few hours mopping up the water all over the flat. The two children were sitting on the bed above the water.

My father was exhausted and had to go to work early in the morning. It took Zoya all night and the next couple of days to secretly clean up the rest of the mess. Fortunately, she was not caught because it was a ground floor apartment and there were no people below her in case water began to drip through the ceiling thus alerting people about her theft gone wrong. Zoya ceased extracting free hot water after this embarrassing incident and remained a good friend. She was eternally grateful for my father's help.

Although encouraged by friends, we did not engage in fiddling with the electric meter, extracting hot water or other devious activities as it would have been disastrous for our cause to leave the country if caught in the act by the authorities. As it transpired, well before Zoya's misadventure, I had already been officially registered as a 'hooligan' (*khuligan*) by authorities at both the local *Raikom* and regional *Obkom* in Simferopol. About a month after we moved into our apartment in the autumn of 1956, I was playing ball with three other Russian boys of similar age who lived in an adjacent building further down the street. Shortly later, the playing turned ugly, when they ganged up on me and began calling me names. One of them hit me in the face and I retaliated in reflex fashion by punching him in the face. His nose began to bleed and as he cried out, his mother appeared on the street and began shouting at me. I immediately started running home as she chased me in hot pursuit. Bolting up the stairs, I desperately banged on our door and shouted to Mum to let me in. Just as the door opened, the furious woman reached our landing and Mum stood there wondering what had happened. I ducked in while my mother incurred two blows on her face and body plus a torrent of abuse that was meant for me. She immediately forcibly shut the door against the body weight of the other woman who angrily tried to push her way inside.

Apart from fighting with Genia, I had never been in a physical fight before and would never be in one again. Despite expecting some repercussions from the altercation, I kept away from the boys and assumed that all had quietened down. It was only months later that my father was informed by authorities in Kerch that the incident had been reported and that at the age of eleven, I was now listed as a hooligan with local and regional authorities. Any further misbehaviour on my part would not be ignored or treated lightly.

Soviet authorities periodically waged 'anti-hooliganism' campaigns. A large one began in the year before we arrived in 1954/1955 and was driven by the Komsomol or young Communist movement. Apart from newspaper campaigns, Komsomols patrolled the streets or cultural institutions and meeting places to see that hooligans did not violate 'socialist norms'. One did not have to engage in criminal behaviour to be classified as a hooligan. A wide range of social behaviours such as listening to rock and roll, school absenteeism, alcoholism, or public disorder and rudeness were deemed to be 'deviant' and undermining the Soviet norm of cultivating useful, healthy, and polite young socialist citizens. In some respects, there were parallel attacks in the 1950s on 'deviancy' in Western countries when a new social cohort called 'teenagers' emerged as a social problem that had to be carefully managed given what conservatives saw as the threat of sexual promiscuity, and other forms of 'immoral behaviour'. The difference in the Soviet Union was that over the decades, thousands of *besprizorniki* or homeless children and young adults were roaming the country in search of shelter, food, and income. They were the casualties of war, or parents sent to the Gulag, or neglectful parents and violent domestic situations.

During the Khrushchev period, extensive reforms were made to the education system, following debates on how to raise orphaned children and how to either prevent or deal with social and criminal delinquents, especially increased working-class violent masculinity driven by drink, fights at the football and attacks on women. The authorities were instructed to crack down on this threat to Soviet order. In Arshintsevo, one response by the authorities was the establishment of dormitories for young offenders from surrounding districts. Every morning, about one hundred of these very tough young men and women in their late teens would march from their living quarters to work at various places, particularly building construction sites. In the wintry weather, they would wear their familiar grey Soviet puffer jackets (now a fashion accessory in many countries) and fur hats *shapka* or *ushanka* with ear flaps. Accompanied by the *militsiia* or armed police, they would swing their arms and sing marching songs as they paraded in disciplined formation along the streets only to return to their dorms after work in the late afternoon.

Advocates of boot camps in America or Australia would have been overjoyed to see such a display of military discipline and daily labour. For most ordinary residents in Arshintsevo, however, it was a daily rousing message and striking reminder not to tangle with these extremely tough reform school veterans and to obey the law unless you wanted to end up suffering the punishment meted out to this hardened mob. I often wondered whether they eventually went on to live ordinary workers' lives or graduated to become professional criminals.

Crime, and the fascination with crime, was another notable phenomenon of Soviet life. In contrast to the media in Australia that were full of crime stories, Soviet newspapers rarely reported crime, even though there was an abundance of individual and gang crimes committed. A new genre of crime stories emerged, especially in pirated editions that circulated on the black market. People couldn't get enough of the tales about violent gangs, blood-curdling murders and associated crimes. On the recommendation of fellow workers, my father brought home a pirated book and read to us some of the horrific escapades that would never have been published in *Pravda*, *Izvestia* or *Literaturnaya Gazeta*. These stories were half fact and half fiction and stimulated the appetite of Soviet readers eager to hear or read more about the unsavoury aspects of life covered up by the authorities.

We didn't need to rely on pirated books to read about crime. Our building had a few characters who filled us with stories of their firsthand experiences. Directly opposite us on the same landing lived a man called Volodya Taras who simply went under the name Taras. He was in his early forties, thin and wiry looking with a large scar stretching from his mouth to his ear. Taras lived there with his wife and child and was one of the many who could not get permission to live in a larger city. He was very friendly when sober but could easily become angry and violent when drunk, which happened at least once a month. Even the *Raikom* authorities were frightened of him when he was out of control.

Taras had already been briefly sectioned in a mental institution in Simferopol after threatening people and eating all the petals on a bush in a state of uncontrolled behaviour. Brought up by his grandfather, as a boy and teenager, Taras was one of the *besprizorniki* or homeless who roamed the country committing crimes in order to survive. Sentenced to a harsh prison life, Taras had killed a man and told us of the violent criminals he had been interned with as well as the fights that he managed to survive. Apart from his knife-slashed face, Taras lifted his shirt to show us a giant scar on his stomach which was the result of another prisoner stabbing him with a screwdriver. Released in one of the prisoner amnesties following Stalin's death, Taras now worked in the same factory as Dad and tried to overcome his violent past. I would occasionally go fishing with him but was always on guard to see whether he was sober or not. I never forgot his role in a memorable incident that occurred on a sweltering summer night in 1958.

Part of the joy of Soviet life not mentioned in their glossy magazines were the regular electricity outages and also the daily rationing of water supply, especially during the summer months. There simply wasn't enough power generated or water available, so residents came second to industrial enterprises that needed to fulfil their planning targets. Water was cut off all day until about ten or eleven at night when we had to fill the bath and pots and bottles for use the next day. On one of these summer evenings, the local *Raikom* erected a screen at the back of their building directly in front of our balcony. They brought out dozens of chairs for viewers to sit on and watch the free public entertainment. We didn't need to go down and sit to watch the films as we could hear the sound system and the images were also visible to us on the back of the screen. First up, were three Charlie Chaplin silent shorts which everyone loved and roared with laughter as Charlie carefully went through his crafted and very physical comic routine. Then the authorities shifted the mood by screening a propaganda film about Soviet agricultural production and the bountiful crops of apples and stone fruit in Crimea which nobody ever saw in the shops.

Suddenly, there was a loud interrupting noise as Taras slammed open the double-glazed windows of his apartment and began screaming: "I want to shit but there's no water. Enough of this propaganda and turn on the water." (*"Ya khochu srat no net vody. Khvatit etoy propagandy i vklyuchi vodu"*) There were gasps and nodding heads of approval amongst the audience until someone sang out: 'Quiet, you ruffian' (*grubiyan*), don't disturb us.' As it turned out, Taras was reprimanded the following day, but they left him alone knowing that it was a brave person who tried to discipline him. What was notable about the incident was that it was the only public intervention we witnessed where someone uttered a criticism of official propaganda. There was no shortage of private criticisms that we heard, but in the Soviet scheme of things it took a very courageous person or a drunk or a madman to challenge the system publicly.

Yet, when it suited them, the local authorities closed their eyes to violations of 'Soviet legality', even when it brazenly occurred on a daily basis in front of the Party's building. Diagonally opposite us on the other wing of our building were the occupants of an apartment that was right next door to the *Raikom*. In this apartment lived a clergyman in his early sixties with his large white beard, as well as his wife and adult son and daughter who were in their mid to late twenties. He was highly respected by many of the older residents who retained their religious beliefs despite decades of anti-religious campaigns by the government. The local authorities left him alone as he didn't have a church building and did not engage in the public proselytising of his faith.

Towards the end of 1957, the Russian Orthodox cleric became ill and died. His funeral took place a few days later but, in the meantime, we observed that his wife, a tough and loud woman of about 50, was laughing and carrying on as if nothing had happened. On the day of the funeral, a truck arrived which would carry the open casket, together with a small brass band which would play as mourners walked to the cemetery behind the slow-moving vehicle. All the neighbours plus mourning parishioners and friends had gathered outside waiting for the casket to be brought downstairs. The grieving widow who had been laughing in previous days, now put on what in our opinion looked like an Oscar-winning performance. Escorted and propped up by a woman and man while she feigned a few near-fainting spells, the widow moaned and wailed so loudly that she caused a number of women and men to instantaneously begin crying. The procession then departed for the cemetery, a scenario of startling performative grief without any Anglo restraint.

Barely two weeks after the funeral, we noticed a regular parade of men visiting the widow's apartment, including quite a few sailors. Together with her daughter and another woman, they became prostitutes and opened a successful brothel with an endless stream of customers having sex and drinking right next to the *Raikom*. Everyone else in the housing estate knew that it was a brothel, but members of the *Raiispolkom*, despite their moral campaigns, did not close it down, even though business a few metres away boomed over the following years. Perhaps the widow and daughter were helping to fulfil the Plan or deliver what was regarded as necessary services for the navy. Meanwhile, the clergyman's son was arrested for raping a woman and was sentenced to eight years in prison. It was as if the death of their religious husband and father had opened the floodgates of crime and amoral behaviour – behaviour that the Party tolerated while simultaneously and hypocritically running campaigns against crime and hooliganism.

Apart from the ex-prisoners living in our town, there were also the political victims who found themselves in the wrong place at the wrong time. Earlier in the book I mentioned the terrible reception that many Soviet prisoners of war received from security forces upon returning home in the late 1940s. Directly opposite Zoya's apartment below us lived a pensioner called Olga and her disabled and middle-aged son Pyotr. Upon returning to the Soviet Union, he was accused of being a traitor and so savagely beaten by security officers that they left him unable to speak properly and barely able to walk or fend for himself. Tragically, on most days we used to see her son sitting around, unable to work and barely able to utter a few disjointed sentences.

By contrast, on the floor above us lived Sergei who had fought in the Soviet-Finnish War or Winter War of late 1939 to March 1940. He told us of the enormous casualties that the Finns inflicted on Soviet troops amidst the snow and ice, and that in his opinion, the Germans were not as good fighters as the Finns. Following the defeat of Hitler in 1945, Sergei was transferred to duty in one of the military units run by the Ministry of Internal Affairs (MVD). He was in Moscow with other troops loyal to Lavrenti Beria, when Khrushchev, Malenkov, Bulganin, the defence minister, and other leaders staged the coup against Beria in June 1953. Sergei and other members of his unit were surrounded by troops loyal to Khrushchev and the anti-Beria instigators of the coup. They were arrested and disarmed in case they tried to rescue Beria. Not being a senior officer, Sergei was eventually dismissed from the military forces and permitted to live in a marginalised town such as Arshintsevo.

Like many others in our building or living in nearby streets, Sergei and Pyotr represented a microcosm of the Soviet Union that made up the one thousand and one tales that tourists would rarely hear or see. We learnt a great deal from the social escapades and about the individual suffering experienced by diverse strata hidden out of view by the Soviet authorities. By contrast, in the 1950s, a majority of people born in Australia had not experienced the destruction of war, starvation, mass repression, scarcity, and corruption. They lived in a state of relative unworldliness and comfort, largely free from the daily struggle governed by obtaining basic food supplies, simple accommodation, or non-back-breaking work. Within the space of a few months, we too had undergone a steep learning curve from childlike innocence in St. Kilda to the knowledge and streetwise premature adulthood acquired by being immersed in the rawness of Soviet life.

12

AN INVALUABLE EDUCATION

While I am not an advocate of home schooling, my years away from formal educational institutions were enormously enriching. What I missed out on in terms of maths, grammar, and five years of conventional, formal education between 1956 and 1961 was more than compensated for by the combined literary, political, and socio-cultural development I underwent due to the life we led in the Soviet Union. Being a keen observer of social life, I took a great interest in the behaviour and social practices of the Arshintsevo community and larger Soviet society. Over the next year or two, I absorbed the Russian language by building up my vocabulary by listening to people speak in shops and in public spaces as well as slowly reading newspapers and listening to the radio. At home, I was surrounded by books in English which unleashed my imagination, and our cherished short-wave radio not only expanded my political and cultural horizons but kept all of us in touch with the outside world.

During the years of our campaign of school refusal in order to leave the country, I became a voracious reader. My parents had brought their collection of books. These included their old copies of Australiana, such as the collected yarns, poems and ballads by Banjo Patterson and various other colonial and early Australian literature, plus post-war social realist novels such as *How Beautiful are Thy Feet* by Alan Marshall, *The Harp in the South* and *Poor Man's Orange* by Ruth Park, *Power Without Glory* by Frank Hardy, *Twenty Thousand Thieves* by Eric Lambert and *Alien Son* and *The Unbending* by Judah Waten. I also devoured many of the European classics, including *Aesop's Fables*, Boccaccio's *The Decameron* with illustrations by Melbourne artist Francis Broadhurst, most of Shakespeare's collected plays and sonnets, and various novels by Charles Dickens.

While my understanding of Shakespeare and other classics was elementary, I nonetheless laid the groundwork in later years for a deeper and more complex appreciation of these and other works. My father had also brought his twenty-volume *Masterpiece Library of The World's Thousand Best Short Stories* which I loved dipping into as I read classic stories by French, German, Chinese, Russian and many other international writers. One of the positive features of the Soviet Union was its large expenditure on the arts and culture. If only their policies had been free of censorship and strict control. Nevertheless, the Moscow Foreign Language Publishing House produced more titles in English annually than in the UK itself. These were simple and cheap productions that my father would order for all of us to read. We enjoyed Americans Mark Twain, Jack London, Theodore Dreiser and O. Henry, French writers such as Victor Hugo, Jules Verne, and Guy de Maupassant, as well as English classics by Sir Arthur Conan Doyle, Lewis Carrol, Jerome K. Jerome, A. J. Cronin, and Sir Walter Scott. Given our knowledge of Russian was still developing, we also read English translations of Chekhov, Gogol, Tolstoy, Turgenev, Belayev and Armenian writer Vakhtang Ananyan. At the time, the Soviets also published entertaining maths books directed at young readers who were given all kinds of puzzles and riddles to solve which made learning maths enjoyable. There was an emphasis in the family on extending our education in areas other than literature and politics.

A few months after we settled into our apartment, our Philips radio kept us in touch with international news and culture. It proved to be a lifeline as the radio could not be jammed easily by Soviet authorities as was the case with all Soviet-made radios. This prized item was the envy of our Soviet friends who consistently offered to buy it. Fortunately, Dad had remembered to pack adaptors for our Australian plugs so that our radio, record player and sewing machine could work in Arshintsevo. The almost overlapping dates of the Suez war and the Hungarian Revolution in October and November 1956 kept us glued to the radio and we were riveted by the daily broadcasts from the BBC. None of our neighbours knew anything about the events in Hungary except the official Soviet account that counterrevolutionaries had been defeated.

Every day, in between reading and going out to shop or doing other essential things, we would listen to the BBC. In the evening our family would discuss the different political implications of global events and why local Soviet accounts were either so different to what we heard from Western sources or why there was non-reporting of crucial developments and conflicts. Bit by bit we acquired an education in politics not offered either in Australian or Soviet schools. Not only did we hear their daily international news broadcasts, commentaries, and feature programs, but we also enjoyed a selection of BBC quiz shows, comedies like the *Goons*, *Take it from here*, *My Word*, and broadcasts of serious interviews, panel discussions on politics, and arts and book reviews. We also loved hearing all the latest pop songs and rock and roll, even though the BBC had its own restrictions on which lyrics could be broadcast.

Sometimes we managed to hear broadcasts from Australia, but these were not always clear and made it difficult to listen to due to time differences. We could also hear Voice of America and European stations but preferred the BBC for its comprehensive broadcasting. While short-wave radio sets became popular in the USSR in the 1960s, few people had them when we lived there. Most people couldn't listen to foreign stations due to constant Soviet jamming. The one exception was Khrushchev's visit to America in September 1959. Not only was the Voice of America not jammed, but the authorities strung up loudspeakers on poles in the main street and square that enabled Russian listeners to hear accounts of highlights of Khrushchev's thirteen-day visit to key American places.

AN INVALUABLE EDUCATION

Frankels in Arshintsevo, 1957.

Life in our apartment also revolved around practices as if we were in the nineteenth century. While my father was at work and Maya was playing with other small children at a neighbour's place, Mum, Genia and I would either sit quietly and read our books or embroider. One could get assorted designs like the pictures on jigsaw puzzles and buy coloured threads for embroidery. I embroidered a portrait of Russian poet Pushkin and also became quite good at embroidering roses and other flowers without any background pattern to fill in. We also embroidered white blouses and shirts with decorative patterns or flowers around the neckline. I now understood the meditative and calming influence that women in earlier historical periods must have felt living in isolated and confined quarters, especially in cold climates while they created items of beauty.

Communist inequality

Earlier I described the social mix living in our housing estate but noted that differences in social class and status were still quite visible.

Class differences in the Soviet Union were not based on Western divisions between the capitalist class which owned the means of production employing and dominating the working class. Instead, power and status were closely related to one's group and individual position in the socio-economic, political, and cultural hierarchy. There were no bourgeoisie in our town and only a small minority of the older population would have been adults during the Czarist days. The vast majority came from former peasant backgrounds and were proletarianized during the rapid industrialisation of the 1930s and post-1945 reconstruction. This was a society based on privileged access to resources and social mobility from the lower rungs of society to the political, economic, and cultural centres of power.

Inequality was pronounced and highly visible, but it was not based on great disparities of privately owned wealth ranging from billionaires and multi-millionaires right through to the destitute as in America, Australia, and other capitalist countries. Instead, it was an integrated technocracy presided over by the Party and military and security forces. The latter exercised their power over workers via upper and middle layers of managers, engineers, and various other professions in the administrative, scientific, educational, and cultural apparatuses. In contrast to official propaganda, social status and material position were constantly emphasised in a mixture of blatant and subtle forms of behaviour and codes of social practice. Everyone in small towns such as Arshintsevo and Kerch knew who had power. They only had to see tin-pot Party officials and managers arrive in their chauffeur-driven cars (I rarely saw any prominent females). In Australia, middle-ranked officials in local government or business would usually drive themselves, but not in the USSR. The main vehicles on the roads in Arshintsevo were several types of trucks, buses, and chauffeur-driven official cars. There were few privately owned cars like the *Moskvitch*. In the rare instances that a tiny minority could afford to buy a car, these people had to wait years for the delivery of their vehicle. Most of the limited car production went to privileged customers in the big cities.

At the bottom of the social hierarchy, apart from beggars, were peasants and rural workers. Forget about fairy tales or Hollywood films about a relationship between a peasant and a princess. As a young person, I didn't realise how elementary class differences were so physically and materially self-evident. Soviet peasants from small collective farms or *kolhozes* often lacked modern living conditions, depending on how isolated or poor they were. It was often the case that when a *kolhoznik* (male farmer) or *kolhoznitsa* (female) came into town and one stood next to them, they had a distinctive smell, the stench of poor hygiene combined with an overpowering musty odour that seemed to reek from their clothing and working with animals. Rural workers on the large, industrialised state farms or *Sovhozes*, also had inferior conditions to those of urban industrial workers. They were no longer peasants but included many young urban recruits to bolster Khrushchev's goal of 'overtaking America'.

One year, my father was sent for a week to a nearby Sovhoz with other workers to do repairs on farm machinery. He was shocked at the poverty and poor facilities and living conditions endured by workers and residents. Many residents had only a few years of education, lacked adequate health and social care and were generally neglected prior to the late 1950s. Tens of thousands of villages were unviable and were eventually closed in later years. No wonder there were restrictive internal passport regulations. Without these restrictions, millions would have left *kolhozes* and *Sovhozes* much earlier to go and live in cities where the standard of living was so much better.

Food was another central delineator of class and status. The ability to afford what were considered 'luxuries' such as white bread, meat, poultry, butter, or fresh fruit and vegetables in winter, were all telltale signs of one's social position. Maria Petrovna, a neighbour who was the wife of Dmitri, a navy captain, was a typical example of the visibility of social class divisions. She would embellish the role of 'Madame' with her snobbish airs. Not only could she afford to buy an elaborate cake with its decorative icing, but Madame would carry it home by holding it aloft in her hands for all the neighbours to see, thus making a statement about her social position loud and clear.

Similarly, when we were occasionally invited to eat at a neighbour's apartment, it was a sign of both Russian hospitality and the great cost they had expended, to put on the table varieties of sausage or *Kolbasa* and several types of canned fish that were still left in their tins so that all the guests could see the labels and the cost of these items. Branding was particularly important in the Soviet Union and not just under consumer capitalism. Needless to say, the amount of vodka and other alcohol one could afford was also a sign of affluence and a mark of one's hospitality.

Given that the shops were often empty, and many food items were scarce, one could usually buy what one needed at the private market stalls or on the black market. The problem was that food purchased outside the state shops was much more expensive and unaffordable as a regular weekly shopping option for most workers. The low wages my father earned and the unavailability of basic items in the shops, meant that my parents were worried that we would become sick due to malnutrition, especially after we all suffered bouts of pneumonia and other illnesses. Tuberculosis or T.B. was still quite common in our town and Dad started selling assorted items of clothing that we had brought with us in order to buy butter, fruit, and other items of food at the private market. The first things to be sold over a period of several months were our specially made leather jackets with lambswool lining.

Minor differences are often magnified in such stratified, poor communities. Those amongst our neighbours who could afford to raise a pig in one of the outside back sheds, enjoyed a bounty not available to others. Over the years we witnessed the routine fattening and slaughtering of pigs. It was an elaborate ritual that went on all day and into the night. Once the pig was stabbed under the left front leg into the heart with a sharp blade, it was blow-torched to clean the skin of hairs. Each section of the pig was elaborately dissected, including stuffing its guts to make sausages. A prized part of the fattened pig was its *salo* or slabs of fat which were salted in layers, stored away, and eaten for up to a year. Unlike bacon or pancetta, *salo* was largely fat with a very thin line of meat. It was so fatty that we never ever became accustomed to eating it. However, for the locals, a slice of *salo* was something that they loved eating and it nourished them throughout the year. Although Arshintsevo was an urban industrialised centre, its proximity to rural communities and the ability of neighbours to raise pigs, chickens and geese or grow food on their allocated plots, gave us a small taste of quasi-rural life not seen in large cities.

The contrast between those who had abundant food and the majority who faced the queues and empty shops was striking. Paying *blat* or key money to get a job in a food shop meant a lucrative income. Shop assistants would earn extra by giving customers a gram or two less on the scales or putting a bucket of water next to bags of sugar so the moisture absorbed would double the weight of all sugar sold. We soon heard about many other tricks deployed or how advanced notice was given to friends and insiders about the impending arrival of milk or meat. Social privilege, corruption and scarcity simultaneously reproduced social division with the one feeding off the other.

Another common feature of how Soviet food was sold was the absence of wrapping paper in shops. Yet, each store had its obligatory complaints book or *zhalobnaya kniga* that citizens could write in if they were dissatisfied with the service. Chekhov's story, *Zhalobnaya Kniga*, was about a complaints book at a railway station that had twenty entries in it which had little to do with its purpose. In a similar vein, an anecdote circulated in Arshintsevo that told of a man who waited his turn in the long queue and eventually asked for a salty herring. The saleswoman reached into the barrel and pulled out a wet herring dripping with brine which she was about to pass to the customer. After being told that she had no paper to wrap it in, the man became furious, banged his fist on the counter and demanded the complaints book. Trembling with fear because most people never used the complaint book, she handed it over to him and hoped that whatever he wrote in it would not result in her losing her job. Instead, he opened the book, tore out a few pages, wrapped up his herring and walked out of the shop looking satisfied with his practical use of the otherwise irrelevant sop to customers called the *zhalobnaya kniga*.

The other key markers of class and status were clothes and material possessions. Whereas street clothing is not always an obvious or consistent indicator of class in Australia, in the Soviet Union it always signified social status. Fur was a clear marker, particularly the type and quality of the fur coat or fur collar which immediately indicated relative affluence and social position. The quality of women's shawls – whether fine wool, silk, cashmere, or coarse fabric – was another instant giveaway. Imported clothing or fabrics for dresses, suits and coats were highly prized as were any foreign goods. Having beautiful wall rugs or carpets on floors, hand-made furniture, ornaments, and jewellery were proudly displayed, as were the number of gold teeth in a person's mouth. We grew to understand that symbols of status and class in Soviet provincial towns were a strange mixture of traditional, pre-revolutionary artefacts of value, alongside access to otherwise scarce goods and services that were regularly made available to those in the political and economic administrative hierarchy.

Nikolai Gogol's 1842 play, *The Inspector General*, about a man mistaken for the inspector coming from the capital to check out whether the administration of a town was in order, certainly resonated with us in the USSR of the 1950s. Following his meeting with President Tito of Yugoslavia in the Crimea in late September 1956, Khrushchev made an impromptu, flying visit to Arshintsevo. The local bigwigs were quite worried as Khrushchev addressed meetings of workers and asked them to inform him of any difficulties concerning work conditions, availability of food and so forth. The responses were muted as everyone knew they would cop it from the local Party officials and managers once Khrushchev left. These anti-corruption visits boosted the popularity of Khrushchev and other leaders, but little changed on the ground despite a few concessions and reforms. As in Czarist times, locals hoped that the leaders in Moscow would one day solve their problems. However, like religious adherents, they were also resigned to their fate on earth. Others quietly and regularly voiced their contempt for the government and its promises. This was no Orwellian society of complete and utter fear and control. On the contrary, there were far more political jokes and dissenting voices amongst ordinary workers than there were in the mostly depoliticised lifestyle of workers in America or Australia.

A few of the following political jokes at the time captured the scepticism and distrust circulating amongst the population.

QUESTION: Is it possible to wrap an elephant in a newspaper?
ANSWER: Yes, if the paper features a speech by Khrushchev.

QUESTION: Why do we need two central newspapers, *Pravda* (Truth) and *Izvestiya* (News) if they both represent the same Party?
ANSWER: Because in *Pravda* there is no news, and in *Izvestiya* there is no truth.

QUESTION: What is the longest joke?
ANSWER: The speech made by Khrushchev at the Party congress.

Next to peasants and rural workers at the bottom of the social ladder, were pensioners. If full-time wageworkers had problems surviving on their wages, the situation for pensioners was often dire, especially for those living alone. One of the endless political jokes that circulated daily or weekly on the underground called *Radio Yerevan* or *Radio Armenia*, was about Ivan Ivanovich who once worked with Khrushchev as a metal worker before the latter began to ascend the political ladder. Now retired as a pensioner, Ivan found that he could not survive on his Soviet pension and decided to go to Moscow, like thousands of others, to seek help from his old mate Nikita Sergeyevich. After waiting for days, Ivan finally met Khrushchev and told him of his plight. "Don't worry Ivan Ivanovich", Nikita Sergeyevich replied, "I've got a good, well-paid job for you here. Tomorrow, I want you to stand on the Kremlin wall with a telescope and let me know when you observe that communism is coming." The next day, Ivan Ivanovich is on the Kremlin wall looking through the telescope that Khrushchev provided for him. A group of American tourists stop and ask him what he is looking at. After explaining his job, the Americans offer to triple his salary if he will come to Wall Street and let them know when the next recession was coming. Ivan thanked them but declined their offer. "Why", they asked. "Because recessions come every few years in capitalist societies", Ivan Ivanovich replied, "however, looking for the arrival of communism is not only a job for life, but is also one for my children, grandchildren and great, great-grandchildren!"

Soviet women, racism and alcoholism

Whether one was a rural worker, a pensioner, or an urban worker, it was doubly worse if you were a female peasant, pensioner, or industrial worker. There were none of the usual ideological defences of patriarchy common in Australia and other countries about how women were unable to do a range of jobs because they were either too weak or lacked intelligence. In the Soviet Union, women did the toughest and dirtiest manual labour in factories, construction sites, road works and in agricultural production. One constantly witnessed women digging up roads and loading the trucks while the male drivers just looked on. In every industry or sector where there were an overwhelming majority of women employed, it was the same hierarchy. Whether in education, medicine, dentistry, chemical industries, transport, machine operators or in a range of agricultural jobs, women laboured away but only constituted a small minority of administrators and managers. So much for socialist equality.

Not only did women do the usual two jobs of paid work and unpaid domestic labour, but domestic violence was rampant. Pay day was the worst. After getting drunk at the workplace *stolovka* or canteen, and sometimes drinking up half or more of their wages, the men would stagger home between eight and ten o'clock in the evening. We would then hear the screams coming from neighbourhood apartments as women were regularly beaten or forced to have sex with their drunken partners.

It felt as though we were still living in pre-modern times. We asked our friend Marusya, who worked on road building, why women wrapped their whole heads up so that you could only see a bit of their noses and eyes. She explained that there was a massive shortage of men due to the deaths of millions of men in the war. If a woman got sunburnt, then men would not look at them as they had plenty of other women to choose from. Galina and Anya, who were factory workers, told us that divorce was widespread and men simply walking out on wives and families was also common. They said that most women had at least two abortions and they knew some who had four or five. Abortion was used as a form of contraception given the expectation that many women would be left on their own should they have a baby. While men in Australia similarly expected to be looked after at home, divorce was harder to get in the 1950s and moral disapproval of men and women living in a de facto relationship was still prevalent. By contrast, in Arshintsevo and other towns, the subordination of women was accompanied by a widespread and much more casual attitude when it came to men living in de facto relationships without making any long-term commitments to their female partners.

Soviet propaganda about women being equal to men was just that, mere propaganda. While the revolution had liberated women from their abysmal conditions as serfs and given them an education and social rights, a new form of inequality permeated women's lives when it came to making decisions, whether at the top in the Kremlin or in the factory or at home. The back-breaking work performed by women and their marginalisation in decision-making in all aspects of social life particularly shocked my parents, who once again were confronted with the gap between the ideology of gender equality and the reality of Soviet Communism.

In contrast to conservative official Soviet morality displayed in films and promoted by the various arms of the moral police against hooliganism and individualism, everyday life was a strange mixture of prudishness and Chaucerian bawdiness or matter of fact, open heterosexual practices. Homosexuality was out of sight, but Soviet films also banned any display of sexual activity. For example, I remember the Soviet audience gasping and making audible noises of part shock or engagement at a local screening when watching the far-from-explicit sex scenes between Lawrence Harvey and Simone Signoret or Heather Sears in Jack Clayton's 1959 film *Room at the Top*. The depiction of class differences in a northern English steel town made this film one of the few acceptable British films imported, despite its sex scenes.

The official culture may have been starved of sex, but it was common to see men and women living together, expressing their sexuality without all the courtship and moralising about no sex before marriage. Public swearing and all sorts of jokes and nicknames infused with explicit sexualised language were something we regularly heard. Political leaders such as Khrushchev or Lenin with their bald heads were usually represented in jokes as penises or Marx and Engels with their beards as pubic hair. It was a crude peasant and working-class humour.

Sexualised references were also applied to locals. One small guy in a nearby building used to be publicly called *Pol Pisda* or half a cunt. Because my mother virtually never went out and became a mystery to many in the housing estate, any glimpse of her was a notable event. One day she got a fish bone stuck in her throat and was standing near the kitchen window chewing on bread in an effort to dislodge the small bone. Just at that moment, *Pol Pisda* walked by in the street and noticed Mum. He was so fascinated, that he kept on looking up at our kitchen window as he walked backwards until he tripped and fell into one of the outside rubbish bins. It was a hilarious moment that we all shared as we watched him get out of the bin.

The other aspect of Soviet life that so disillusioned my parents was the prevalence of anti-Semitism and racism. Once again, the chasm between official propaganda that combatted all forms of racial and ethnic discrimination, and the unofficial everyday practices of cultural and social discrimination, were stark. At one level, since 1917 there had been dramatic social revolutions in most of the Republics of the USSR. Much had been done to integrate various nationalities. Tens of millions of people of non-Russian backgrounds had been educated and enjoyed social mobility from their former peasant illiterate backgrounds or so that they would feel committed to the political system, military forces, and industrial production system. Yet, at the unofficial everyday level of lived experience, old prejudices were hard to eradicate.

It was not just the pervasive anti-Semitism expressed by so many people, but the failure of the authorities to curb racist expressions and behaviour. Radio Yerevan was continually full of racist jokes that usually featured a Russian, a Ukrainian, a Georgian, a Jew or an Armenian, or other variations of ethnic stereotypes. People from the Caucuses such as Georgians were called *cherniye zhopa* or black arse, while Ukrainians were derided by Russians and others as *hohols* (a derogatory term derived from the traditional haircut of shaved head with single tussle). Jews were called *gryaznyy zhyd* (dirty or filthy Jew) as well as other abusive adjectives added on, even though the term *zhyd* was banned in the 1930s after its original neutral connotation was converted into a swear word. Many of the political jokes involving Georgians were based on stereotypes as they were cast as either sexual predators trying to seduce Russian women or commercial thieves. Ukrainians were depicted as slow or thick, Jews were cunning and deceptive, and similar pejorative characteristics were attributed to other national groups.

Our experience of the Soviet Union in the late 1950s meant that we were not surprised to read about the revival of religion, racism, superstition, fascism, and rampant nationalism after the collapse of the regime in 1991. Personal subjective experiences are often inaccurate and unreliable. However, when our family regularly would discuss what we observed in social and political attitudes, we were very much aware that Soviet values were only championed by about a quarter of the population. Another third was indifferent or unenthusiastic but went through the motions in order to avoid trouble, and about a third to forty percent were either openly critical or barely disguised their hostility and prejudices in private settings. It was little wonder then that millions of people discarded any vestiges of Soviet official views on religion, racism, and collective social behaviour once the USSR was dissolved.

Of course, nationalist pride was still overwhelmingly and genuinely evident in Soviet sporting achievements and especially after the launching of Sputnik in October 1957, together with other scientific developments. The government could always rely on patriotic fervour when encountering foreign threats during the Cold War. Hence, there was always tension and contradictions between widespread dissatisfaction with so many aspects of daily life, and the ever-present hope that perhaps one day life would be much better, and that the Soviet regime would deliver on its promises. This is why after moving away from the years of terrible repression under Stalin, the government needed to deliver on improvements in wages, consumer goods and social welfare. Without these improvements and reallocation of production from heavy industry to providing more consumer goods, there would be falls in productivity and discontent would spread and destabilise the regime.

However, the increased production of consumer goods did not always alleviate social discontent, especially if factories produced thousands of lamps but they were all coloured orange, or just a few unpopular styles of shoes and jackets simply because they were easy to produce and fulfilled the plan. The shops always had various such items that couldn't be sold because the public had no direct input into what they wanted factories to produce.

We were always incredibly careful not to openly criticise the regime for fear that as foreigners we would be reported. Instead, we listened to the life stories and experiences of our neighbours and visiting friends. When asked, we would tell them about life in Australia but not in a manner to make them feel even more despondent about inferior living conditions in Arshintsevo and Kerch. Nonetheless, there were grave events that brought home the harshness and irrationality of the central, undemocratic, command planning system that angered the whole community. In the winter of 1958/1959, the large processing plant had a disastrous industrial accident. Apparently, men working in the furnace area were trapped as gas fumes threatened their lives. Other workers ran to management to beg them to shut down the machinery to save the men's lives, but the director didn't act quickly enough because he was worried about disrupted production and failing to fulfil planning targets. Seven men died. Virtually the entire population of Arshintsevo turned out for the mass funeral as the dead men in their open caskets were followed by thousands of mourners as they slowly proceeded towards the cemetery. Ironically, the loss of life caused more disruption than if management had acted immediately and put workers' lives ahead of production targets.

There were many similar incidents, strikes and stoppages across the country over the years we were living in Arshintsevo, despite these events and incidents never being reported in the Soviet media. News eventually circulated to other cities, carried by relatives, visitors, and others. Soviet workers also engaged in their own 'silent' sabotage when working conditions became unbearable. Sheila Fitzpatrick in her book, *Everyday Stalinism*, describes how this tradition of resistance went back to the 1930s when Stakhanovite workers (named after Alexei Stakhanov, who exceeded the level of production required of workers) were hated for setting intolerable work regimes and for the privileges they received. Other workers would attack and injure Stakhanovites so that zealous managers would not maintain excessive work practices.

It was one thing for intellectuals in Moscow and Leningrad to circulate critiques of the system through what was later called *samizdat*, or the underground printing of censored and dissident material. However, for workers in provincial industrial towns such as Arshintsevo, these modest or more dramatic practical acts of resistance had to be carried out at significant risk in order to make life bearable. Resistance usually involved devising methods to protect workers from exhaustion, stealing supplies to ease hardship and collective go-slow measures.

Outside of work, attempts to evade the lucrative and giant revenue-earning state monopoly of alcohol production often ended in disaster. It was not unusual for those workers who ventured into making bootlegged spirits at home, to become disabled or die from alcohol poisoning and other negative consequences. The authorities faced a losing battle against alcoholism. Education was ineffective against the harshness of life, the meaningless of long and draining work conditions and the general culture of drowning one's sorrows in drinking. Whereas basic food items were in short supply, vodka and other drinks were always available in the shop and at work in the *stolovka* or at kiosks in the streets. Closing or slowing down the alcohol pipeline was politically explosive and avoided in the first two years we were there. However, in 1958, Khrushchev launched a massive anti-alcohol campaign. The price of vodka was increased by 21% and banned from sale in food shops, near schools, factories, and sports facilities. In restaurants, the price of vodka was increased by 50% and limited to 100 grams. Unsurprisingly, in response to government restrictions, the illegal production of alcohol skyrocketed with many casualties. The public also switched from vodka to other sources of alcohol such as wine or beer.

No leader from Khrushchev to Gorbachev succeeded in ridding the Soviet Union of the scourge of alcoholism. By the time Yeltsin took power (himself an alcoholic), such were the shocks from the big bang introduction of the capitalist market, that the drop in living standards combined with alcoholism led to the biggest fall in life expectancy in the second half of the twentieth century. Male life expectancy in Russia fell by an incredible six years between 1991 and 1994, from an already-low 63.4 years to 57.4 years, while female life expectancy fell from 74.2 to 71.1 years over the same period.

My father was also a victim of alcohol, although never an alcoholic who drank every day. There was much social pressure from his workmates and friends to drink with them on pay day and on other occasions. Vodka was not like beer, and it would only take several rounds of drinks to negatively affect one's health if consumed at that rate over a longer period of time. During his three years of living by himself in Arshintsevo, between 1960 and 1963, when his application to return to Australia was repeatedly refused, alcohol must have contributed to him later developing cancer of the pancreas. Although he drank much less upon returning to Australia, the damage had been done. Like millions of Russians before and after him, his life was shortened by a combination of the everyday trauma he suffered in the Soviet Union and the alcohol he probably consumed to make his lonely life bearable.

Boris, Maya and Genia with their father, February 1958.

Each of us learned something different from the society we were forced to live in. Although I was only fourteen when we finally departed the Soviet Union, my age was not a true measure of the processes of maturation that I had undergone. The combined experiences of closely observing and engaging in daily aspects of Soviet life while also reading extensively and acquiring an education and exposure to global politics via the radio, meant that I was richer in knowledge and life skills than others of equivalent age. It was as if my childhood had finished in St. Kilda and the years in Russia had leapfrogged me into adulthood with a new set of responsibilities. Occasionally we would dress up in our clothes from Melbourne, have a photo taken, and imagine that we would soon be going home.

Of course, knowledge of the world and personal emotional maturity do not develop at the same pace. Sometimes one or the other remains relatively immature or permanently undeveloped. Our isolation was not easy to endure, and arguments would often break out between one or another of us. During 1956 and 1957, Genia and I would occasionally fight with a broom or mop due to boredom or frustration. We were no angels. After one such fight, we realised that we could seriously hurt one another and reached a truce where we decided to confine our arguments to verbal rather than physical conflict. We needed to conserve our energy for the larger fight ahead. Our struggle to leave the Soviet Union would test our emotional determination, resilience, and endurance in the face of demoralising and damaging setbacks.

13

WE REFUSE TO ACCEPT YOUR REFUSAL

When we embarked on our concerted campaign to get out of the Soviet Union in August 1956, we were not optimistic that the Soviet authorities would let us return to Australia. Following our refusal to go to school for the new school year beginning in September, my parents made official applications to the Kerch officials in September requesting exit visas to return to Australia. These Kerch officials eventually contacted their superiors in the *Obkom*, Simferopol, the regional administrative centre in Crimea.

In Simferopol, it was a branch of OVIR (*Otdel Viz I Registratsiy*) or Visa and Registration section of the Soviet Ministry of Internal Affairs that together with the Directorate of Police in the Ministry of the Interior of the Ukrainian Soviet Socialist Republic, that managed applications to leave the country. They instructed my parents (via Kerch officials) to contact Comrade Barannikova of the *oblast* or regional Directorate of Police. My father made a special journey to Simferopol and met Comrade Barannikova at the end of November. She informed him that if the family wished to leave the country, we would first need a document from relatives in Australia stating that they agreed to sponsor the whole family. Dad was also told that the Soviet government did not believe in splitting families and was unconvinced by the reason that we were unhappy about living in Arshintsevo simply because the children were born in Australia.

Nevertheless, we were pleasantly surprised by this favourable reaction to our application and naively assumed that once we received a statutory declaration from our relatives, filled in all other documents and paid our 400 roubles for the exit visa, that we would soon be on our way back to Melbourne. How very wrong we were.

The truth is that we simply did not understand the different methods deployed by Soviet authorities, depending on how they were trained. On the one hand, there were still many security officials who had learnt their 'administrative techniques' during the darkest days of Stalin's terror. Although officially restrained in the Khrushchev era, it didn't take much for them to revert to the old script of hurling abuse and making violent threats such as, 'we have the power and you will obey, or else...' On the other hand, there were the modernised or de-Stalinised officials who were polite, listened to what you said but ultimately denied your application by using all kinds of delaying and other bureaucratic strategies. Occasionally we encountered a sympathetic official who tried to either explain that they would try their best to help or else directed you to those who had ultimate decision-making power.

Since my two sisters and I were born in Australia, the Soviet local and regional authorities wished to avoid any international or unforeseen complications. Hence, our parents' application was not instantaneously dismissed but instead were told to get supporting documents for their exit visa. Consequently, Mum wrote to her uncle and aunt in Melbourne requesting their support. We also wrote to various friends in Melbourne including Reg and Joan Brettargh telling them of the terrible mistake we had made leaving Australia and requesting their help. Mum also wrote to Joan and Reg asking whether they would be prepared to foster Genia and me in the event that the Soviets would only permit the Australian-born children to leave. Maya was only two years old and too young to be separated from her mother. In response, Joan and Reg made the extraordinarily generous offer of agreeing to foster us in the event that our family had to split up.

In the first two years of our struggle to return, in 1956 and 1957 Joan and Reg were incredibly supportive and would be our main connection to the Australian Department of Immigration. Meanwhile, two weeks after my father's visit to Simferopol, regional Police and Party headquarters sent Inspector Sinitsina and another Party woman from *Obkom* in Simferopol to our place to interview my mother in December 1956. They wished to know why we wanted to leave the USSR and why we were unhappy. It was dawning on us that getting out of Russia might be much harder than the original favourable instructions about simply providing supporting documents from Australia.

The painful truth is that hardly anyone with a Soviet passport was permitted to leave the Soviet Union in the 1950s. We heard of an Italian who married a Russian woman while she was living in the West after the war. She and her husband returned to a town near us. He was desperate to get back to Italy and made a failed attempt to hang himself after authorities refused all his applications to leave the country.

Yet our case was considered more unusual. The authorities did not initially simply reject our application for an exit visa. Rather, they adopted two strategies simultaneously. One was to offer us more attractive options. As a sign of the seriousness of the case, the Party head of the *Obkom* in Simferopol made a special trip of coming all the way to Arshintsevo to talk to Dad at his workplace to enquire about why we wanted to leave. First, he ordered the manager of his factory to increase my father's wages. Secondly, they asked if perhaps a better job in Kerch or moving to Moscow would help, especially for the children's education. It is important to understand that across the Soviet Union, parents dreamed of getting their children into the leading institutes, artistic academies, and university in Moscow. Mothers hoped their sons or daughters would become famous ballerinas, pianists, or soloists while fathers desired that their sons attend the best technical and scientific institutes in Moscow. Dad told the party chief he was not interested in these incentives as his wife and children were so unhappy and they wanted to return to Australia.

The other strategy was to isolate us from communicating with the outside world. Prior to this official overt and covert response, we had been corresponding with friends in Melbourne. Mum even wrote to Russian friends in Melbourne called the Barskis, requesting a food parcel to be sent to us from Melbourne. They organised a parcel of mainly tinned food which arrived a couple of months later via a Swedish organisation. A blindly loyal supporter of the Soviet Union, Mr. Barski wrote an abusive letter to Dad for criticising conditions in Russia. Four years later we found out that our letter thanking them for the food parcel never arrived and that the Barskis thought we were ungrateful. Mr. Barski died before we returned to Melbourne.

Shortly after arriving in Baku and seeing the awful conditions in the USSR, my parents warned other Russians not to come. Dad wrote to the Popovs in Melbourne telling them not to leave Australia, but they ignored his advice and returned to the USSR only to bitterly regret their decision. The same was true of Nikita Pivniyev and his Yugoslav-born wife Mira and son Victor who returned to the USSR from Melbourne in 1957. Remarkably, ASIO were unaware of my father's warnings to these other Russians and instead reported the malicious falsehood that he was a 'subversive', on the gravy train, and giving lectures all around the USSR. Ironically, in 1958, it was ASIO and the Department of Immigration that would jointly consider our application to return to Australia along with the Pivniyev's and another family's application.

The strategy of isolating us meant that most of the letters we wrote from Arshintsevo from 1956 to Mum's relatives, our friends and the Australian government were seized at the Arshintsevo post office. A few got through if posted from Kerch, and we know that some got through in later years if carried by sympathetic Russians and posted from other cities they were visiting. We knew this because, strangely, the local *Raikom* and *Gorkom* in Kerch permitted us to receive letters from Australia and other countries, but not to send them to Australia or elsewhere. The replies we got indicated that our friends, such as Reg and Joan, knew of our plight and kept us informed about the extremely slow machinery of the Australian government. We also sent letters to Australia via Dad's sister and husband Misha in Baku. A few of these did manage to arrive in Melbourne.

Unfortunately, from about December 1956 to 1959, we were subjected to a near-total blockade as far as any communication with Australia. No wonder we didn't hear anything back from our relatives about providing a statement of support. Nor did we have any news directly from the Australian government. In late 1957, after complaining about the censorship and seizure of our outward mail, the post office in Arshintsevo denied this and informed us in late 1958 that, 'regrettably' there had been a 'malfunction' in the mail system. They compensated us 200 roubles for the money we had spent on stamps. Of course, none of our seized letters were ever found or returned to us, let alone posted to Australia.

In the midst of this mail blockade, we received a post card from our extremely eccentric friend Ted Harvey. Ted was a cross between a nutty professor and Jacques Tati's character *Monsieur Hulot*. He used to drive a three-wheel bubble car in Melbourne in the 1950s that would send the kids wild with curiosity when he arrived at our place in East St. Kilda. A bachelor and a communist fellow traveller, Ted also did business importing goods from East European countries, like Bulgarian ceramic coffee sets. Unbeknown to us, Ted was travelling through Japan and sent a typed postcard in 1957 that simply stated:

> Arrived Japan 11th July and have visited Tokio, Sandai, Matsushima, Nikko, Kamakura, Nagoya, Giru, and now Takayama. Will then go to Kyoto, Osaka, Hiroshima, Miyajima, Beppu, Nara and Toba.
> —Ted (handwritten in Russian letters)

The Soviet authorities must have thought that it was a message written in code and they possibly spent weeks trying to decode it. We were expecting trouble from hostile and suspicious local officials. However, knowing Ted, (combined with our grim situation at the time) we all fell about with a laughter that would not stop. Genia laughed so much that she lost control of her bladder. I still have Ted's postcard and still laugh every time I read it.

ASIO is fed lies

Most of us have little idea of what it is like to be a refugee or political dissident and be caught between a repressive government that seeks to persecute you and other governments that refuse to let you into their country. In response to desperate situations, honest people continue to be forced to become streetwise, economical with the truth and develop levels of resilience and patience as well as skills that they never before needed to acquire, let alone exercise. We were not refugees, but we might as well have been, given the way we were treated by both the Soviet and Australian governments. We did not face the prospect of being sent to the Gulag or detention in a refugee camp for years. Yet, just like refugees and political dissidents, we knew what it was like to have our lives kept in limbo for years, with no access to what was in the files kept about us by Soviet security agencies and by ASIO and the Australian Department of Immigration. We also knew what it was like to experience the occasional glimmer of hope only to see it fade or be abruptly extinguished by another refusal of our applications by either the Soviet or Australian governments. Our long struggle to leave the USSR and to reunite our family in Australia would take a total of nearly seven years from 1956 to 1963.

While we were all too soon made aware of the hostility to our case by local and regional Soviet officials, we completely underestimated ASIO's opposition to our return to Australia. It was not just their long-held view that my father was a pro-Soviet subversive and threat to Australia's security. After we left Melbourne in May 1956, ASIO continued to be supplied by its local informants with misinformation about my father's activities and position in the Soviet Union. It was only four years later in 1960, when my mother, Genia, Maya and I returned to Melbourne and our old ASIO 'companion', Ernest Redford, interviewed us, that we learnt about some of the complete falsehoods that informed ASIO's view of 'Frenkel'. We all laughed in disbelief, when asked if we could confirm the reports to the Victorian branch office of ASIO and circulating amongst local Russian emigres, that he was now either a commander of a Soviet submarine or working in the submarine base in Kerch. It took decades later, reading the secret classified files that were released, for me to learn the extent of the lies about him in reports, so absurd that they too would have been laughable, if they had not had such dire consequences.

There was so much in these malicious reports that was taken as fact and neither questioned nor adequately investigated for verifying evidence by ASIO. The files mentioned that a supposed Soviet newspaper had reported that my father was on a tour of Soviet cities in his capacity as President of the Australia-Soviet Friendship Society, giving lectures about Australia. Not a shred of evidence backed up this claim. The Soviet newspaper was not named, no date was given, and no corroborating evidence was provided. None of the ASIO officers who handled their informants could read Russian, and they, therefore, relied on absurd rumours spread amongst their paid contacts in the Russian émigré community.

A case in point was a secret Memorandum sent to ASIO Headquarters concerning the subject of Abraham Frenkel and Tania Frenkel Applicants for Re-Entry Permits, which was stamped URGENT and dated January 6, 1958. It was written on behalf of ASIO Regional Director, Victoria, T. E. Nave (but the author's name remains redacted). The three-page Memorandum outlined my father's relationship to Petrov, his pro-Soviet activity and why ASIO should oppose granting him a re-entry visa. The Memorandum relied heavily on two reports from ASIO informant or employee, Alex Scheback, dated February 7, 1957, and March 5, 1957. Scheback claimed that Dad was a member of the St. Kilda branch of the CPA, went to a social function organised by the St. Kilda Branch on November 14, 1953, and that at another meeting of the St. Kilda Branch they mentioned Frenkel as "having made progress in certain activities on behalf of the C.P. of A." What these 'activities' were is not mentioned by Scheback. My father was never a member of the St. Kilda Branch and never engaged in conspiratorial or subversive activities. Once again, no corroborating evidence was provided.

Remember, ASIO had already sent a report from informer Scheback in 1954 who claimed that my father was the 'top man' in Melbourne and that Vassilieff worked for him in repatriating Russians. Scheback had been a friend of the Barskis (who had sent us a food parcel) and Ben Stokalin (Stocklin), a Russian who had come to Melbourne from China after the war. Stokalin would visit us with his big Alsatian dog and tell us that despite several years passing, he still suffered from the jet engine noise in his ears after flying from Shanghai to Australia. My father met Scheback via Stokalin. Now, in 1957, Scheback continued his false reporting. He told ASIO that Wassileff (Vassilieff) had seen Frenkel in Russia and according to Vassilieff, the Frenkels may soon be back in Australia. This was untrue. No such meeting in Russia ever took place between my father and Vassilieff. In addition to these rumours and falsehoods, Scheback also reported that:

> FRENKEL believes that because of his membership to (sic) the C.P. of A, he expected to obtain a good position such as attache in Russia. Further, FRENKEL hoped that Russia would appoint him Russian Commercial Attache in America. SCHEBACK said that as this did not eventuate, FRENKEL now wishes to return to Australia.

The notion that my father wanted to be an attache and especially Russian Commercial Attache in America was fanciful and completely at odds with his long-held desire to live as an ordinary worker in the 'workers state'. We witnessed his rejection of any special favours on our arrival in London when he turned down the trip to East Germany, and in Leningrad when he declined the offer of a comfortable non-factory job. He also had a profound dislike of American capitalism. Only the ignorance within ASIO's hierarchy could account for their belief in the fabricated fictions supplied by a dishonest, and possibly paid liar. ASIO Regional office in Victoria sent all Scheback's fabrications to ASIO headquarters and didn't even correct or question his various claims, including that we were supposedly living in Yacta! As there is no town in Crimea called Yacta, which ASIO could have easily checked, perhaps this was just an uncorrected typo or ASIO misheard 'Yalta', especially if Scheback had been feeding an ASIO officer rumours and lies over the phone.

Instead of living in the tourist resort of Yalta or being a submarine commander or expecting to be appointed as an attache, my father was working as a humble electric welder in Arshintsevo. Unfortunately, these lies combined with ASIO's incompetence and their determination to prevent our return, meant that another one of our applications to return to Australia was torpedoed.

Spry's obsessive interventions

One of the letters that my mother wrote to Joan and Reg Brettargh in late December 1956 was somehow lucky to get through the blockade. In this letter, she also included an additional letter which she addressed to the 'Emigration (sic) Authorities of Australia', dated December 21, 1956. The letter briefly outlined details about our family and that she and the children didn't ever want to leave Australia. Dramatically, she then painted a picture of extreme pain and suffering. It was a style of letter designed to 'tug at the heart strings' in the hope that Australian Immigration officials would be favourably disposed to our case.

> Since we arrived in the Soviet Union the children have been terribly sick, demanding all the time to be taken back to their homeland Australia. It is already 8 months since they are without school; they sit home crying night and day, wanting only one thing, to return home to their native land, to their schools, friends, and relations. They have been accusing the father for everything that happened. My husband is suffering terrible agony and pain and regretting the terrible mistake he has made. Several months ago, we applied to the Government here to let us return back to Australia ... A few days ago, we received a reply from the authorities here, that we shall be

allowed to leave the Soviet Union only if we produce a document from the Australian Government that we together with the children are permitted to re-enter Australia ... I believe with all my heart that you will put an end to the sufferings of Australian children and their parents by granting us the only document that we need to leave this country for which we shall be grateful all our life. It is impossible to explain everything in a letter, but we shall answer all questions as soon as we meet the Australian authorities.

After receiving this letter in January 1957, Reg and Joan waited for about six to seven months for us to send photos and copies of birth certificates needed for any official application to Immigration. Due to the mail seizures, various attempts to forward these to Reg and Joan failed. Eventually, they received additional supporting photos and wrote to their local Member of Parliament, Sir Wilfred Kent-Hughes, requesting his support for our case.

Politically, when we lived in Australia, Kent-Hughes was regarded by my parents as beyond the pale. Like Menzies, Kent-Hughes admired the industrial relations system in fascist countries that suppressed free trade unions and kept businesses profitable. Unlike Menzies, Kent-Hughes proudly declared his support of Fascism and in 1933 wrote a series of articles for the Melbourne *Herald* entitled '*Why I Have Become a Fascist*'. It is important to recall that in Australia, between 36,000 and 80,000 ex-soldiers and businessmen belonged to the secret and not-so-secret armies of the pro-fascist New Guard. In 1930, *The Bulletin* had called on ex-General, Sir John Monash to become *Il Duce* or dictator to save Australia from the Bolsheviks. As a Jew and constitutional monarchist, Monash rejected these pleas from business groups.

Later on, Kent-Hughes was a prisoner of war, Deputy Premier of Victoria and then a member of Menzies' federal cabinet. He was even more anti-Communist than Menzies. However, a year before Reg and Joan wrote to him, Menzies had dropped him from cabinet as his calls to bring back conscription, spend more on defence, and his leadership of the 'Taiwan lobby' in the Liberal Party proved to be embarrassing for Menzies. In 1955, Menzies went to see President Eisenhower to persuade him not to go to war with China over Taiwan. If he were alive today, Kent-Hughes would have loved AUKUS and spending $368 billion on nuclear submarines.

Sir Wilfred's rabid anti-Communism meant that he took up our case and on October 9, 1957, wrote to Athol Townley who had succeeded Harold Holt in October 1956 as Minister for Immigration.

> I have no reason to believe that the application is anything but 100% genuine, so, unless there are any reasons which are unknown to me, I wish to support the application.
>
> If I remember rightly, there was some propaganda with their return to Russia, but the counter-propaganda on their return to Australia would be of much greater value if, as I believe, the request is as genuine as the letter from Mrs. Frankel would appear to be.

Mum's letter had clearly persuaded Kent-Hughes. However, Townley merely replied that he would look into our case. Director-General of ASIO, Brigadier Spry, was asked by Minister Townley whether ASIO had any objection to the return of the Frankel family. Spry's personal reply would be a consistent and obstinate objection during the next three years. His reasons were based on a set of fanciful and paranoid arguments which I will discuss in what follows. Spry's clearest objection to my father was stated in a letter to the Secretary of the Department of Immigration, Tasman Heyes on September 8, 1958.

> You will realise that I am most concerned in this case in view of FRANKEL's record, which I made available to you in my memorandum Serial 3866, dated 11th April, 1958, and in which I mentioned FRANKEL's repatriation activities which, I would stress, amounted to sabotage of your Immigration programme. (My emphasis)

While the Director-General's view was countered by senior officials in Immigration and other departments in 1958 and 1959, his veto power was only partially overruled in 1959. In the meantime, Joan Brettargh wrote to Minister Townley on December 3, 1957, expressing her concern and anxiety about the welfare of the Frankel children. She also emphasised that a considerable amount of time had passed since Sir Wilfred had submitted their letters on behalf of the Frankel family. Athol Townley could not inform Joan about whether Immigration had agreed or refused to issue a re-entry visa for us as the long delay involving ASIO and Immigration continued well into 1958.

Such were the static wheels of government, that although my mother had written her letter in December 1956 and Townley received it in October 1957, he still failed to give Joan and Reg an answer before he was replaced as Minister of Immigration by Alexander Downer Snr in March 1958. After submissions from ASIO, another year went by until Minister Downer notified Sir Wilfred Kent-Hughes on January 12, 1959, (and the Brettarghs a week or so later at the end of January) that the Frankel family had been refused re-entry visas by the Australian government. Downer also instructed G. C. Watson, the Chief Migration Officer at Australia House, London, to notify the British Embassy in Moscow that "it had been decided not to readmit the Frankel family to Australia." The reason why the British Embassy was asked to communicate this refusal to us in Arshintsevo will be explained shortly. We were shocked to receive the unwelcome news from the British Embassy dated March 10, 1959.

Our experience, and the experiences of thousands of immigrants and refugees subjected to the feet-dragging slowness of government decision-making, could be characterised as cognitive dissonance or parallel realities. In one reality, we and others were desperate to hear about a government decision that often took a minimum of one to two years of agonising waiting time before a case was even considered, let alone decided upon. However, in the world of Ministers and senior bureaucrats, each calendar year was somehow reduced to the equivalent of a mere 24-hour day.

Even though some officials had empathy and tried to prevent unnecessary suffering, most Ministers, while formally acknowledging the suffering of people kept in limbo, continued to delay decision making, blind to the human consequences. It usually took external action in the form of protests, legal action, and media publicity to shake up these slothful, dehumanising timetables and attitudes. One only has to look at the recent suffering of countless refugees in detention in Australia or offshore to realise how little has changed since the 1950s.

ASIO, and especially Brigadier Spry, constituted the major obstacle for our family. Fuelled by years of negative reports and false information with no attempt to substantiate what was fed to him by ASIO regional officers, Spry was adamant that he would not budge on his refusal to let my father back into Australia. While he grudgingly acknowledged that we children were Australian-born citizens and that my mother was not involved in the repatriation of Russians prior to 1956, he used the so-called 'humanitarian' card of not wishing to split the family. This was the ostensible excuse for why he would not let the rest of the family return after he denied my father a re-entry visa.

Spry's decisive intervention in April 1958 was delivered in conjunction with responses to the applications made by the Pivnijev family and by Joseph and Olga Mikhailoff and their daughter Margarita who came to Australia from China but returned to the USSR in 1957. "There is only one safe way of dealing with all these applications and all similar ones", he declared, "and that is to refuse them without any exception."

Alexander Downer Snr, who was the father of Alexander Downer, Foreign Minister in John Howard's government, ultimately agreed with Spry's security assessment to exclude all three families. Yet, he covered his own tracks by adding a note of caution. "In future, each application should be decided, as in this instance, on its merits. Otherwise, some serious injustice might occur." By contrast, Spry's prejudgment of migrants from Eastern Europe constituted the equivalent of racial profiling by police forces. He argued that there are migrants who come and find conditions difficult and return home. No objections can be made to such migrants from the UK or other democracies. "In the case of persons who wish to return from the U.S.S.R., however, the risk to the security of the Commonwealth is so great, that no other considerations, compassionate or otherwise, should be allowed to weigh."

The Director-General of ASIO never spelt out what this extreme risk to Australia could be. Instead, he painted implausible scenarios where my father could engage in espionage or propaganda for the Soviets. Ignoring the suffering of my father and other returnees, Spry's mind worked overtime to come up with any confected reason to oppose my father's re-entry to Australia. He went so far as to assert on April 11, 1958, that:

> There is first the possibility that a repatriate's return to Russia may have been organised with the intention from the outset, and with his knowledge, of training him in some particular role and then sending him back. Frenkel, with his many years of pro-Soviet activity, is an obvious candidate for this category.

The National Archives also contain files where other senior officials in Immigration at the time actually questioned ASIO's logic. Surely, these officials argued, ASIO could monitor a few Russians and these returning people would be too well known to engage in espionage. Also, their propaganda value in Australia would be nullified, especially amongst the ex-Soviet emigre community, by the mere fact of their return to Australia from the so-called Soviet paradise. Spry countered these arguments with the paranoid claim that the Soviets had no compassion, could easily deal with a nuisance problem, and therefore would only permit my father to leave if they could still control him and he would remain useful to them in Australia. ASIO was still labouring under the gross lie and distortion that my father was a subversive, receiving special treatment and lecturing across the Soviet Union, and trained by Soviet intelligence.

While Spry and ASIO justifiably assumed that Soviet intelligence was adept at deception, they were nonetheless essentially ignorant of how the Soviets responded to returning Russians and why their repatriation was not designed to get ex-Soviets in the West to return home *en masse*. Instead, ASIO worked on the absurd logic that my father, the Pivnijevs and Mikhailoffs could become dangerous undercover plants like Philby, Maclean and Burgess. It only required a simple question about what access to vital government information or military secrets could these suffering individuals and families establish upon return, to dismiss Spry's spy-obsessed scenario as nonsense. None of those returning Russians could have gained jobs in sensitive areas of government. They certainly were as far as it is imaginable from being members of a Cambridge-like elite such as Philby and company.

As to fomenting pro-Soviet propaganda amongst Russians, even this exaggerated and unrealistic fear could have been easily nipped in the bud. For example, in exchange for re-entry visas, each of the small number of persons seeking re-admittance to Australia could have been required to sign a document that they would be deported back to the USSR if they engaged in pro-Soviet repatriation propaganda. Instead, the reality was that Spry was heartless and showed less compassion for us than his de-Stalinised Soviet contemporaries, and that is saying something. Soviet security eventually agreed to let us out with no strings attached, yet it took Spry and ASIO another three years to reluctantly agree to my father's return. They refused to acknowledge that Dad was not an agent of the USSR. It took a further four years before ASIO approved my father's application for Australian citizenship in 1967.

Isolation and Arrest in Moscow

In fact, ASIO's obsessive and unwavering hostility caused us to suffer enormously and unnecessarily for an extra two years. As decision-making dragged on at a snail's pace within the Australian government from late 1957 until we heard the negative news of our application being rejected in March 1959, we continued to struggle to get the Soviet authorities to let us out. We did not know that we were simultaneously fighting two enemies. Instead, we mistakenly thought – during the period from August 1956 until March 1959 – that we were only struggling against the Soviet authorities.

The problem in our case was that we were thoroughly isolated in Arshintsevo. We were kept in the dark. Prisoners in foreign prisons are entitled to consular visits, but we didn't even have this minimal contact with the Australian government as they had no embassy in Moscow since the Petrov affair. Joan and Reg had also explicitly asked Kent-Hughes not to make our case public, as my parents expressed their fear of retaliation by the Soviets. So, all through 1957 and 1958 we laboured under the illusion that help would come from Australia once we overcame Soviet refusals to give us exit visas.

Prisoners in jail develop coping strategies to survive physically and mentally. Days and months are counted until the next visit from a family member or friend, years are counted until parole hearings and so forth. The years in Arshintsevo were broken up by several key events and setbacks. In between these new developments were endless days of reading, going out to shop or perhaps fishing and occasionally seeing a visitor or two. Many weeks were filled with despair that we would never get out and we would then discuss Plan B, such as which city should we try to move to before we became adults and tried to leave for Australia again.

In January 1957, my parents were called to the *Gorkom* in Kerch and told to translate all their documents (marriage and birth certificates, former employers, and Australian places of residence) into Russian. They spent all day filling in forms and translating these into Russian. At the end of all of this bureaucratic detail, the official called them illiterate and said to get a translator. This was a ruse but cost them a lot of money and was not the end of the document process. For the next few weeks, they had to travel to Kerch to answer questions and clarify details repeatedly.

After all of this, they called my father into the Kerch office and told him that he and my mother's exit visa application had been refused. Dad was then called into another section of security and ordered to sign a document that we had been refused permission to leave. My father refused to sign knowing that once he signed, it would be taken as evidence that he accepted and couldn't ever re-apply. The charade of OVIR simply requesting documents and statements, including one from our relatives in Melbourne that they would support our return, was now over.

Following this major setback, we embarked on a letter-writing campaign that would go on for at least another one and a half years. On an almost weekly basis either myself, my mother and father or Genia would write letters appealing to one or other of the Soviet leaders. Apart from Khrushchev, we also wrote to Nikolai Bulganin who was Prime Minister or Chairman of the Council of Ministers until removed by Khrushchev in March 1958. We also wrote to Kliment Voroshilov who was the Chairman of the Presidium of the Supreme Soviet or President. Each of these letters would be a variation of themes about how we were born in Australia and wanted to go back home. As parents, Mum and Dad would appeal for help to end their children's suffering.

I lost count of the number of letters we wrote. Most were either ignored without even a formal acknowledgement of receipt as perhaps they were also seized by the Arshintsevo post office. Miraculously, Genia did receive one formal response from the Ministry of Foreign Affairs stating that they did not deal with individual applications and directed her to the local OVIR or passport office. Months went by without hearing from any senior official, let alone re-opening our case. But we knew that a persistent campaign of letter writing would still register our determination to leave with the local *Raikom* and regional *Obkom*.

Given that our condition was unchanged, and that we had heard nothing from the Australian government, the next significant development was Dad's decision to go to Moscow to try and meet two Melbourne friends who had written to us that they would be attending the World Festival of Youth and Students to be held in Moscow beginning on July 28, 1957. Paul Key was an Australian of Chinese background who worked as a high school teacher. Nancy, his wife, was also involved in Left student and post-student politics. She had written to us in early 1957 saying in memorable words that Melbourne "had become little Chicago with all the crime and police sirens making lots of noise at night."

The Youth Festival attracted about 34,000 visitors from abroad. Delegates were housed in a specific area similar to an Olympic athletes' village. Moscow had never seen so many foreign visitors and security forces were extensively mobilised to keep an eye on them. Dad briefly met Paul and Nancy to arrange to see them that same evening and pass on letters we had written to the Australian government. The meeting never happened. When he returned to see them, security forces arrested my father for having contact with foreigners and took him to a building, probably Lubyanka, for interrogation. He was kept there for several hours and was very shaken by the guards with machine guns, the prison cells, and the netting on some of the staircases to prevent people from jumping off and committing suicide. It was a terrifying ordeal for him.

In 1983, I was on a tour of Moscow and Leningrad with a group of foreign tourists, including a large contingent of American students from Stanford University. As our bus passed Felix Dzerzinsky Square (where Lubyanka was located) the students kept pestering our Soviet guide whether that was in fact Lubyanka. Unruffled, she answered yes, and repeated the old Soviet joke that 'one could get a good view of Siberia from there'.

My father was strenuously questioned, had all his documents checked with local authorities in Kerch and Arshintsevo, and threatened not to contact foreigners. A mere five or six years earlier, he could have literally been shipped off to Siberia. Luckily, they ordered him to immediately return home on the next available train. When he returned a couple of days later, I had never seen him so distressed and frightened. It was not for nothing that the KGB and other security forces had such a notorious reputation. Dad also whispered to us not to talk freely as he said the authorities knew everything and he was sure our place was bugged. He also wondered whether Paul and Nancy had reported him to Soviet officials.

Paul Key and Tania, St. Kilda, 1961.

When we returned to Melbourne in 1960, my mother renewed contact with Paul and Nancy to hear their version of what happened in Moscow. They were genuinely surprised and wondered why Dad had not turned up to have dinner with them. We accepted their explanation and remained friends with them over the years going to films and having dinner together. It was also in 1960 that Nancy had an affair with the political satirist Tom Lehrer when in Australia on his controversial three-month tour. Her relationship with Paul never recovered and they separated a year or so later. A photo from 1961 entitled 'two pals with broken hearts' showed Mum without Dad and Paul without Nancy. Years later in the 1970s and 1980s, Nancy, who had remarried and done a political 'about turn', would come to visit us, and bring newspapers by the Right-wing Lyndon LaRouche Citizens Electoral Councils movement. This led to arguments, and she stopped visiting. Like many former Communists in Europe who now support Right-wing nationalists such as Marine Le Pen in France, Nancy had made the full crossover from Left to Right.

Stubborn resistance versus intelligence

Between August 1957 and about July 1958, we made no headway with our case at all. Ten years earlier in 1947, the Frankfurt School philosophers, Theodor Adorno and Max Horkheimer had published their classic, *The Dialectic of Enlightenment*. In a concluding section on 'The Genesis of Stupidity', they argued that:

> The true symbol of intelligence is the snail's horn with which it feels and (if Mephistopheles is to be believed) smells its way. The horn recoils instantly before an obstacle, seeking asylum in the protective shell and again becoming one with the whole. Only tentatively does it re-emerge to assert its independence. If the danger is still present it vanishes once more, now hesitating longer before renewing the attempt. In its early stages the life of the mind is infinitely fragile. The snail's senses depend on its muscles, and muscles become feebler with every hindrance to their play. Physical injury cripples the body, fear the mind. At the start the two are inseparable.

These insightful observations emphasised how children governed by fear and constraint were likely to develop psychological scars and social pathologies in the process of becoming 'hard and able' people attracted to authoritarian leaders and solutions. However, what these philosophers ignored is that no social change would have been possible in the world if society relied solely on intelligence. We were certainly fearful of the Soviet authorities. However, we also learnt that intelligence on its own also got you nowhere if you let fear overwhelm you. Hence, we refused to recoil into our shells and pushed on with our campaign to get out of the country. Despite being initially severely shaken by his arrest in Moscow, Dad soon recovered his drive a few weeks later and we continued to write letters to Soviet leaders and to friends in Australia. Of course, one could expect a letter directly addressed to the Minister for Immigration in Australia to be seized, regardless of the city in which it was posted.

What seemed like an eternity was the routine of everyday life in Arshintsevo as 1957 slowly ebbed away and 1958 rolled on in a strange stalemate. It was as if we were forgotten or abandoned. Under these circumstances of falling back on our own psychological resources, we were sustained by literature, music and being connected to the outside world by our invaluable radio. We were free to go about town or explore the sea and the nearby fields, so our situation was not comparable to politicians in some countries who were kept by the military under house arrest. Nonetheless, our isolation invariably took its toll.

During this period, Dad's sister Nusia was dying, and he received an urgent cable to come to Baku. Earlier in 1958, the local Party head of the *Raiispolkom* had called him to come in to discuss his troubles. The Party secretary then referred to his wife, our mother, as a 'mad woman'. Things were beginning to deteriorate as officials in Arshintsevo and Kerch started to put pressure on both my parents to accept that there was no way that permission to leave the Soviet Union would be granted.

While he was away in Baku, two officials came and ordered Mum to go to the mayor's office in Kerch. She refused but they came with a car the next day and drove her to Kerch. The third senior official in charge at the *Gorkom* ordered her to sign a document that permission to leave for Austria had been refused. Mum refused to sign and told them she had applied to return to Australia, not Austria. After several earlier attempts to browbeat us into attending school, they now told Mum that Genia and I would be put in boarding school as it was unacceptable for us to refuse to attend school. When my father returned from Baku, he found Mum ill in bed, in a terrible state because they intended to split up the family.

Each member of our family experienced despair and depression at various stages of our ordeal to get out of the Soviet Union. Nevertheless, we would each eventually recover and reignite our determination to not succumb to our isolation and the hostility coming from local authorities. As a family we would regroup, plan our next move and endeavour to give one another essential support. Although we refused to give in to the pressure to attend school and abandon any hope of leaving the country, by August 1958, it was clear that outside help was needed to force the Crimean regional and local authorities to change their minds. Friends and workmates suggested to Dad that he should go to Moscow and try to see President Voroshilov.

At the end of September 1958, my father managed to arrange time from work and travelled to Moscow. Like thousands of others making the pilgrimage to Moscow, there was little chance of seeing Voroshilov. One official in Voroshilov's office told him that he should go to see Comrade Tulotski who was a senior official in the head office of OVIR. My father managed to see Tulotski who was very nasty and told him directly that his application to return to Australia had been refused. He then went to the Soviet Red Cross in Moscow. A sympathetic official listened to his story but told him that he must go back to OVIR. Dealing with the hierarchy in Moscow was a dead end. And all the time while this was going on throughout 1958, ASIO and Immigration were sitting on their hands and delaying making any decision regarding our case.

At the same time that my father was in Moscow trying to see Voroshilov, another order came from Kerch *Gorkom* that a car would be sent for Mum and we three children. We were driven to Kerch with a Party official and taken all around Kerch to see the sights before going to the mayor's office. Once again, it was a stalemate with pressure being put on us to attend school. One official screamed at my mother, "how it is possible that your children are still not in school." She replied, "how is it possible that the children are suffering so much because they are not allowed to return to Australia." Another official began shouting that her permission to leave had been refused. He also said that when Genia turns sixteen next year in August 1959, she will be issued with her own Soviet passport which will end any claim she has to return to Australia. Once my father came back from Moscow and we exchanged the depressing news from Tulotski and the local *Gorkom*, it was time to bypass Soviet authorities and try another approach and see if we could get the British Embassy to intervene.

WE REFUSE TO ACCEPT YOUR REFUSAL

Seeking help from the British

The British had acted on behalf of Australia in the absence of an Australian Embassy since 1954. We planned that Mum and the three of us would go and seek help from the British Embassy while my father remained at work. Where could we find the location of the Embassy, as we did not have access to a Moscow telephone book or street maps? Fortuitously, we heard a broadcast on the BBC about a protest outside the British Embassy on *Sofiyskaya Naberezhnaya* (Sofia Embankment). We now had the vital information we required. The Embassy, which Queen Elizabeth in 1994 described as the most beautiful of all her embassies, was built for a sugar merchant and allocated by Stalin to the British in 1931. Situated directly on the river opposite the Kremlin, the Soviets had tried to get the Embassy back without success.

After leaving Kerch by train, we arrived in Moscow on October 27, 1958, after the long, two-and-a-half-day trip. There are several bridges along the Embankment and Mum asked the taxi driver for the wrong one. Nonetheless, he took us to *Sofiyskaya Naberezhnaya*, and we asked him to stop after seeing the British flag flying atop the Embassy. As we were dressed in our best clothes from Melbourne which still barely fitted us, we didn't look like local Russians. Genia and I got out of the taxi first and walked through the guarded gate and Mum and Maya came after us. Fortunately, the police did not stop us as we looked like foreigners. Walking through the door to the front reception, we were greeted by a Scotsman who was difficult to understand, and my mother got a fright because she thought he was a Russian speaking English with a strong accent. All the consular staff were out at a meeting.

Following their return, we were lucky to be taken into the office of Mr. Muston, the Vice-Consul. He was an exceptionally nice and sympathetic person who listened to our history of arriving in the Soviet Union and all the details of how our applications to leave had been rejected, how our mail was blocked and other details. My mother also provided him with copies of passports, birth certificates and other documentation. We requested that the British Embassy issue us with British passports and visas in lieu of the absence of an Australian Embassy. Although sympathetic to our plight, Muston informed us that as we were underage, no separate passports or visas could be issued as we still belonged on our mother's passport. However, he assured us that he would write to both the Australian and Soviet authorities and strongly support our case. In the meantime, we had to return to Arshintsevo and wait for an answer from the Australian government.

True to his word, after he arranged for us to be driven in the Embassy car to catch the train back to Kerch, the Vice-Consul wrote the next day to G. C. Watson, the Chief Migration Officer at Australia House, London. In a lengthy, four-page detailed letter (plus copies of all our documents), Muston concluded: "This is a long and rather complicated letter. I should, however, be most grateful if you would give it urgent consideration and let me know, as soon as possible, what, if anything, can be done to help the Frankels." Muston's letter and attached documents were communicated to Minister Alexander Downer. ASIO were also informed of this new development. However, our pleas and Vice-Consul Muston's efforts to help us were to no avail. It took another four and a half months before we heard in March 1959 of the Australian government's refusal to issue us with re-entry visas. After the initial shock of hearing that the Australian government had washed their hands of us, we decided that what was required was a last drastic act in order to change their minds.

14

DESPERATE ACTION

SEPARATIONS AND SAD FAREWELLS HAVE BEEN PART OF our family's history. This is why I almost invariably begin to cry in response to scenes in films that show the characters having to say goodbye to each other. Both my father and mother had two agonising farewells before I experienced these tear-filled events. They had to leave their respective families in Poland and Palestine in 1937 and 1938, never to see them again once they departed for Australia. My first emotional farewell was when we set off for the British Embassy in October 1958. We were all aware that there was a chance that the four of us might not see Dad again if we were granted British passports. This proved to be fruitless, and our visit turned into an attempt to get the British to put pressure on the Australian government which had kept us in the dark for over two and a half years.

Following the great disappointment in March 1959 of learning that we had been refused re-entry visas to Australia, we were confronted with two basic options: either give up hope of leaving the Soviet Union in the short-term and find a better city to live in than Arshintsevo, or Genia and I could go to Moscow by ourselves and through a bold act, draw attention to our case by seeking asylum in the British Embassy. After careful consideration, we decided on the latter option, even if it involved splitting the family for an unknown period of time, perhaps many years.

We were familiar with the location of the Embassy and knew that Vice-Consul Muston was still working there. I was thirteen and Genia was fifteen. It was three months short of three years since we had arrived in the Soviet Union. Although it was still winter at the end of March, we decided to travel without extra clothing apart from a change of underwear. This would fit into a small carry bag and arouse less suspicion. Our small bag accommodated enough food for the two-and-a-half-day journey, plus two books to read and toiletries. The one minor miscalculation we made was that we overlooked that it would be the Easter holidays in Western Europe when we arrived on Monday March 30, 1959. Orthodox Easter in Russia would be almost two weeks later. Fortunately for us, there were still a few staff on duty at the Embassy.

Before we left Arshintsevo on Friday evening, we had an emotional farewell with Dad and Maya. Dad had bought the tickets a few days earlier but could not accompany us on the bus to the train station in Kerch because he wouldn't be back from work in time. Also, we agreed that all five of us would not go to the railway station as this would draw attention to us. So, Mum went with us to Kerch while Maya played at the neighbour's place. It wasn't a busy time of the year and we had just one other person in our compartment. Mum spoke to him and asked him to look after us until we got to Moscow. We then bade our mother an emotional farewell as she waved us goodbye, all being conscious that perhaps she would never see us again. As a parent myself now, I have often reflected on the courage it must have taken for my parents to have said goodbye in these drastic circumstances. At the time, this departure seemed to happen so quickly, that the momentous consequences of leaving were overshadowed by the fear that our plan might not succeed.

Inside the compartment, our fellow traveller turned out to be a Siberian from the area near Novosibirsk. He was about 30 years old and was very friendly. We spoke Russian to him and could not believe his name when he told us that it was Semyon Rasputin. He did not know whether he was a distant relative of the infamous Grigori

We then returned to Freddie's apartment where he lived on his own. He was 42 and had sailed the world four times while working on ships for fourteen years and also cooking in regional hotels. In 1957, he accepted the chef's job in Moscow and told us about living within the foreign diplomatic enclave. Staff at different embassies constituted a separate community that would compete in tennis and other competitions, put on plays and performances, and generally try to entertain one another in a world largely separated from Soviet life.

Freddie gave us British newspapers and magazines to read as we relaxed and awaited further developments. At around four o'clock in the afternoon, we were told by a member of staff that Consul Raymond Muston had been called at home and was now downstairs and able to see us. He was very sympathetic to our case and upset that the Australian government had refused us re-entry visas since our last discussion with him in October 1958. We also passed on a letter written by Mum to Muston. In it she expressed her shock upon reading the negative news from Minister Downer conveyed by Muston's letter dated 10th of March. Mum then declared:

> My children are perishing, they do not belong here, and they shall never be happy here.
>
> I am appealing to you Mr. Muston, hear the voice of a broken-hearted mother – save my children. Please do everything possible, that they shall return to their beloved homeland Australia, the only place where they belong, where amongst their friends and relations they shall continue their education and be happy as they were before. I shall always be grateful to you.

After an appeal like that, we were convinced that Muston would help us. Nonetheless, he reiterated that it was out of his power to grant us asylum and that we would have to return home. We steadfastly refused to go and insisted that we speak with the British Ambassador who, he said, would not be in until the next day. On seeing our determination and not wishing to create a scene, Ray Muston then left the room to make further enquiries and deliberations. He returned to let us know that he would do his utmost to arrange for the Ambassador to see us. In the meantime, Freddie had agreed that we could sleep in his apartment overnight.

Later in the evening, Freddie cooked dinner for us. He then took us up to his apartment where we spent the evening talking until he then prepared a couch and bedding for Genia to sleep in his lounge room. As there were no other beds, Freddie said that I would sleep with him in his large bed. He gave me a set of his pyjamas and we went to bed. Neither Genia nor I slept well as we were both so worried about the possibility of not being able to stay at the Embassy and dreaded having to return to Arshintsevo with no resolution to getting out of the country. It had been an anxious day that required all our courage and determination.

The next morning, after showering, Freddie prepared us another hearty and enjoyable breakfast. We then sat and read in the apartment while we waited for an audience with the Ambassador. At about 11 a.m. we were informed that he was now able to see us. When we descended the staircase, Ray Muston was there to greet us and said that we were lucky to see the Ambassador as he had a full schedule of meetings. In the previous weeks, for instance, he had hosted Prime Minister Harold Macmillan on his visit to Moscow.

As we entered his office, Muston introduced us. Sir Patrick Reilly was polite and expressed concern over our predicament. He had just turned fifty, was very pale with a sad face. Prior to Moscow, he had held senior positions such as Minister in Paris, and deputy under-Secretary of Foreign Affairs. One of his jobs was to co-ordinate British intelligence services. In later years he believed that he had played a role in preventing Soviet spy Kim Philby from being appointed head of British intelligence services, thus thwarting what would have been a real coup for the KGB.

Sir Patrick listened attentively as we outlined the detailed history of our case and the responses of the Soviet and Australian authorities. While Genia and I spoke, his secretary took notes. He then asked what we would like him to do about it. We answered that we would like to be granted asylum. He said that this was out of the question as we were not British-born. We then asked him to intervene on our behalf by writing directly to Prime Minister Menzies and External Affairs Minister Casey to reconsider their earlier rejection so that our family could return to Australia. We also asked that he attach to his letter a direct appeal to the Prime Minister from me and Genia. Sir Patrick agreed to our requests and promised that he would definitely write to Prime Minister Menzies.

Sir Patrick Reilly

On departing his office, the Ambassador shook our hands and wished us well. He told us to be patient when we returned to Kerch as a decision may not be made by the Australian government for months. Although he meant well, this was a gross understatement as we knew from painful experience that it took more than two years for the previous application to be rejected. I then sat down with Genia, and we wrote a letter to Prime Minister Menzies. Having written countless letters before, we were well-practised in the art of appealing to leaders. Apart from too many commas and not enough full stops in the long last sentence, we emphasised that:

Our father under the influence of Soviet propaganda and letters from his sister, made a terrible mistake and ruined all our lives, this he is regretting now.

We do not belong here! We are Australians! Our life is full of misery without school, friends, or any joy of life for nearly 3 years now....

We are appealing to you Mr. Menzies not to destroy our family, to have mercy and to pardon the terrible mistake made by our father who was misled by his sister. Please give our parents a chance to correct their mistakes, let them return to Australia together with us and they shall be loyal Australian citizens, as they have already been severely punished by life, sometimes grown ups make bigger mistakes than children, please pardon them.

The Archives show that our letter was circulated by the Prime Minister's Department to the Minister for External Affairs, Minister for Immigration, and ASIO. There is also a handwritten comment from Immigration (possibly by A.W. Bazley) claiming that we didn't write this letter and that it is in our mother's handwriting – a heartless attempt to discredit us in any way possible. The original of our letter is held in the National Archives, and readers can easily see that it is Genia's handwriting and can compare it with letters written by our mother.

Consul Muston told us that he would book berths for the evening train. We said we only had ten roubles as we had not intended to return. The Embassy then paid 320 roubles for our train fares to Kerch which is mentioned in Sir Patrick's letter to Menzies. The saga of the fares continued throughout 1959. One of the letters in the National Archives July 28, 1959, is from Australia House in London which enquires as to which departmental account they should use to refund the British government for the princely sum of £11. 8s. 7d. sterling (equal to 320 roubles) spent on our train tickets. "Perhaps it would be possible to recover the amount from their sponsor Mrs. Joan Brettagh (sic) in Melbourne." A handwritten note on this letter from someone in Immigration states that "We can hardly ask this woman to reimburse us. She is no more than a friend who made reps on behalf of the family."

Before leaving, Muston had arranged with his wife to have us come to their apartment to have an early evening meal before catching the night train. At first, we expressed our reluctance to leave the Embassy. We were terrified that Soviet security would arrest us once we left the building. Muston assured us that this would not happen and, as we would travel to his apartment in the official chauffeur-driven car, diplomatic protocol would ensure that we would not be interfered with by the Soviets.

We said goodbye to Freddie and thanked him for all his kindness. He had thoughtfully packed a bag of food and English snacks for our trip back to Kerch. He also included *Punch* magazine and the *Daily Express*, true examples of the conservative establishment media. I always remember looking at the picture of the starlet on page three. In 1959, it came as a shock because the woman in a bikini not only aroused my pubescent sexual curiosity but was the complete opposite of the dull, desexualised publications and films offered in the Soviet Union. We then got with Muston into the Embassy car which was parked in the Embassy grounds. As we left the Embassy for Muston's apartment, a security car immediately began following us. Muston was familiar with them and told us not to worry. Soviet security had obviously been alerted that we had been in the Embassy overnight and were curious to find out who we were and why we had come to the Embassy.

After a short trip, we arrived at Consul Muston's apartment building where other diplomats lived. It was a better-quality building than the usual Soviet apartment blocks. We went up in the lift and were greeted by his wife. She had cooked a lovely meal and the four of us relaxed over dinner as they both asked us about our life in Arshintsevo. I can't remember what we ate but we were struck by the affluent comfort of the residence compared to the way we lived in Arshintsevo. They had been in Moscow since 1957 and would leave in about six months' time to take up a new posting in Geneva. We thanked Mrs. Muston and Ray Muston escorted us in the Embassy car to the railway station.

Our train was due to leave at 9.30 in the evening and Ray Muston came to ensure that we boarded the train safely. Despite our car being followed again by Soviet security, there were no incidents as we boarded our train. Both Genia and I expressed our deep appreciation to Consul Muston for all his help and personal warmth. It was with mixed feelings that we travelled back home. On the one hand, we were disappointed that we were returning to the old depressing routine in Arshintsevo. On the other hand, we felt more optimistic and were stimulated by the exposure to people in the Embassy and contact with British food and popular culture, no matter how conservative and mediocre we viewed it in retrospect. At the time it was wonderful compared to the Russian food we ate, and we understood why Western popular culture was so dazzling to people living under censorship and restrictions in Communist countries.

We took the bus to Arshintsevo on Thursday April 2nd after leaving Kerch railway station. When we arrived home to the surprise of Dad, Mum, and Maya, they were overjoyed to see us, as they had not heard anything for almost a week since we departed. Of course, they were disappointed that we were not granted asylum, but were also more optimistic after they heard about the promise of the British Ambassador to intervene on our behalf.

The Ambassador's impact

At the time, we did what we set out to do with all the courage we could muster. Imagine it as a movie about the Cold War. Far from Australia, in a repressive Communist country, a thirteen and a fifteen-year-old brother and sister take a secret train trip lasting over two and a half days. For us children to quickly pass the guards, enter a foreign embassy and claim asylum must have been a historical first in the Soviet Union and rarely if ever repeated thereafter in most other Communist countries.

The day that we arrived back home was also the day that Sir Patrick Reilly wrote a personal letter to Menzies as well as including our letter to the Prime Minister. The British Ambassador also adhered to diplomatic protocol by despatching his letter to Menzies via the Department of External Affairs with a copy and separate letter for the Minister, Richard Casey. Sir Patrick opened his letter with diplomatic niceties, by seeking forgiveness from Prime Minister Menzies for taking "the unusual course of bringing to your attention" the despatch he had sent to the Minister of External Affairs about the Frankel children and Frankel family. He then proceeded to give a summary of our arrival in Kerch and contact with the British Embassy since October 1958. In separate letters, Sir Patrick provided Menzies and Casey with a detailed account of our arrival at the Embassy the previous Monday and Muston's and his own dealings with us. In his words:

> They are a very determined pair of young people and we found it quite impossible to induce them to leave the Embassy and to return to their parents without promising that we would bring their appeal to your personal attention. As reported in my despatch, I saw them myself. It seemed to me really out of the question that I should hand over to the Soviet police two children who were patently young Australians. I therefore thought it right to give them an assurance that I would bring their appeal to your personal attention and on the strength of this assurance they agreed to go home to the Crimea.

The dispatch continues:

> In general they gave an impression of having considerable intelligence and strength of character and they gave every appearance of genuine antipathy to this country and sincere affection for Australia: but although they complained bitterly of their conditions of life and of the food which they had to eat, they did not look unhealthy or undernourished. Their clothes were respectable and almost certainly had come from Australia, though their outdoor coats were inadequate for this climate. They are convinced that their father is

no more than a simple misguided man who made an awful mistake for which forgiveness should not be irrevocably denied ...

I think that for children of their age, who say that they have had no schooling since they came here because they refuse to make any sign of accepting "Sovietisation", their appeal is very well put. They are well versed in current affairs, no doubt because, they say, they listen all day to broadcasts from Britain and Australia.

In his letters, the Ambassador canvassed both sides of the argument by trying to strike the right tone for Menzies' conservative government. Yet, Sir Patrick also revealed his own conservative politics and personal prejudices.

No one can have much sympathy for Mr. Frankel, even if his activities in Australia had been respectable; but I have some sympathy for the children whose lives have been blighted in this way. For their age they are rather remarkable, although not particularly attractive people: and to the best of the judgement of members of my staff and of myself, given a chance and with this wretched experience behind them, there is every likelihood of their proving good and loyal citizens. I feel justified, therefore, in recommending that the appeal of the two children (but of course not their parents) should be considered.

What did Sir Patrick mean by describing us children as 'not particularly attractive people'? After singing our praises about our 'strength of character' and how 'remarkable', and 'intelligent' we were, did he simply mean that we were not physically attractive, or did he express his own barely disguised anti-Semitic prejudices about us? As to his lack of sympathy for my parents, perhaps the Ambassador was cleverly using this to indicate to Menzies and Casey that if they chose to split the family then it is doubtful that the Soviet authorities would give just the two children exit visas. "Indeed" he declared,

I am bound to say that the odds seem against it, particularly if the parents must remain in the Soviet Union. But, unless the children are consummate actors, they have certainly now had a strong inoculation against Communism and to the best of my judgement they should prove loyal citizens of Australia, where their hearts belong. In all the circumstances therefore, I feel justified in recommending that their case should be reconsidered and for the reasons explained above I feel myself under a moral obligation to bring it to your personal attention.

Like Menzies, Casey was a devoted Anglophile and more British than Australian in his mindset. Also, like Sir Patrick's Reilly's father who had been a senior official in the Indian civil service, the British Government had appointed Casey as Governor of Bengal in 1944 where he presided over the aftermath of the devastating famine. Almost a year after he received Sir Patrick's letter, Casey was made a life peer or Baron Casey and later became Australia's Governor-General between 1965 and 1969. Later, Casey had difficult relations with other senior Liberals, particularly Treasurer Billy McMahon for the latter's refusal to work co-operatively with Deputy Prime Minister John McEwen. Menzies' successor, Harold Holt, drew up papers for Casey's dismissal due to his undue interference in the political process. These were not acted upon as Holt drowned in December 1967. Casey appointed McEwen as caretaker Prime Minister to prevent McMahon from succeeding Holt and thereby triggered a crisis in the Coalition government. McMahon withdrew from the leadership ballot and Gorton became Prime Minister in 1968.

It is evident that Casey was not afraid to disagree with some of his Liberal colleagues. On April 15, 1959, he made a formal interim reply to Sir Patrick and informed him that the Prime Minister would duly consider his letter. He also instructed the acting Secretary of External Affairs, W.G.A. Landale, to forward the Ambassador's lengthy despatch to both the Department of Prime Minister and the Department of Immigration. On April 22, 1959, Landale informed the Secretary of Immigration that External Affairs was not consulting ASIO, and presumed Immigration would do so if they thought it was necessary. Casey also instructed Landale to inform Immigration that:

> We have no knowledge of the record of affiliations of this family in Australia but we feel that provided they were not considered a serious security risk, a case could be made out on humanitarian grounds for reconsidering the application of the whole family for permission to re-enter Australia. If the father's record in Australia was bad, we suggest that thought be given to re-admitting the two older children.
>
> If you were to decide that the whole family or alternatively the two older children could be granted permission to re-enter Australia, we would be prepared to approach the Russian authorities with a view to obtaining exit visas for them. However, we realise that these might well be refused.

Clearly, Sir Patrick's letter was already having a positive impact. Nonetheless, any decision would still take another five months and we would still be caught in the crossfire between the different attitudes and agendas of Ministers, senior departmental officials and ASIO.

Menzies was ill with influenza and could not personally answer Sir Patrick. Instead, his Private Secretary, William Heseltine, wrote to the British Ambassador on April 22, thanking him for his letter and informing him that the Prime Minister was shortly off to America and England and that our case would be examined. In the meantime, Chief Migration Officer at Australia House, G.C. Watson, informed the Secretary of the Department of Immigration, Tasman Heyes on May 26, that the British Embassy had recently heard from the Frankel children that their parents had been called to the passport office in Kerch on April 28, to fill in visa application forms marked 'British Embassy, Moscow.' These are forms which the Soviet Ministry of Foreign Affairs sends to the Embassy when they allow people to leave the USSR. However, the Embassy was suspicious that the local Kerch authorities were aware that the Australian government had rejected the Frankel's re-entry application in a letter sent to them by Soviet post.

There is no doubt that Kerch officials had seen Minister Downer's refusal in the letter that was posted to us on March 10, 1959. However, they were also aware that we had gone to the British Embassy at the end of March and so were preparing visa applications in case there had been a change of mind by the Australian government via the British Embassy. It is also important to remember that just over two weeks before we secretly travelled to Moscow, the Australian and Soviet governments re-established diplomatic relations on March 13, 1959, almost five years since they were broken off over the Petrov affair. While the Australian Embassy was only reopened later in 1959, perhaps the Soviets were giving us permission to leave as a sign that they did not wish to start a new dispute with Australia in the event that we were issued with re-entry visas and the Soviets refused us permission to leave. Whatever the reason, it will remain a mystery as to why the Soviets granted us exit visas.

Given the extremely slow machinery of Ministerial decision-making in Canberra, Menzies did not reply to Sir Patrick Reilly until August 28, 1959. One of the reasons for this was that Alexander Downer was overseas and Brigadier Spry was also on leave. In their absence, the Secretary of the Department of Prime Minister, E. J. Bunting, wrote at the end of April to the Acting Minister of Immigration, Frederick Osborne, who was Minister for Air. Despite passing on the British Ambassador's letter and the secret folder on our family, F.M. Osborne replied to Secretary Bunting in Menzies' office on May 22, that he would seek the advice of Acting Secretary of the Department of Immigration, A.L. Nutt. On June 4, Nutt wrote to Osborne stating that:

> Whilst I support the recommendation that the Frankel family be now allowed to return to Australia, I feel that the case is of such possible public importance that it would not be advisable to so decide in the Minister's absence.

It is unclear whether the recommendation to readmit the whole family that Nutt referred to came from Minister Osborne, or from Minister Casey, or from Secretary Bunting or from other senior Department of Immigration colleagues. Nutt also informed Minister Osborne that Mr. Bazley from the Department of Immigration, had prepared a comprehensive submission on the Frankel case. In fact, six months after Minister Downer, on ASIO's advice, had refused us re-entry visas, the Department of Immigration responded to Sir Patrick's letters to Menzies and Casey, by reopening our case for review on June 18, 1959.

Judging from the submissions made by senior officers within Immigration, there was clearly a division between those who favoured that the whole family be readmitted and those who sided with ASIO to only re-admit the three Australian-born children and their mother. Acting Secretaries Nutt and H. McGinness favoured the whole family. McGinness stated on June 2, that: "It could do a great service to other Russians and satellite nationals here if the Frankel family were re-admitted and could be persuaded to tell their story publicly. This would be out of the question if any member of the family were left behind at the mercy of the N.K.V.D." He also stressed that it was unlikely that the Soviets would use Frankel as a spy.

On July 2, Acting Secretary of Immigration, McGinness wrote to ASIO requesting their response to the reopening of the Frankel case. Acting Director-General of ASIO, Ron Richards, responded to Immigration on July 3. Ignoring information communicated by the British Ambassador, Richards' antipathy towards my father is revealed for all to see.

> I have seen no evidence that FRANKEL would be willing to engage in anti-Soviet propaganda, or that he is personally dissatisfied with the Soviet regime or any aspect of it. The stories about his representations to the Soviet authorities, his attempt to visit the British Embassy, his arrest by the Soviet police and present fear of being arrested again, all come from Mrs. FRANKEL, not FRANKEL

himself. FRANKEL has played a singularly passive part in all the agitation for his return.

Reading ASIO's wilful distortion and discounting of the truth about my father's endless risks and ceaseless sacrifices and trials in his attempts to get us out of the Soviet Union still makes my blood boil. Richards and other ASIO officers were both ignorant of Soviet conditions and wilfully callous. They dismissed the real dangers my father faced of being sacked from his job for going to Moscow on our behalf. We could have literally been kicked out onto the street from our apartment without income if the local authorities had decided to severely punish my father for travelling without management's permission and trying to see a foreign embassy.

Today, this gross insensitivity and disregard for the risks so many people take in fleeing repressive regimes, crossing borders, and paying people smugglers are still displayed by Immigration officials and ASIO. It is a perverse form of bureaucratic 'proof seeking', devoid of human compassion that requires a detailed documentation of claims that are not readily able to be produced by countless victims.

Richards informed Immigration that ASIO would only agree to the return of Frankel's wife and three children. Ironically, after years of rejection, he adds:

> that action in the case of the daughter Genia especially calls for some urgency, in view of her age. Otherwise, according to the British Vice-Consul, she will be compelled to take out a Soviet passport. Such an event could, I think, have unfavourable repercussions if it became public.

Given that Genia was to turn sixteen on August 26, little urgency was shown by Immigration and Prime Minister Menzies who, notably, only replied to Sir Patrick on August 28th!

Acting Secretary Nutt was not happy with ASIO's response. On July 9, 1959, he wrote to Secretary Landale at External Affairs stressing that in the interests of the three children "we should be prepared to stomach the father if necessary." Moreover, Nutt suggests:

> I think that this should be admitted to whomever is to negotiate this further with the Russians (Sir P. Reilly or Mr. Cutts) so that they will have discretion to do everything possible to get the children out.
>
> If we will only accept the children (with the mother) without the father, the Russians will be able to refuse on the ground that we are breaking up the family. If that happens, our negotiator should have discretion to say – all right, we'll take the man too.
>
> Surely ASIO can take care of one ratbag (and probably a chastened ratbag at that) in the interests of getting these Australian-born children out of an appalling fate.

Alas, Nutt's more humanitarian response was rejected by his superior. On July 16, Secretary of the Department of Immigration, Tasman Heyes, sided with ASIO. While he doubted that Dad would constitute a serious risk to the security of Australia, he said that "there is no reason why we should take any risk whatever with him." So much for compassion or commitment to the idea of family and the significant role of the father which was the dominant ideology of the time.

As to the Minister for Immigration himself, following his return to Australia, Alexander Downer sent a handwritten memo to Heyes dated July 27. In it he said that in light of the new facts presented by Sir Patrick Reilly, he was prepared to authorise the admission to Australia of Mrs. Frankel and the three children. However, he could not consent to admitting Mr. Frankel "on account of his subversive activities only a few years ago ... the interests of the nation, and its safety, must be regarded as transcending the welfare of any individual."

It was now clear what Downer's advice would be to Prime Minister Menzies and what Menzies would later communicate to Sir Patrick. However, before this occurred, a serious mistake occurred that infuriated the British Embassy. Apparently, a migration officer in Australia House mistakenly sent the British Embassy a telegram informing them that the Minister for Immigration had rejected our case. This was actually the decision made by Downer eight months earlier, in January 1959.

On August 14, the Department of External Affairs received a cable from Australia's new *Charge d'Affaires*, Bill Cutts, who had recently arrived in Moscow.

> British Embassy has received from London telegraphic advice in the baldest terms of your decision. In view of the personal interest shown by the British Ambassador (who is at present absent on leave) I presume he will be given some explanation of the rejection of his representation. I think that you should know that the British Embassy are rebuked by the terseness of the advice they have received.

Cutt's cable was also sent to Immigration, P.M.'s Department and ASIO. Frantic handwritten notes on the cable indicate that telephone calls were exchanged between the Secretaries of three Departments to ascertain what was sent to the British Embassy. On August 18, External Affairs sent a cable to Cutts instructing him to convey to the British that "Australian authorities are still considering the United Kingdom Ambassador's representations sympathetically..." After investigating this diplomatic blunder, Chief Migration Officer, Watson, wrote to Secretary Heyes on the 9th of September confessing to the mistake emanating from his office. "Any embarrassment caused by our reply to Moscow is very much regretted..."

Cutts' cable must have jogged Immigration into action. On the same day, August 18, Minister Downer wrote to Menzies informing him of the decision he had made on July 27 in his Memo to Secretary Heyes. Anxious to rectify any damage done with such a senior representative of the British government, ten days later on August 28, 1959, Prime Minister Robert Menzies replied to 'My dear Sir Patrick'. In it he conveyed Alexander Downer's decision to admit Mum and the three of us but to refuse my father permission to return on security grounds. The Prime Minister repeated word for word what Downer had written in his Memo to Heyes one month earlier.

In a final paragraph that could be read as either paternalistic or fawning deference, Menzies wrote:

> You asked my forgiveness for bringing to my personal attention the copy of the despatch which you had sent to the Minister of External Affairs. If forgiveness is required I certainly give it; and I thank you for your personal interest in what is, of course, a most appealing human case. Now that we are once more represented in Moscow we should be in a position to carry on the matter for ourselves, and I shall pass on copies of this correspondence to the Minister for External Affairs, the Right Honourable R.G. Casey.

On September 17, Sir Patrick replied and thanked Menzies very much for his letter and for his interest in this case. He expressed his understanding of why "this is not a suitable time to permit the re-entry of Frankel himself." Sir Patrick added that since his earlier letter, "the Soviet authorities have forwarded to us visa applications and Soviet passports for the whole family. We shall now of course issue the necessary documents to those members of the family whom you have authorised to go and it is possible that they will be able to travel within the very near future."

Re-reading the files in the National Archives, two things stand out. Firstly, there is no doubt that without our getting Sir Patrick to promise to intervene on our behalf by writing to Prime Minister Menzies, we would never have been able to leave the Soviet Union. During the 1950s, such was the servile colonial mentality of Menzies, Casey, Downer, and senior officials to a representative of the British Crown, that displeasing the Ambassador was out of the question. As the Ambassador had not pleaded for my father to be granted an entry visa, Menzies, Downer and Casey could save face and still please the Crown.

Secondly, the divisions between ministerial advisors over whether to re-admit all of us or not, was indicative of how the fate of so many people can hang in the balance once caught in the maze of competing interests and career-motivated, trouble-avoiding strategies. Humanitarian responses by a minority of officials to my father's plight were overruled by spurious excuses made by ASIO and several Ministers all falling under the bureaucratically convenient but heartless umbrella of 'national security'. In recent years, watching thousands of refugees incarcerated or then kept in limbo for years on temporary visas, it is clear that these same heartless and groundless claims of a risk to 'national security' continue to be invoked by Australian governments.

Irreversible decision?

The period between our return from the British Embassy and our eventual departure from the Soviet Union in March 1960, was a highly stressful roller-coaster of fluctuating emotions. Not knowing about our fate and waiting to hear from the Embassy about Canberra's decision produced alternate waves of depression and optimism. Our mood was not helped by the Kerch passport office via OVIR in Simferopol calling my parents into the office during April and May to fill in two different sets of visa application forms with additional photos and application costs. We did not know whether this was genuine or another way of pretending to grant us exit visas only to then refuse us as they had done two years earlier.

The months rolled on. In late September 1959, we received a letter from the British Embassy informing us that we could return to Australia but that our father could not. We were both elated and distraught. Being a Friday, Genia went to Dad's workplace to tell him the news. After work, he decided to head to Moscow to see if the British Embassy could do anything about his refusal. Without telling his management, he departed on Sunday night and made his way to the Embassy a couple of days later.

Ray Muston's successor, Consul A.J.V. George met with my father and in lengthy Minutes dated September 29, informed Canberra that

Frankel pleaded with them not to destroy his family. He said he felt the government's decision was like a death sentence if he remained in Russia. He told Consul George about how he had made a terrible mistake believing Soviet propaganda and that he would be prepared to sign a written declaration that he would become a loyal Australian citizen if granted permission to re-enter the country.

In his Minutes of this meeting, George stated that he explained to my father why he could not reverse the decision but that the refusal was not permanent. He then described how my father came to realise that the present decision was final, and they then discussed which route Frankel's family should take back to Australia. George suggested that flying to London was the best route and that he and Mr. Cutts would assist his family with tickets when they came to Moscow. Dad left full of gratitude for the help and consideration given to his family.

Upon returning to Arshintsevo later in the week, my father was not only extremely disappointed but was also greeted by a terrible uproar at work. The manager demanded to know where he had been for almost a week and that absence from work without a doctor's certificate is regarded as traitorous. Some of the other workers told him they knew that he had been to the British Embassy, and he continued to be harassed in the coming weeks and months. He refused to provide a written statement to the manager and his pay was cut significantly.

In November, we were informed that the Australian visas were sent and were ready to pick up from the passport office. However, we waited for weeks, and they still hadn't arrived. Dad went to the passport office in Kerch and complained that we had not received the passports with the visas. We were all quite upset but couldn't do anything as we were at their mercy. Eventually, on January 4, 1960, OVIR contacted us to come in and pick up our passports. We were elated but unfortunately, the drama continued. When we arrived at the passport office in Kerch, we were informed that our passports had been sent back to the British Embassy because an error had occurred, and Genia was registered as a boy.

DESPERATE ACTION

More than a month of agonising wait ensued. It was not until February 10, that our passports came back with the corrections made to the visas. Mum and Dad went to the passport office and paid 400 roubles. On handing over our passport, the old-style Stalinist official told my parents that: "if I had my way, I would just put you against the wall and shoot you. Clear out, as you have one month to leave the country."

We now had the arduous task of raising sufficient money to pay for our fares. We began selling household items that the local people were keen to buy. By the end of February, we had about 4,500 roubles, but at an exchange rate of 28 roubles to the pound it wasn't enough for our fares to Australia. We would have to sort out our financial issues in Moscow at the British and Australian Embassies.

Before we left Arshintsevo on Monday, February 29, 1960, we packed our bags with essential clothing. We also took our photo albums, as well as a Russian cookbook and three Russian books on smoking fish that Dad asked us to take. He was optimistic that he would eventually gain re-entry to Australia once the rest of us returned and campaigned with the Australian government on his behalf. The train to Moscow departed in the early evening and Dad would accompany us to Dzjankoi which was the junction point in northern Crimea before the train headed for Moscow.

We said goodbye to our neighbours and waved farewell to Arshintsevo as the bus drove through familiar streets that had been our life since 1956. Genia was both happy to leave but also sad to say goodbye to her friend Sasha who was a chauffeur for an official in the *Raikom* that would park its cars at the back of our apartment building. Although I had turned fourteen, Genia was sixteen and Maya was five, it had been a life-changing experience that would resonate with us for the rest of our lives. At this point of time in February 1960, we were focussed on the trip ahead rather than on the deeply embedded psychological and social impacts of Soviet life that would remain with us in the future.

On the brief trip from Kerch to Dzjankoi we were all incredibly quiet. Engulfed by the intense emotion of having to say goodbye to our father, few words were exchanged. There was much crying as we hugged and kissed for what may have been the last time. Dad ran alongside the train in the dark as it departed the platform. It would be three awfully long years before we would see him again.

Last days in Moscow

Upon arriving early in the morning on March 2, 1960, we waited at the station in Moscow until the British Embassy opened. The taxi driver took us to the back of the Embassy where there were guards posted. They demanded to know what our business was with the Embassy and ordered my mother to hand over her passport with our exit visas. We waited for what seemed to be forever, and worried that they could seize the passports and that would be the end of our ability to leave. Instead, they returned them, and we were instructed by Mr. Wood at the Embassy that Richard Woolcott, the recently arrived First Secretary at the Australian Embassy would come to assist us.

Shortly later, Richard or 'Dick' Woolcott arrived. He had been fully briefed about our case and drove us to the Australian Embassy. Woolcott was extremely friendly and had returned to Moscow after being expelled in 1954 over the Petrov affair. Educated at Geelong Grammar and obsessed about sport, he proudly showed us his Richmond football club jumper. Over the years I would observe how Woolcott would become one of the most influential diplomats and public servants shaping Australian policy towards Indonesia and the Asian-Pacific region. I shared his vision of integrating Australia into the Asian-Pacific region, rather than clinging to the old British colonial past. However, I strongly disliked his policies that tied Australia to President Suharto and other dictators in the region, both before and after he eventually took charge of the Department of Foreign Affairs and Trade.

At a personal level, Woolcott was incredibly supportive, and we may not have been able to leave without his decisive actions and invaluable help. The first thing Woolcott organised was our accommodation at the Hotel Ukraine for two nights. This was comfortable but expensive. The main problem was that we didn't have sufficient funds to travel onwards to Melbourne whether by Air India to Sydney via Delhi or by ship from the UK. How would we obtain the money to pay for our fares? Woolcott agreed that the option of going back to Arshintsevo to save more money was out of the question as that could take years given Dad's low wages. Importantly, the Soviets might also annul our exit visas which were only valid until the 18th of March.

Before booking our flight to London on British European Air, he urgently cabled External Affairs on March 3, requesting whether funds for fares could possibly come from the 'Distressed Australians' fund or whether we were eligible for the ten pounds assisted passage scheme for British people. The Department of Immigration refused on the grounds we were not eligible and External Affairs and Department of Finance instructed Woolcott that Mum would have to agree to repay the shipping fares once in Australia.

After much to-ing and fro-ing, he got confirmation that Australia House would advance a loan for the return shipping fares when we arrived in London. As we could not convert roubles into pounds, 3550 roubles (or £84) were left with the Embassy and would be deducted from the government loan of £476 (or 3.5 berths at £136 each) leaving a debt of £392. This was a considerable amount given that wages for many female workers in Australia in 1960 were between £10 and £20 a week.

After we left, all these details were outlined by Woolcott in a long letter to the Secretary, External Affairs, dated March 8, 1960. He also covered various aspects of our case, such as the concern that my father had been denied a visa for past mistakes. Woolcott specifically warned us against making any anti-Soviet comments to the Australian media once we left as this would jeopardise our father's potential future exit from the USSR.

He stressed that the actions he took in arranging our flight and loan were governed by humanitarian considerations of getting the children out of the country rather than by "the letter of the regulations applicable to such cases." Woolcott then added:

> The two eldest children in particular have had a very difficult time here during the past three years and, on numerous occasions, attempts were made either to frighten, cajole, persuade or trick them into signing documents renouncing their Australian citizenship. At other times they allege that threats and lengthy interrogations were also employed. The persistence and fortitude which the two eldest children have shown in the face of the continued pressure to which they have been subjected by the Soviet authorities has, as you know, won the admiration of the British Ambassador and members of the British Embassy who are familiar with this case. For our part we consider that their attitude is worthy of high praise and fully justifies the opportunity of resuming their lives in Australia which they will presumably now have.

Such was Dick Woolcott's concern that there be no other financial or security threats to our departure on March 4th, that he accompanied us to Moscow airport to see us actually board the plane. At the airport, apart from the coolness of the Soviet migration officials, there was another obstacle. We couldn't board the plane because our vaccination records were out of date due to a recent outbreak of smallpox. Fortunately, a Soviet doctor rectified this on the spot and administered our smallpox inoculations. After we surmounted this obstacle, we thanked Dick Woolcott for all his vital help, said goodbye and boarded the flight. Unfortunately, before taking off from the runway, the pilot announced that there was a problem with one of the engines and that we would have to return to the terminal and disembark. This was our first flight ever and the stress of hearing this announcement only added to the cumulative tension of the past few days. After nervously waiting a few hours in the waiting lounge, we got the 'all clear'. This time, we re-boarded with great trepidation. So, instead of departing at 12 p.m. lunchtime we left at 4 p.m. The flight was less than half full and we got much attention and service from the flight attendants.

As the plane finally took off from Moscow and climbed high in the air, we were cautiously happy but still tense. We were on our way to London via Copenhagen. A brief time later, the pilot announced that we had left Soviet air space and we began to relax. However, the pilot then announced that we had been diverted from Copenhagen to Hamburg. As we made our descent into Hamburg, I registered an incredible sense of joy and relief. If freedom was more than a concept, but also a deep emotion, then I certainly felt it there and then. We had departed Moscow on a grey day with snow all about on the ground. As we flew over Hamburg, the physical contrast could not have been greater. Everything looked so green and lush even though there were still trees without leaves. It was a spectacular sight that I will never forget.

Following our stopover, we boarded for the last leg to London. By the time we arrived it was 8 p.m., but we could still see the green lawns and bushes from the air. We were all overjoyed at being in London again. It was almost exactly three months short of four years when we first arrived here on June 4, 1956. Now we were back under quite different circumstances. After what we had been through, and despite not having any material possessions or knowing what would happen to us, we felt optimistic that we would be able to cope, survive and flourish.

15

FREEDOM AND ITS DISCONTENTS

BEFORE FLYING US OUT OF MOSCOW, RICHARD WOOL-cott had arranged with Australia House for someone to meet us at the airport in London. He informed them that we only had a small amount of money after leaving the balance of our roubles at the Australian Embassy. The social worker at Australia House, Miss Friee, met us and then took us to the Salvation Army hostel for women in Marble Arch, a wholly inappropriate place given that there were no men allowed. The Salvation Army officer, Sister Durrant, reluctantly agreed to admit me after being told that we had just arrived from Moscow and had nowhere else to stay. She allocated us a family room with a few beds. It was an austere place and very cold after central heating in Russia. London can still be a cold and miserable city. In 1960, many places still had no heating or hot water apart from a tiny radiator or putting a shilling or two in the meter.

In the morning after breakfast, we decided that this was not the place to stay given that it could be weeks before we boarded a ship for Melbourne. The only other people we knew were Joan Brettargh's parents in Leyton, whom we visited in June 1956, but they had moved somewhere else unknown. By chance, at the hostel we read in the newspaper that Rabbi Israel Brodie, the Chief Rabbi of Great Britain and the Commonwealth, had presided over some function the previous day. Brodie had previously been rabbi to the Melbourne congregation (based in Bourke Street and then South Yarra) between 1923 and 1937. He had also championed East European Jewish migrants against the wishes of the more conservative Anglo-Australian members in his congregation.

My mother had the idea that we should try to see him to ask for help. Fortunately, his home address was in the phone book and located in the nearby affluent suburb of St. Johns Wood. Genia and I asked her, what on earth are we going to say to him? She replied that we will tell him that we bring a message from Soviet Jews. "What", I said, "you only met a few Jews on the train from Kharkov!" "Don't worry", she replied, "leave it to me". On Saturday afternoon, the four of us made our way by bus to his home. When we arrived, he was still at the synagogue but after being told what our 'mission' was, his brother asked us to come in and wait for him. When Rabbi Brodie arrived with his wife, he asked about us and we told him that we were originally from Melbourne but had just arrived after years in the USSR. He then asked Mum, "What is the message you bring?" Mum replied with a straight face, "The Jews in the Soviet Union need help as there is a lot of anti-Semitism." This was actually true, even though nobody had deputised her to convey this message. Yes, Brodie nodded, "it is a very sad and difficult situation."

After a few more questions about our experiences in the Soviet Union, we told him where we were staying and why it was unsatisfactory. He then took our details and said that he would arrange for us to move to the Jewish Shelter on Mansell Street, Aldgate, near the Tower Bridge. True to his word, we stayed over the weekend at the hostel in Marble Arch and moved to the Shelter on the Monday. The Jewish Shelter was set up in 1885 and by 1939 had helped about 1.2 million people including many refugees. It was located in a poor and dingy area of East London that was later demolished to make way for a new council housing estate. In the nearby streets Jack the Ripper once roamed in Whitechapel and at one end of Mansell Street was Petticoat Lane with its colourful market and at the other end on the Thames was the Tower of London.

The Shelter couldn't be more different from the Salvation Army women's hostel. It was divided into men's and women's dormitories on separate floors that could each hold one hundred plus beds. These were only half occupied when we stayed there. It was a revelation to see Jews from across the world. Religious Jews, secular Jews, families, single men and women, all colours and nationalities from Europe, Africa, Asia, and Latin America. They had no common shared culture except those who were religious or those who were persecuted or in desperate need of support. Moreover, there was no so-called common ethnicity or race, a concept usually applied to Jews by non-Jews. I would defy anyone to identify a secular Indian Jew from Bombay or Iraq as having anything in common with a Polish or Irish Jew, other than their common humanity.

It was fascinating to hear their individual stories. Some wanted to live in Britain, others were in transit to a new country. The place was clean, warm, and served good and plentiful food designed to meet the variety of cuisines desired by its residents. This was a truly cosmopolitan world without any required religious observation or exclusion based on political beliefs. No wonder the German writer, Stefan Zweig described the Shelter in 1935 as the 'House of a Thousand Destinies.' We would stay there for two weeks before departing London.

A few days after we moved into the Shelter, a young lawyer, called Greville Janner, visited us. He was in his thirties and active in various charities and youth clubs. Janner asked how he could help us and also offered to show me various aspects of London. Janner, later Lord Janner, had a thriving legal practice in the Inner Temple and later rose to be the most important Jew in Britain. He 'inherited' his father's Labour seat of Leicester West and held it for 27 years from 1970 to 1997. Janner also became chair of the British Board of Deputies of British Jews and played leading roles in numerous other British and international Zionist organisations.

A postscript to this encounter was that in 1991 and until Janner's death from dementia in 2015, he was charged and investigated in relation to numerous counts of child sex abuse with males under the age of sixteen from care homes and elsewhere. The crimes were committed between the 1960s and the 1980s. Due to inadequate police investigation and his failing health, Janner avoided being convicted and his victims never received justice in the courts. Luckily, I escaped his clutches unscathed. This was the era when so many victims of sexual abuse by prominent public figures were hushed up by police and religious authorities. I was never alone with him long enough and we were only in London for two weeks.

In London, we were grateful to Janner for making our stay so enjoyable while we organised our passage home to Melbourne at Australia House. He invited all of us to his home one Sunday for lunch where we met his Australian-born wife, Myra, and his young children. Janner kept in touch with us for a few years after we returned to Melbourne and even visited us a couple of years later on one of his official visits to various Zionist functions, even though we were anti-Zionists. While in London, he also organised and paid for me to have a haircut and purchased a ticket for me to see a matinee performance of *West Side Story* at Her Majesty's Theatre. This was, for me, a breathtaking production that had an enormous impact in terms of opening up a world of theatre, music, and dance.

A few days later, he phoned the Shelter to ask me whether I would like to meet him at Earls Court tube station at 11 a.m. and we would then go to the Exhibition Centre in Earls Court. I agreed and waited at the entrance to the station for over 45 minutes, but he was nowhere to be seen. I thought that something at his work prevented him from coming, and not having his phone number, decided to go and see something at a nearby local cinema. Arriving back at the Shelter at about 5.30 p.m. I was greeted by my mother who had been crying inconsolably. The police were also there, and all of them wanted to know what had happened to me. Apparently, while I was enjoying seeing two films, all hell had broke loose.

I thought that Earls Court station only had one entrance and was unaware that Greville Janner had been waiting at the other entrance to the station. When I failed to turn up, he called the Shelter to ask where I was. Mum replied that I had gone to meet him. Janner then panicked and let his imagination run riot. He said that the KGB had probably kidnapped me and were taking me back to the Soviet Union. Janner called again at 3 p.m. and I had still not returned as I was midway through the second film, as in those days you got two feature films in a session! He then called Scotland Yard and reported me as missing, presumably kidnapped by Soviet agents. They arrived at the Shelter and asked my mother for a photo of me. They were going to broadcast this on the BBC television evening news if I still hadn't turned up by six o'clock. Thanks to Janner's fertile, Cold War imagination, I received a stern lecture from the police and was told to act more responsibly in the future.

Our brief stay in London was filled with visiting museums, galleries, and historic places. We had brought a small amount of money after the balance was left in Moscow with Woolcott and had to carefully reserve this to spend on bare necessities such as public transport. The Jewish Shelter generously did not charge us for our stay or meals. It also provided temporary residents with a choice of good, second-hand clothing and shoes donated to it by members of the London Jewish community. We selected a range of clothing that were luxurious items compared to Soviet clothing. As to the department stores and shops in the West End, we were truly dazzled by capitalist consumerism. Despite our window shopping being all look and no buy, one had to have experienced life in the Soviet Union to get a sense of how staggeringly different London was from Moscow, let alone Arshintsevo.

On March 20, 1960, we said goodbye to our fellow residents, thanked David Gedalla and other staff at the Jewish Shelter for their wonderful support and departed London on the *Orsova* bound for Melbourne. Australia House had arranged our booking relatively quickly and we were on a ship full of ten-pound immigrant Poms and assorted returning tourists. The *Orsova* would reverse the route taken in 1956 by her sister ship *Orcades,* except that this time apart from Gibraltar and Naples, we didn't stop in Marseilles and added Rhodes to pick up Greek migrants before going through the Suez Canal. In 1960, the Canal still had evidence of the fighting in late 1956 such as damaged cargo ships stranded there. After Aden, we called into Bombay (offshore) before heading for Colombo and then across to Fremantle.

Once again, I loved being on the ship and enjoyed all the social activities and the sea air and marine life. There were no major storms like on the *Orcades*. What actually disturbed me were the crass Australian magazines such as *Pix* and *Australasian Post* that we read on board. They were full of trivia, and apart from articles on celebrities, essentially promoted affluent Australia in a brash and crude manner. I remember in particular an article about a man who bought a shirt made out of gold. A few of the English and Scottish migrants I made friends with on board were equally dismayed by the material vulgarity of Australian life as presented through the eyes of these commercial media. After London with its rich offerings of culture, it was as if we were heading for an Australia that was denuded of cultural choice and I worried that it could be little more than a place where one accumulated wealth and possessions.

When the four of us arrived in Fremantle, ASIO field officers continued their monitoring of our movements. Archive files show that they reported on which shops we went to in Perth, what Genia was wearing and whether we contacted any local persons in Perth. We were still viewed as possible subversives. Our arrival at Station Pier in Port Melbourne on Saturday April 16, 1960, was exactly three weeks short of the four years when we departed from the same pier in 1956. Mum's cousin Riva Wittenberg and her husband Julius 'Ginger' Wittenberg welcomed us. Reg Brettargh also met us as Joan was at home with their children. We expressed our sincere thanks to Reg and Joan for all their support during the past four years. The Wittenbergs first took our luggage to a house owned by a Mr. Joel in Pine Avenue, Elwood, who was a friend of our uncle Samuel Strelec. Then they returned to drive us to this temporary accommodation until we got jobs and could rent our own place. ASIO reported on who met us, what clothing we wore what we had in our luggage (after secretly inspecting it at migration clearance), and where we were taken.

Re-adjusting to Melbourne

We were both relieved and extremely happy to be back home in Melbourne after our four-year ordeal. Our main problem was that we had arrived in Melbourne with only one pound left in Mum's purse! Without any money or material possessions other than our clothing, we were totally dependent on the generosity of our relatives whom she had been relatively estranged from before departing for Russia.

St. Kilda looked familiar and yet it was not quite the same. Unsurprisingly, we now saw it through the eyes of people who had lived in the Soviet Union and who had also visited a range of countries in Europe and Asia. Although Mr. Joel was a nice person who lived on his own, his house was not suitable for another four people. After discussions with our relatives, it was agreed that Riva and her sister Ann would accommodate us for a few weeks. I went to Riva's house in Kew where her son and daughter, Ron and Yvonne were also living. The others went to Ann's place in North Balwyn with her husband and daughter. During the next few days as we recovered our bearings, we were taken around Melbourne to reacquaint ourselves with the city. We also checked out work and accommodation options. Genia got a job in a sandwich bar and later in a small belt factory in Oliver Lane off Flinders Street.

Reg told me that there was a job at the *Herald and Weekly Times* (HWT) where he was a printer. Years later, Joan and Reg separated, and Reg would move to a small flat in St. Kilda. The last time I saw Joan was in 1979. As a 'mature age' student, she, and thousands of others, especially a large contingent of women, benefitted from the Whitlam reforms of providing free education. Joan was now studying Social Work at Monash University. Many students were unhappy with the narrow case-work focus of their course and demanded that the Department introduce subjects that linked social work to the broader political, economic, and social issues affecting Australian society. The Head of Department agreed to their demands and asked whether they knew anyone who could teach such a subject. My name was put forward, and in 1979 I taught a course on Australian political economy and social work. Joan, who could have become my foster mother twenty years earlier, was now one of my students. It was an awkward situation. She was now 56 and had become a conservative Christian who didn't agree with the more Left-wing students who were at Monash at that time.

Back in April 1960, I would travel in the Wittenberg's car to their small clothing factory in Flinders Lane right near the back of the old *Herald and Weekly Times* building. On my first nervous day at work, Reg met me and showed me the Personnel office as it used to be called. I was assigned to the sub-editors' office as a copy boy where I would see the editors behave like children and constantly throw paper planes at one another, whether they had messages on them or not. I was also instructed to deliver and pick up the tray with morning tea for Sir John 'Jack' Williams, the Managing Director of *HWT* which was the most powerful media group in Australia. Williams had succeeded Keith Murdoch (Rupert's father) and *HWT* controlled half the papers in Australia plus television and radio stations. When the Hawke government changed its media policy in 1986, Rupert exceeded his father's power over Australian media by taking control of *HWT,* thus giving him 70% of Australia's print media.

One day, when removing Sir John's tray, I tripped and broke the fine-bone china teacups. However, I suffered no repercussions. Downstairs was radio 3DB which used to run the Phoenix Biscuit footy quiz. Each week, one had to select the winners of the 12 teams in both the firsts and reserves of the Victorian Football League – before the advent of the AFL – for a jackpot of £25. After working there for three weeks as a junior for only £4.17.6 a week, this jackpot was more than five times my wage. Not knowing anything much about football, I filled out the competition form in the staff canteen and forgot about it.

I was bored with my job and decided to leave. The following week, I got a job in the Myer basement as a salesman for an extra pound a week. A few days after leaving the *Herald*, I received a letter from *3DB/HWT* and thought it was a cheque for the backpay owed to me.

I then read the enclosed letter and got a pleasant surprise. I was the winner of the Phoenix Biscuit jackpot of £75 which had not been won in the previous two weeks. This was a small fortune. At this point, my mother had found a flat to rent at 20 Mary Street, St. Kilda. We had no furniture, so I kept £5 for myself and spent £70 on furniture for all of us.

Jewish Welfare in Melbourne had been notified by our uncle that we might need help resettling in Melbourne and also that our father was still denied permission to re-enter Australia. They contacted us and were generous in their provision of household items, clothing, and general assistance. They also gave my mother a loan of £100 for furniture and helped find work for her as a machinist in a clothing factory. Overall, conditions were quite difficult for us during 1960 and 1961. The social worker at Jewish Welfare kept a log of the various health and financial problems we experienced. On May 5, 1960, she recorded that our mother had found a job in a factory but due to lack of childcare, was thinking of putting Maya temporarily in the Frances Barkman House in Balwyn for Jewish orphaned children such as survivors of the Holocaust. This was merely a strategy and tactic to convey to Jewish Welfare that things were tough, and that we needed help. My mother never had any intention to put Maya in a home. However, according to the files sent to the Department of Immigration, the social worker stated that she persuaded Mrs. Frankel that this would not be good for Maya who had already been separated from her father.

Despite such survival tactics (still adopted by many refugees), the reality was that things were indeed tough. At varying points during the next three years, one or more of us were out of work. We fell into arrears on our rent, and Genia was sick with asthma and kidney problems. Tania was depressed without Abrasha and found it hard to manage. We were like millions of other low-income Australians with hire purchase debts on our H.G. Palmer TV set, and other appliances, such as a second-hand fridge and washing machine. Without my father's income, it was a struggle to survive on our three low wages.

Genia had worked in a couple of sandwich shops and the belt factory but didn't like it. She was described by the social worker in reports sent to the government, as "rather cheap looking and her speech very uneducated." The social worker's moralistic, judgemental views belie the fact that Genia could write detailed, persuasive letters to the Prime Minister and other Ministers. There was no acknowledgement of Genia's self-education, and later her work in film and the arts. Remember, this was the era when government bureaucrats, ambassadors, security officers, doctors and even social workers gave gratuitous descriptions of people based on prejudices about their appearance that had nothing to do with the legitimacy or justice of their case.

After leaving our cousins in Kew and North Balwyn, we slowly started to re-establish our life in Melbourne again. With our father isolated in Arshintsevo, it was already financially difficult for us to survive without the additional burden of having to repay £392 to the Australian government. A great deal of correspondence and communication between Mum and the Department of External Affairs and Department of Social Services took place over the next decade or so concerning her ability to repay the debt. Despite being in the so-called 'Free World', the Australian government kept monitoring us in a manner that was little different from Soviet bureaucrats. The National Archives contain detailed assessments by Departments of Social Services and External Affairs outlining each and every pound, and later dollar, of our income, and also itemising all expenditure of our household to see whether we had the capacity to make regular repayments. With more than half still owing, and my mother on a widow's pension in the 1970s, it was eventually written off by the government as the repayments were small and intermittent due to Mum's inability to pay.

Changing jobs and studying

In the four months after the *Herald*, I worked in retail, an office, a factory and two milk bars. Although I earned double what I was paid at the *Herald*, I was generally bored with these jobs and only lasted a few weeks in each one before moving elsewhere. My main objective was to earn more income given our difficult financial situation. However, a brief period of unemployment followed. I even applied for a job selling tickets at Victorian Railways, yet this basic job required a minimum education qualification of the Intermediate Certificate (Grade 9) and I had not even completed Grade 6 before departing for Russia in 1956. I enquired about night school, but classes would not begin until February 1961.

The three years between arriving in Melbourne in April 1960 and finally being reunited with our father in February 1963 were both unsettling as well as a period of exploration. Although we missed Dad in our lives and were in regular postal communication with him, Mum and all three of us learnt to fend for ourselves and establish new interests and social relations. Alongside our preoccupation with campaigning to get the government to let our father back into the country, Genia and I were also trying to redefine and reorientate our lives after the four-year interruption. This was 'freedom and its discontents'. There were new challenges related to finding satisfying jobs, earning enough and yet being limited and restricted in our opportunities by our lack of formal educational credentials.

We found Melbourne wonderfully comfortable compared to Russia, but also provincial. Genia would constantly devise imaginative plans to open all kinds of money-making businesses which eventually came to nothing. She also began hanging out with a bohemian crowd of painters, lovers of jazz and filmmakers while continuing to work in the belt factory. These interests would later lead her to have incredible overseas adventures in Europe and Asia and work in the film and television industry in the US and Australia over the following decade or so. Genia also had a fertile imagination and would love telling tall tales to gullible listeners about her time in Russia, including how she supposedly worked on a chain gang with other delinquent youth repairing roads and bridges. Genia's real-life experiences were extraordinary enough without these concocted stories.

Soon after arriving back in Melbourne the impact of seeing *West Side Story* in London motivated me to look for work in television or in the theatre. I saw an ad for a studio in the city that offered training for aspiring TV actors. It was a scam set up by a guy who had been in a few TV commercials. I was so excited that I forgot to take off my make-up after the audition and, on the way home on the tram in conservative Melbourne, I was the object of attention for passengers and the conductor who couldn't stop staring at me. Fortunately, I didn't have the money for a full course but attended a couple of sessions. I remember a German man called Werner who also worked there. He was a decent person and must have had a guilty conscience as he drove me home and told my mother that nothing would come from this course and to not waste my money.

About two months later, the producers of the Melbourne production of *The World of Suzie Wong* announced auditions for their coming season at the Palais Theatre. Although fourteen, I looked a few years older and auditioned for one of the roles as a sailor. At the time, I didn't realise that *Suzie Wong* was an Orientalist depiction of Asian women. The producer told me and several others that we were hired and would begin rehearsals in a few weeks' time. Instead, he returned to Melbourne with a cast that he had hired in Sydney. I then realised that acting was a precarious occupation and decided to go back to studying. In later years I would confine my performances to lecture theatres and classrooms.

Meanwhile, after a brief stint in a machine tools factory, I found a job as a storeman and packer in a clothing factory at 100 Flinders Lane. The factory with showrooms was A. Frankel Pty Ltd owned, by coincidence, by Akiva Frankel and his son Morris. They were not related to me, but I was treated better by people who thought I was their son or grandson. Akiva had probably arrived in Melbourne in the 1920s or 1930s and Mum knew Morrie and his brother Max from Left circles. In the mid-1970s, I would teach Max's son Michael who was a radical student at Monash and would later become a film lawyer in Sydney.

Flinders Lane was at its peak of activities in the 1960s and I would work at this job until A. Frankel Pty Ltd went bankrupt in 1963. As a storeman, I packed all types of dresses that were made by the women in the factory behind our packing room door. Occasionally I would hear the screams of women who got a needle through their finger as they rushed to make enough money on the piece work wages, they were paid. The whole row of sewing machines would have to be stopped in order to extract the needle from the woman's finger as she sat screaming or crying or had already fainted.

From the factory, the finished garments were then hung in the stock room. Depending on sales made in the front showroom, or by our travelling salesman making orders in country shops, we would then pack them in boxes and couriers would collect them for delivery. Flinders Lane was buzzing with the activity of all the couriers picking up and delivering garments and fabrics, buttons, belts, zips, and other essentials. Only New York's garment district centred around 7th Avenue was larger than Flinders Lane and all the tiny lanes running off it. I would also carry rolls of dress material on my shoulder as I delivered it to other nearby factories or showrooms. Over the next three years, I would learn to negotiate all the lanes, staircases and nooks and crannies of the rag trade or *schmatta* business.

Boris, 15 years old, St. Kilda, 1961

In 1961, I began studying at Swinburne Tech night school. They put me in grade 8 and our classroom was in the kitchen of a disused old terrace house that would later be pulled down. Public education facilities were in a parlous state. I would rush from the city by train to Glenferrie Station for the classes beginning at either 5.30 or 6 p.m. three and four nights a week. I breezed through grade 8 and over the summer holidays decided to jump years 9 and 10 and study for my Leaving certificate in 1962. I fantasised about becoming an industrial chemist and discovering some new chemical formula. These dreams soon evaporated as I swotted the maths and chemistry books over the summer and quickly realised that the humanities and social sciences were more to my liking.

I spent five years at night school between 1961 and the end of 1965 completing my Matriculation certificate. Initially, I had no intention of going to university, but by 1964 I developed a strong appetite for further study. My intellectual curiosity was in marked contrast to the profound anti-intellectualism of many of my workmates who were mainly preoccupied with how many beers they had knocked off the night before, sport, the latest car or consumer fashion item and so forth. The truth is that I disliked most of the jobs I worked at and suffered mentally and physically. Each month I would develop a severe migraine, almost like a regular period, and would vomit and have to lie down with a terrible headache. When I started university in 1966, my migraines virtually disappeared except for one or two per year. I still get migraines, but they have lost all their severity. After working six years full-time before university, I made a vow never to work full-time on any job I disliked. I was able to keep that vow for the rest of my working life.

Before 1966, each day was incredibly full. Mum and Genia would leave home early in the morning to get to their jobs by 7.45 a.m. and 8 a.m. I would start later between 8.45 and 9 a.m. and would get six, seven and eight-year-old Maya dressed, make her breakfast and also her lunch, and then leave her at St. Kilda railway station where I took the train to the city. She would wait there for about 15 minutes before walking to nearby St. Kilda Park primary school. There was no pre or after-school care in those days and while we would worry about her getting there safely and walking back home which took about 15 minutes, we had no choice if we wanted to keep our jobs and survive. After working all day, I would go to night school from Monday to Thursday nights and get home between 9.30 and 10 p.m. and eat a late meal before rising for work the following morning. After this routine, I found full-time study at university a breeze. It was like being on holiday.

In addition to my work and study, I got a part-time job at the Palais Theatre St. Kilda on Friday and Saturday nights as well as Saturday matinees and occasionally other nights if there was a big star in town. This was wonderful as it enabled me to see all the films and live performances. I started on a Saturday matinee and apart from ice creams, my tray was loaded with all kinds of kids' sweets such as liquorice straps, chocolate frogs and so forth. As the lights went up, I was suddenly besieged by an army of kids who began trying to pull sweets from my tray. It was sink or swim as I was paid a mere 10 percent commission on anything I sold rather than wages, and anything stolen would have to come out of my earnings. I immediately shouted out in my loudest voice: "Everybody stand in line!" Lo and behold, they all obeyed my order.

Serving adults in the evening was easy, except for the danger of tripping on the steep stairs in the lounge and dress circle. The Palais held over 3,000 seats and one had to be a mountain goat in the dark negotiating each step blocked from view by my tray loaded with ice creams and boxes of chocolates. My first big show was Harry Belafonte in August 1960. I went backstage and got an autographed photo of him but was sacked by the manager for this indiscretion. Not having a replacement, he soon rehired me and over the next few years I covered Margot Fonteyn and Rudolf Nureyev, comedian Shelley Berman, popular singers like Pilita and touring Soviet shows brought out by impresarios Eric and Michael Edgley. The night Shelley Berman performed to a packed house, there were four empty seats in the very front row. After interval, he shouted to all the people in the very last back row upstairs in the gods, "the first four people who come down can be my guests." What followed was a stampede with people running down and falling over in the dark and nearly breaking their necks just to get to those front row seats.

Apart from the Palais, I was also sent to the bar next to the Giggle palace at Luna Park where live comedians would perform from the balcony. On quiet nights at the Palais, I would also work in the Palais de Danse which was one of the largest ballrooms in the world before it burnt down in 1969. On a couple of occasions, I managed a bar in the Palais de Danse in 1960 on a Saturday afternoon when an attempt was made to foster a regular rock and pop festival by one of Melbourne's radio stations. Local pop stars from Channel Nine's *Bandstand* such as Lucky Star, The Delltones and Billy Thorpe performed, but poor attendance killed the venture.

Politically, the three performances of Paul Robeson in November 1960 made me uncomfortable. His magnificent voice thrilled me and the packed audiences at the Palais. I had listened to his recordings for years. Physically he was a towering figure. Yet, at a meeting for Communists and fellow travellers on a Sunday afternoon, Robeson's cringing apologetics for the Soviet Union were too much for me to stomach. He was a courageous giant fighting racism in America and suffered much for his defiant politics. However, in the Soviet Union he was a coward as he closed his eyes to the terror and the repression of people he knew personally. This silence probably tormented him in his final years. Most of the people attending this function were the same type of uncritical supporters of the Soviet Union that we used to mix with before we discovered the reality of the so-called 'paradise' in the USSR. My lived experiences in the Soviet Union made me suspicious of blind ideological positions and allegiances and any type of groupthink whatever its political colour.

Twelve years later in 1972, I was in San Diego visiting radical philosopher and hero of the 1960s student movement, Herbert Marcuse, whose work was the topic of my Master of Arts thesis. He had just received a letter from Angela Davis, his favourite student, who was on a tour of Eastern Europe to thank people for the mass support she had received during her notorious trial on charges of murder and kidnapping related to the escape of the Soledad Brothers. Acquitted in June 1972, Davis wrote to Marcuse about how impressed she was with the Communist countries. As he read her letter to me, he was clearly dismayed at her apparent loss of critical judgement. I replied that like Paul Robeson, it was no surprise that Angela Davis ignored the repression in these countries because while these two black Americans were feted by Communist regimes, they were treated like social pariahs in their own country.

Observing wealth and power

After I lost my job due to A. Frankel Pty Ltd collapsing in May 1963, my experience in Flinders Lane helped me to get employment in the fabric department of Hicks Atkinson, one of several department stores that no longer exist, such as Ball & Welch, Foy & Gibson, Mutual Store and Buckley & Nunn. I must have been bad luck because five weeks later, Hicks Atkinson, also went bankrupt. In the reference for me provided by the staff manager at Hicks, it stated: "Very keen, anticipate a very bright future as a businessman." How ironic! It did, however, convince Georges to hire me in July 1963 to work in the silk and lace department.

If my previous jobs had given me an insight into working-class conditions in factories, offices, and shops, working at Georges gave me a front row seat view of the class structure of Australian society, especially the incredible wealth and power enjoyed by a small minority of the population. Georges was the finest department store in Melbourne and Australia and catered to the bourgeoisie and wealthy country cockies. This was the era before the affluent began doing their shopping in Paris, London or Milan. I served everyone from the Governor's wife to the Toorak and Brighton elite, TV celebrities and countless 'commoners' (as the conservative staff called them) who, after their first date, asked for samples of the finest French and Swiss silks, wool lace, or Thai silk for their imagined dream wedding. With my tape measure handy and familiarity with how much material was required for all styles of dresses, I was actually a highly successful salesman. I had increased my age to gain an adult wage and management threw in a bonus of ten shillings for the grand total of £19.14 shillings per week.

To give one a sense of the disparity between the wages paid and the cost of goods in Georges, a mere yard of fabric was often more expensive than a male adult's weekly wage. I would also usher fashion parades and assist in so-called charity nights where the wealthy elite would drink French champagne and donate to their tax-deductible favourite causes. At Christmas time, I was set up with my own trolly of expensive gifts for customers who had everything but had run out of gift ideas.

The store had certain similarities with the TV show *'Are you being served?'* Like other British department stores, we had our own colonel. Ex-colonel Forbes was a dour Scot who would stride through the store followed by his chauffeur. Each year he would select one of the more outwardly effeminate male salesmen and send them to the Outward-Bound Australia training camp on the Hawkesbury River to 'toughen them up'. They would come back four weeks later looking emaciated. He told me that there was no need to send me there but wanted me to be trained as a buyer and go to Europe on trips to select new season fabrics for sale. I politely declined and informed him that I was studying at night school and would not be ready for training until I finished my studies.

In early 1965, I got tired of selling fabrics and asked for a transfer to another department. I asked for George Jensen silver, but they put me in shirts in 'Georginas', the nickname for Georges' men's store. Like the other floors of Georges, the price of clothing downstairs was astronomical. I always remember that a pair of English-made quality shoes were the equivalent of more than three weeks' wages. Even so, a number of fellow salesmen purchased these on lay-by and paid them off over a period of six months or more. One day in 1965, the cultivated tranquil atmosphere policed by the shop floor supervisors was shattered. Pandemonium broke out in Georges as young female salespersons ran through the store. News had quickly spread that the Rolling Stones had arrived to do some shopping. Old wealth and the new cultural politics of the 1960s were strange bedfellows. Perhaps their visit to Georges was a foretaste of how the Stones would themselves become wealthy conservatives in later decades.

The novelty of Georges with its bourgeois customers and celebrities had long worn off. It was a relatively easy job while I was studying. However, I also decided to leave because the Menzies government had introduced conscription in 1965 and I feared that my real age would be discovered if I was selected in the first ballot. In June 1965, I moved to the Victorian head office of the Commonwealth Bank of Australia at 367 Collins Street, a few blocks away from Georges. I was placed in the Security Department which was where applicants for loans had their collateral assets checked at the Land Titles Office and the old Companies Office. On my first day I was asked whether I was a 'Mick', or a 'Mason' as religious sectarianism was still prevalent in workplaces. My job was hardly stimulating and was similar to conveyancing work done at the time by aspiring lawyers to gain their Articled Clerk certificates. The good thing about the job was that one could be out of the office for more than half the day, and there was also a fine, subsidised staff dining room with white linen tablecloths providing good meals.

At the end of November 1965, our small group of employees were joined by two second-year law students from the University of Melbourne who came first and second in their class. The first was Kenneth Hayne who would become a High Court justice and later preside over the Banking Royal Commission, and the second was Robert Richter who would become one of Melbourne's leading criminal lawyers. Together with a couple of others, we would take Ken and Robert to the Titles and Companies office and show them the ropes. Ken was reserved and conservative but in recent years has become more progressive. Robert, whom I was friends with in the 1970s, was always flamboyant yet, unfortunately, later became the sought-after barrister defending too many business and conservative establishment figures.

Following the introduction of decimalisation in February 1966, I left the Commonwealth Bank in March and started studying at Monash University. I was rejected at the University of Melbourne and just scrapped into Monash on the second or third round of offers. My exam results were quite poor after getting shell shock sitting with thousands of others in the Exhibition Building and barely finding my seat number, let alone being able to focus on the exam questions. I knew nothing about Monash which was a new university and far away in Clayton. But I grabbed at the chance to study full-time.

I had applied for a bonded teaching studentship that paid all university fees in return for three years teaching at any post allocated, usually a country town. However, I didn't get one and was told by a clerk in the Education Department that I wasn't cut out for teaching. While initially disappointed, this turned out to be my lucky day as I could now select subjects that would not have been approved had I obtained a studentship. Fortunately, I had just managed to save the annual fees for university which were quite high and had to be paid upfront. No wonder few working-class students could afford to study. Monash and the University of Melbourne had only between 6,000 and 10,000 students in the late 1960s compared to their mass education industry numbers of 55,000 to 85,000 students today. They were far from socially and culturally diverse, had a heavy presence of private school students straight from school, most of whom lacked any experience of work or hardship.

For income, I took up part-time work at Leo's Spaghetti Bar in St. Kilda on Saturday and Sunday mornings and helped make the minestrone with Mario and gelati with Nino. I also worked three nights a week managing the squash courts and over fifteen tennis courts near St. Kilda railway station, at the end of Mary Street where we rented our flat. I began my sixty years of playing tennis at these courts in 1963 as a member of Middle Park Tennis Club (which was located on a few of these courts in St. Kilda) and led a campaign that saved them from developers in 1971. Unfortunately, they were later sold off in the 1990s for private property development by Jeff Kennett's government. Few non-privatised local tennis clubs remain in Melbourne as property developers and governments destroyed them in many suburbs over the past thirty years.

At Monash, I was a few years older than most first year students both in age and experience. In History, my tutor in Renaissance and Reformation history was Dorothy Fitzpatrick, mother of Sheila Fitzpatrick and widow of the socialist civil libertarian, Brian Fitzpatrick who had recently died. The department was full of people such as Ian Turner, Alan McBriar, Geoffrey Serle, and others who had been active former Communists or members of the Labor Club at the University of Melbourne in the 1940s and 1950s. In the Politics Department, the Vietnam War and student radicalism would create sharp divisions among the staff. B.A. Santamaria had his spies in the lecture theatres and *News Weekly* labelled the Politics Department the 'Monash Soviet' even though all staff members were critical of the Soviet Union.

Actually, many students became more radical than most academics. While we learnt much from our teachers, their battles were still mainly directed against the last vestiges of the conservative, authoritarian Menzies era. Students, by contrast, were pointing to the conservatism of liberal social democrats in the ALP and the need to bring about much more radical social change.

At the end of first year at university, my results were good enough to get a Commonwealth scholarship plus an independent scholar living allowance which students received if they had worked full-time for at least five years. This made life easier and enabled me to participate in a new and exciting world which I loved. I was one of three students who started the first combined honours degree in History and Politics at Monash. The other two were Alan Blackman who became a lawyer and Mark Raper who left the course to help refugees during the war in Biafra, and later became president of the Jesuits in Oceania and Asia Pacific.

Compared to the University of Melbourne which was largely a tired and conservative institution in the 1960s, Monash was one of the most stimulating places to be in Australia during the late 1960s and early 1970s. The challenging new courses taught by many younger academics, and the vibrant atmosphere generated by student politics and a myriad of activities, debates, and protests all combined to make Monash an exciting and life-changing place. While this book is not the place to discuss these exciting years, let me simply note that my life moved in a different direction due to my experiences at Monash.

At the completion of my Honours degree in 1969, I joined the Commonwealth Public Service as I had not yet heard whether I had secured a post-graduate scholarship. I was appointed as the first 'humanist' working on projects with the PMG's (Postmaster-General's Department) leading team of engineers and telecommunication planners. Sir Frank Packer had made an application to start a cable network. My task was to analyse the social, economic, and cultural aspects of cable TV and whether or not the PMG should grant a license to Packer's Australian Consolidated Press. I have written about this experience in 'Boris Bites Packer: How I accidentally thwarted Sir Frank and discovered Madame Blavatsky' (*Arena Magazine*, September 2011). Hardly anyone in Australia knew anything about cable TV in 1969. In my March 1970 report about cable TV, I advised that Sir Frank Packer's application be rejected, as cable was too valuable a media platform to be handed over to private companies before the PMG had even worked out the future of public broadcasting or its own future media policy. I do not know what happened to my report. It may have been accepted as PMG policy or pigeonholed like so many other reports. Whatever its fate, two things were confirmed by history: Packer never opened a cable TV network, and it was a quarter of a century before cable TV began operating in Australia between 1993 and 1995.

Returning to Monash on a post-graduate scholarship, I was told that I would most likely become the next scholar on the exchange scheme that Monash had with Leningrad University. I was going to research something non-controversial such as the application of

Hegelian philosophy by nineteenth-century Russian writers such as Chernyshevsky and others involved with the literary journal *Sovremennik (The Contemporary)*. I was not enthusiastic about reacquainting myself with Soviet society, but other academics suggested that it would help me develop an academic career in Russian politics. Due to mass student protests and the need to pay for guards to protect the Administration building, the exchange scholarship in 1970 was cancelled. With great relief, I then changed my thesis topic to something that was much closer to my interests, namely, Marcuse's critical theory. Radical critique, the study of the political economy and social structure of capitalist societies would become my passion in the following decades and help fuel my political engagement.

In hindsight, my work and study experiences in the decade between 1960 and 1970 proved to be decisive. Had my father not taken us to the Soviet Union in 1956, I would have stayed at school and perhaps started working at age 14, 15 or 16 like most of the other kids in St. Kilda. I may have possibly finished high school or even more remotely, gone to university. Undoubtedly, I would have been quite a different person without the invaluable cultural and political experiences of living in Russia. I may not have followed an academic path. Despite coming from a family that greatly valued knowledge and ideas, formal study at university was not a foregone conclusion as evidenced by the work in film, photography and design taken by my sisters. The experience of living in Russia followed by six years of full-time work and five years at night school set me apart from my contemporaries. I was simultaneously Australian and yet a fish out of water. My ambitions and values were unlike those held by most of my workmates and the vast majority of university students. The limitations of the world of material possessions, dominant cultural priorities, class power and social inequality were starkly apparent in Australian and Western society as was the travesty of Soviet Communism. My political and cultural ambitions were thus driven by the desire to radically restructure or replace the glaring deficiencies of both systems.

16

'ASIO DOES NOT CONCERN ITSELF WITH COMPASSION'

WHILE WE ALL WERE HEADING IN NEW DIRECTIONS, our father remained trapped in Arshintsevo. He continued to work at the same gruelling job, but his workmates were more friendly to him now. They may have felt sorry for him being left alone without his family. The housing authority put pressure on him later in 1960 to give up our apartment. He refused to leave but had to agree to other people moving into the room which we children previously had as our bedroom. Dad kept the front room and balcony and shared the kitchen and bathroom. He would have been constantly reminded of our absence and his difficult circumstances.

Over the next three years, Dad would send parcels of books that we had originally brought from Melbourne plus many others that he had purchased in Russia. Sea mail was slow but relatively cheap, and the authorities did not block these parcels after checking them. Slowly, over the next three years we re-acquired our old library. He was also a regular weekly writer of letters and cards and also sent photos of himself taken by his friends. We would send photos of us and fill him in on what we were doing, as well as any developments in his case.

From our arrival in April 1960 until the end of the year, nothing changed as Minister Downer refused to budge and turned down all our written appeals to him as well as to the Prime Minister and the Minister for External Affairs in April, May, June, August, and later months. John Gorton, who was Acting Minister for External Affairs, wrote to my mother on June 9, 1960, that his colleague, the Minister for Immigration "regrets that he feels unable to alter his previous decision, of which you were aware before you left the Union of Soviet Socialist Republics to return to Australia."

Gorton was communicating Alexander Downer's decision on May 24, 1960, in which he personally wrote to one of his senior officers, A.W. Bazley, that "I do not think we should alter my previous decision at this stage: but F's position should be reviewed on some later occasion in the light of his conduct, and international relations." The 'international relations' mentioned by Downer were the extremely heightened tensions between the US and the Soviet Union after American pilot, Gary Powers, and his U2 spy plane were shot down on May 1st over Russia. This led to the collapse of the summit conference in Paris between the USSR and the US, UK and France.

In May 1960, there was also an exchange of correspondence between the Director of Naval Intelligence and Brigadier Spry at ASIO and the Department of External Affairs. Naval Intelligence informed ASIO and External Affairs that they had no knowledge of a large submarine base in Kerch where my father was supposedly working in a secret capacity. Notably, in this recorded exchange, he was not referred to as the 'Soviet subversive', but now as the 'Australian welder'. In fact, there never was a submarine base at Kerch or Kamysh Burun. The nearest thing was a base making small gunboats. In believing in and amplifying the misinformation about 'Frenkel' working in submarines, ASIO's geopolitical and cultural ignorance was on full display with disastrous consequences. To put it in the vernacular, ASIO couldn't tell the difference between its arse and its head. One thing is certain, the Soviets would never have given Dad an exit visa had he actually been working in stringently controlled areas such as submarines or any military base.

In 1958, ASIO officer E.V. Wiggins asserted that "FRENKEL could be described as an opportunist of limited intelligence, who, having been built up and exploited by the Soviets, aspires to the DJILAS 'New Class', has not quite made it in the U.S.S.R., but still holds some long-term hopes." What Wiggins referred to is former Deputy leader in Yugoslavia, Milovan Djilas, who was jailed in 1957 for publishing his best-selling critique of Communism as developing a 'new class' of privileged party bureaucrats. Wiggins' assessment was a complete distortion of my father's disillusionment with the Soviet Union. As an idealistic true believer, he never aspired to join the privileged elite. Recall that he turned down the offer of a better job when we arrived in 1956 because he thought he was returning to an egalitarian socialist society.

Actually, ASIO could not agree on whether my father was a naïve simpleton or very astute and being trained by the Soviets for subversive work if re-admitted to Australia. On May 20, 1960, Deputy Director Operations at ASIO issued a Minute Paper in which it stated: "The case against FRENKEL, on his record in Australia, is serious and not lightly to be offset by reported disillusionment..." Hence, throughout 1960, ASIO kept monitoring our activity, especially as we were actively engaged in a campaign of writing to Ministers about our father's case. Later in the year, on September 28th, and October 7th, 12th, and 20th, 1960, we were called in four times for interviews/interrogations by Ernest Redford and other ASIO officers at their office next to the Regent Theatre at 187 Collins Street. They wanted to know all the details about our experiences in the Soviet Union. ASIO concluded that their four interviews with Mrs. Frankel and two of her children "failed to reveal any attempt to fabricate, nor are there any reasons to doubt the genuineness of their statements."

It was at these interviews that we first learnt about the falsehoods that were still believed by ASIO, including the absurd claims that he was on a lecture tour of the USSR or working in submarines. When we asked the name of the Soviet newspaper that reported his supposed lecture tour, they didn't know, confirming our suspicion that it was based on a rumour from local informants. In fact, ASIO was little better than a 'Dad's army' of ill-trained and largely politically ignorant officers. It was an organisation that knew little or nothing about these societies and the cultures of migrants from these countries. Yet, ASIO was quick to make ill-informed judgments on many Australians that caused untold pain and suffering. They blocked career paths, led to the loss of jobs, and deployed anti-democratic tactics against legitimate civil society groups and movements. Today, ASIO continues to be awarded massive budgetary outlays and the public is deprived of any serious accountability or knowledge of an organisation that is so lightly monitored and remains largely a law unto itself.

Lobbying to change Canberra's mind

Walter Lippman, who ran Jewish Welfare in Melbourne, also actively lobbied Canberra to let our father return. However, Syd Einfeld, President, of Federation of Australian Jewish Welfare Societies, based in Sydney, was unsympathetic to our case. Nonetheless, he arranged for Mr Brand from his Sydney office to send to A.W. Bazley of the Immigration Department detailed notes on our case (including the social worker's log, mentioned in the previous chapter). This was after he met Bazley at a citizenship ceremony in Sydney. In one of his letters to us in September 1960, Dad also enclosed a letter that he wrote directly to Minister Downer which we then forwarded to Immigration. In it, he appealed to Downer to reconsider his earlier decision in July 1959 and to grant him a re-entry visa.

On Christmas day 1960, we all travelled by public transport to Seaford beach for a Christmas picnic. The weather was hot and sunny, and Seaford was still a little-developed suburb with pristine water. We all had a wonderful day, as this was the first time my mother had been out in the sun after spending nearly four years indoors, refusing to go outside, in Arshintsevo. Soon after we got home at about 8 p.m., she collapsed. I ran to get the local doctor who lived at his practice a street away. Luckily, he managed to come and wanted to put her in hospital as she was badly sunburnt and suffering from heat stroke. She resisted but spent the next two weeks in bed recovering. She never went sunbathing in bathers at the beach again.

As the months rolled on in 1961, we also approached Frank Galbally, who was Melbourne's leading criminal lawyer with an interest in immigration issues. He took on our case pro bono and kept us informed about any developments in Canberra. Strangely, there is no record or mention of his name in the hundreds of National Archives papers, whereas all others connected with our case are cited and filed. After a year of agitation through collective letter writing by all of us to the Prime Minister, Minister for Immigration, Minister for External Affairs as well as Dad writing to Richard Woolcott and Keith Waller, Australian Ambassador in Moscow, the government was starting to slowly reconsider its refusal to re-admit him to Australia. Liberal Party member, William Haworth, was our local MP for the seat of Isaacs. Our uncle approached him on Dad's behalf and Haworth then contacted Immigration to examine his case. Genia also wrote again to E.J. Bunting, Secretary of the Prime Minister's Department in April 1961, reminding him that he had informed us in January 1961 that enquiries were being made into our father's case, but months had gone by, and the matter was urgent. Bunting replied on April 12, stating that Immigration had been contacted and as they had also received other representations on behalf of 'Frenkel', his case was now being actively considered and a decision would be made soon.

Abraham Frankel, alone in Arshintsevo, 1962.

During May 1961, senior officers in Immigration, External Affairs and the PM's Department met and discussed what to do. The handwritten notes on May 22, testify to their desire to resolve this 'extremely difficult case' but also their reluctance to decide without Minister Downer. Officials P. Lawlor and P. Manton of the Department of Prime Minister were concerned about unfavourable publicity should he be refused entry again. They acknowledged ASIO's objection on security grounds but also noted that "ASIO does not concern itself with compassion." Bazley also confirmed that Immigration was aware that "since Mrs. Frankel came back with her children, that the case could easily develop into one of considerable public importance, and be aired in Parliament, and in the press."

Manton suggested that "perhaps we could let Frankel come back to Australia, ostensibly to visit his family, and let him stay here permanently..." Bazley from Immigration objected and said that this would form a bad precedent for other applicants from Soviet countries. Moreover, "if Frankel refused to depart voluntarily, as would probably happen, it would not be practicable for us to deport him to the U.S.S.R. Therefore, the decision will have to be either to allow him to come back to Australia without limitations, or to deny him re-entry – and if we deny him re-entry, there is bound to be a public outcry."

Bazley and Nutt would be the two key Immigration officials drafting reports on his case for Minister Downer. Arthur Bazley was an interesting character. He served at Gallipoli and assisted Charles Bean as librarian in the team that wrote *The Official War History of Australia in the War of 1914-1918*. During the next twenty years he became chief clerk and librarian at the Australian War Memorial in 1940 and then joined the Department of Immigration in 1946. The other official, crucial to our case, was Acting Secretary A.L. Nutt, a strange mixture of political and bureaucratic values. In 1955, the media had criticised Immigration for bringing in very dark-skinned Greeks, Cypriots, and Lebanese. Nutt suggested in a memorandum to Minister Harold Holt that "anyone who in appearance shows any marked departure from the 'white' European type, should be refused entry ... even though they and their families may have lived in Europe for generations". In other words, Nutt upheld the racist White Australia immigration policy.

Meanwhile, Secretary Landale at External Affairs had discussions with Ralf Harry who was Australia's most senior diplomat and foreign affairs official. He had helped draft the UN Declaration on Human Rights as part of Evatt's UN delegation and was also involved with drafting the ANZUS treaty and several other significant treaties. Harry was also secretly involved with the Australian Security Intelligence Service for many years. Even his family were unaware of this role until it was exposed in 1989 in *Oyster*, a book by Brian Toohey and William Pinwill on Australia's intelligence organisations.

Landale and Harry from External Affairs effectively washed their hands of my father and told immigration that they had no particular interest in him coming back. However, External Affairs would do everything necessary if Minister Downer decided to re-admit him. It was thus left for Bazley and A.L. Nutt in Immigration to present the case to Downer. In two separate and lengthy discussion papers on May 19 and June 27, 1961, Bazley documented both the case history and discussions held in the various departments as well as recommendations for Nutt to present to Downer. In points 14 and 15 of the second report in June, Bazley warned that:

> I think the time is fast approaching when the two elder Frankel children may come to Canberra and go to Parliament House in an attempt to see the Prime Minister, with the hope of receiving an assurance that their father will be allowed to come back here to them. Indeed, I understand (from correspondence with Jewish Welfare) that they have been thinking of doing this for some time ... However, if they decide to come to Canberra and do not see the Prime Minister personally and receive some sort of assurance, they will probably refuse to leave Parliament House. In that event the pressmen at the House will be sure to get hold of them, and their story, with all the sentimentality attached to it, will be published from one end of Australia to the other.

These are the tactics (without resultant publicity) which these children followed in 1959 when they went to the British Embassy in Moscow... No doubt they feel that this demonstration resulted in permission being given for their own return to Australia with their mother and younger sister – and that by following the same line in Canberra they might succeed in getting their father here.

Bazley concluded by quoting Sir Patrick Reilly about Genia and I being 'very determined, remarkable, but not particularly attractive people.'

The upshot of all this conferring by the three Departments was that Minister Downer instructed Acting Secretary Nutt on June 17, 1961, that 'Frenkel' be called to the Australian Embassy in Moscow to be interrogated by a senior diplomat on questions formulated by ASIO. This would then be scrutinised to see whether he had changed his views or not and whether to issue him with a re-entry visa. After Immigration contacted the PM's Department and External Affairs, it requested Brigadier Spry and ASIO in July to prepare a lengthy case history and series of questions. These were dutifully prepared by ASIO that covered my father's years in Australia since 1938, his involvement with Communist and pro-Soviet activities, contact with Petrov and other Soviet Embassy officials in the repatriation of Russians, plus all details of his current views and activities in the Soviet Union since June 1956.

Bill Morrison's report

The task of interviewing my father was assigned to Bill Morrison, who succeeded Richard Woolcott as First Secretary. Earlier in 1954, both Morrison and Dick Woolcott were junior diplomats before being expelled from Moscow over the Petrov Affair. Morrison became famous for losing a bet with Woolcott and having to drop his pants and 'moon' the Kremlin on the night before they departed. He later held three ministries in Whitlam's government including Minister for Defence, and like Woolcott became Ambassador to Indonesia after his parliamentary career ended in the mid-1980s.

My father took unannounced leave from work and arrived in Moscow on September 28, 1961, after receiving an official invitation from Morrison which was held up by Soviet authorities for over two weeks. Soviet security police were aware of his visit and Morrison wrote that he and his wife and child accompanied him to the taxi stand about half a mile away. They believed that my father was eventually picked up by security after he departed. His description of my father is in some respects, an unusually nuanced psychological portrait.

Morrison noted that Dad was dressed in clothing purchased in Australia and that his disillusionment did not stem from inferior economic conditions in Russia. Rather,

> he is a gregarious type, a lover of organised activity and one who is prepared to do a lot of hard work in return for recognition by his friends of his achievements. His activities in repatriation could, I believe, be explained by his proclivity to be regarded as one to whom people looked for advice and assistance. I would say that he was a generous man and that this generosity was motivated, perhaps unconsciously, by a desire to purchase if necessary the esteem of others. He is a man of interests and tastes somewhat above the people with whom he would normally associate in his work. He is possibly somewhat too aware of this and the opportunities given by the Australian/Soviet Society to indulge himself in the literary group and to tutor people in the Russian language must have been eagerly grasped. In short, Frankel is the type usually found in organisations, and the Communist Party and its subsidiary activities provided an outlet for his energies. The enthusiasm which he undoubtedly showed could, depending on the use of words, be regarded as fanatical. His main disillusionment on returning to Russia was that he was not incorporated into any organisations and that his services were and abilities (of which I suspect he has an inflated opinion)

were not used. He found himself very much on the outer and this, coupled with the discontent of his wife and children, was the main reason for his disillusionment.

While Morrison's insights captured something of my father's personality and behaviour, he was profoundly wrong about the main reason for Dad's disillusionment being that his services and abilities were not used. Like the analyses by ASIO and other department officials, Morrison had no experience of and little understanding of what it was like for a true believer to have his ideal and cherished image of Soviet Communism shattered when confronted by the realities of repression, inequality, and corruption. These were the factors that so shocked Dad in the early weeks of his return and not that his 'talents' were somehow not recognised or used. My father was not conventionally ambitious but guided always by his deepest values rather than by pragmatism or financial or reputational gain.

At the conclusion of his report, Morrison attempted to answer the question of what is likely to happen if Frankel (the correct spelling now) returns to Australia. My father had signed a pledge at the Embassy that he would not engage in political activities and would be a loyal Australian citizen. Morrison added that:

> The main guarantee of Frankel keeping his pledge is his earnest and sincere desire to be re-united with his family. From the photographs he showed me and the discussions we had over lunch, the family seems to be one of which any man could be proud and his separation from them is obviously a cause of great grief. That he was prepared to sacrifice himself by this separation so that his children could grow up in Australia is, I think, the acid test of his attitude to the Communist regime. It must have been an awesome decision.

In early October, Morrison sent his lengthy report on his interview with Dad to Canberra. On October 23, 1961, Secretary Landale of External Affairs was the first to respond to Morrison's report by notifying Immigration that External Affairs "can see no objection to the re-admission into Australia of Frankel, should the Minister for Immigration decide to do this." In the following two months, correspondence between Immigration and other Departments showed them also agreeing with External Affairs. Unsurprisingly, Brigadier Spry and ASIO were the very last to hold out.

On November 21, 1961, Spry stated that he was "not over impressed" by my father's story and by "the apparent activity of the Soviet Security Authorities against him. This could well be aimed at giving cover to his story of intimidation. Nevertheless, as his family has now returned to Melbourne, I do not wish to press the security objection to Frankel's admission." Spry's grudging refusal to say he approved of his return, meant that Immigration had to write to ASIO to clarify their position. Five days after Spry's reply, Immigration called ASIO and were informed by Ron Richards, Deputy Director-General, that Spry "has withdrawn his objection." On December 5, 1961, the new Secretary of Immigration, Peter Heydon, wrote to Alexander Downer informing him of Spry's new position. Downer replied that he would discuss the case in January 1962. Actually, Downer must have been confident that the Menzies government would be re-elected on December 9, 1961. As it turned out, Menzies just scraped in by a bare majority of one seat.

Towards the end of December, Dad wrote a moving card to Mum about how they couldn't be together to celebrate the twentieth anniversary of their marriage on December 26, 1961. I still have that card. A month later, and almost two years after we were separated from our father, Minister Downer approved his re-admission to Australia at the end of January 1962. Secretary Heydon notified all Departments and the Australian Embassy, as well as our mother, her uncle (via MP Haworth) and all others making representations to Ministers in Canberra. We were overjoyed to hear the news but there would still be a long haul of another protracted year before he was able to leave the Soviet Union.

After being interviewed by Morrison in September 1961, my father's return from Moscow was once again greeted with outrage by management at his factory. He was tried by a trade union committee and accused of consorting with a foreign government. As punishment, his bonus was withdrawn. This was his final warning. If he left work again without permission, he would be sacked.

My father was elated to hear the news from Morrison and from Mum that he would soon be travelling to Australia and would be reunited with us all. If only that had been true. Instead, 1962 turned out to be an excruciating year of endless delays by both the Soviet and Australian authorities to finalise the attachment of his re-entry visa. It is difficult to describe the many sleepless nights, bouts of anxiety and depression that we all felt at various stages of the year. After two applications were filled out, statutory documents from Australia were needed for an exit visa. This process took seven months, and then all went quiet. Dad had to enquire at the Kerch passport office because he still hadn't received his visa.

Internal and external events only complicated this delay. On June 2, 1962, several thousand people marched on Communist party headquarters in Novocherkassk, a town in the Rostov region, to protest national price increases for meat and dairy products. They were also protesting changes to work conditions. Twenty-four people were killed by troops and dozens injured. Seven people were later executed and 114 convicted of causing 'mass disorders' and 'banditry'. The Novocherkassk massacre was covered up, but news got out. It was part of a much wider call for strikes with leaflets across the USSR denouncing price increases for food. This was not an ideal time for authorities to give an exit visa to my father.

A few months later in October 1962, the much more serious Cuban missile crisis threatened not only the world with nuclear catastrophe but once again derailed Dad's application to leave. There was no movement on his exit visa in November and December of that year and our hopes waned. Then, surprisingly, on December 17, 1962, Second Secretary, R.S. Laurie at the Australian Embassy reported to the Secretary of Immigration that the Soviet Foreign Ministry had issued Frankel with a visa and to please inform his wife.

My father was given the news at the end of the year and then began selling all his furniture such as the Laminex table and chairs, our beloved Philips radio, and other things to raise enough money for his fares. In January 1963, those at work who remained his friends, secretly prepared a photo album (with the approval of management) as something by which he could remember them as a token of their happiness that he would soon be re-joining his family. Over the year they had taken photos of him at work and at places in Arshintsevo and Kerch as well as at public celebrations of May Day and the Revolution Day on the 7th of November which all workers had to attend.

After making final preparations, Abrasha or Abraham Frankel, my father, departed Kerch in early February and arrived in Moscow where the Australian Embassy organised his flight to Sydney via Delhi on Air India. He arrived in Melbourne on February 6, 1963, three months short of seven years since departing on May 7, 1956. We all took the day off work and school to greet him with much crying and celebration.

EPILOGUE

It would take a couple of months for my father to settle back into life in Melbourne. He had just turned fifty-five and was brimming with excitement and energy to be back in Australia. He hoped to re-establish himself both within the family that he loved so much and also begin working once again, perfecting the traditional art of smoking and curing fish. Over the years in Arshintsevo, he had studied the latest techniques of smoking fish, a topic on which the Soviets had published numerous technical manuals. Alas, all this additional study came to nothing as his former employers were not interested in having him back. They had learnt to produce smoked fish without him. Therefore, Dad went to work as a welder in a repair garage in South Melbourne. He was pleased that wages, conditions and working hours were much better than in Arshintsevo, but I know that he was quite disappointed that he couldn't work in the area of his choice where his knowledge and expertise could be utilised, refined and developed.

Re-establishing himself within the family was also not straightforward. We all loved him being back, but Genia and I had turned into adults during his absence and now had our own interests, needs and friends and did not rely on him as in the past. The pecking order had changed. In the second half of 1963, Genia moved out to live with her boyfriend. Mum and Maya were incredibly happy to be with

Dad again, but the years of separation had made my mother more independent. Consequently, while they loved one another, there were more arguments and tension between my parents in the short years of life that remained for him.

We were all extremely interested in politics and social issues and continued to have many discussions and arguments over local and international events and policies. My father had signed a pledge that he would not engage in pro-Soviet politics. As it turned out, this pledge was unnecessary. He was not afraid of ASIO. Rather, my father had no interest whatsoever in mixing with people from his former life in Australia, such as those active at the Australia-Soviet Friendship Society or his former Russian émigré acquaintances.

On June 21, 1963, Ernest Redford from ASIO interviewed him about his political activities and his life in the USSR. When asked about his views on Communism, he replied that he was interested in music and literature and stated: "I won't go for politics because I told you straight, I was a maniac. You still have many maniacs here." In other words, he didn't want to mix with people who, in his opinion, were still deluded by refusing to acknowledge the reality of life in the USSR. Discussing *Revolutionary Desire in Italian Cinema*, Italian film analyst, Luana Ciavola observed that 'excessive political faith works as a straitjacket'. My father's ideological blindness certainly prevented him from seeing the reality of Soviet Communism clearly. Perhaps a straitjacket in 1956 would have restrained the 'maniac' from returning to Russia? But then how poorer all our lives would have been if we had not gone through both the traumas and the enriching experiences of witnessing Soviet life.

Although my father acknowledged his former political fanaticism, he nonetheless upset ASIO in this final interview by speculating that if Communism changed in the future, as he once believed it might, then "I will again be a Communist." Asked to clarify this, he professed a utopian hope that if there was a change to a genuine form of communism, like genuine Christianity, where "one will give to another and that one will look after another and so on, educate him and so on,

I will believe, but at the present time I cannot." ASIO misunderstood this honesty and instead reported that 'Frenkel' had lost none of his former arrogance. Victorian Regional Director of ASIO, Redford, reported that "Frenkel proved a very difficult person to interrogate due to his domineering attitude and by his refusal to listen carefully to questions." Actually, Dad simply refused to give ASIO the conventional anti-Communist answers they wanted to hear.

In February 1965, Director-General Spry informed Immigration – after both of my parents had applied for Australian citizenship – to grant it to my mother but withhold a security clearance for my father as, quoting Redford's October 18, 1963 report, "it cannot be said with any degree of certainty that he gave a full and truthful account of his activities in the Soviet Union." Spry's antipathy towards my father continued to the very end. However, on April 4, 1967, Peter Barbour, who was now acting Director-General of ASIO, gave him a security clearance for naturalisation. By the time he attended the citizenship ceremony later in the year, he was already showing signs of the cancer in his pancreas and would only live a brief time longer until April 1968.

Between arriving in early 1963 and becoming ill in 1967, my father spent the next four and a half years living a quiet life based on work and family. His main passion was literature and music as he built up his classical music record collection. He also purchased a tape recorder and would sit at night recording music from the radio even though before FM radio was introduced, the sound quality was not particularly good. By the middle of 1967 he suffered increasingly severe pains in his stomach, chest and back and was eventually diagnosed with what they thought was pancreatitis. In November 1967, they operated on him at the Alfred Hospital but discovered that there was little that they could do as the cancer had spread extensively. They gave him only three to six months to live.

When Dad recovered from the exploratory surgery, he seemed to briefly acquire a new burst of energy. He would walk from St. Kilda to Port Melbourne and talk about returning to his job. At the time, there was a division amongst doctors as to whether they should tell patients that their condition was terminal or leave this decision to family members. While my father was still in hospital, we discussed the issue as a family but could not agree on how to proceed. I thought that he should definitely know but Mum thought that he wouldn't cope well and would rapidly decline. Yet, this was going to happen whether he knew the diagnosis or not. Out of respect for her wishes, we didn't tell him. It was a decision I deeply regret. Instead, I accompanied him one day to his workplace where he joked with his workmates and told them he would be back in a few weeks as soon as he felt in better shape. While he was talking with his workmates, I took the manager aside, explained his condition and told him that he would not be returning. The manager was shocked and cried.

Just at the time when Harold Holt drowned on December 17, 1967, Dad was beginning to go downhill. He was confined to bed most of the day and after Mum finished her few weeks of Christmas holidays in mid-January 1968, the main task of looking after him fell on my shoulders during the day, as I was on summer break from university. We had barely any income and my mother could not afford to stop working as a machinist at Keith Courtney's clothing factory in Flinders Lane. I would go to the Alfred Hospital to pick up bottles of morphine to try to alleviate the pain my father experienced. Medical solutions were grossly inadequate in those days, and he spent most of his last three months in a stupefied condition or sleeping most of the day due to pain-killing drugs. It was simply a terrible way to die.

I worked at home until Monash classes began in March, many of which I missed for the first few weeks. 1968 would be both a depressing and an auspicious year for a range of personal and broader political reasons. In January, I went to see if my new lecturer was in his office. Austin Gough was a former newspaper man turned academic who arrived at Monash to teach 19th century French history. Although a conservative who hated the radical left, Gough was an inspiring teacher who enriched his classes by illustrating his historical interpretation with lectures on art and literature. Despite our opposing politics, he encouraged me by suggesting that I analyse the

1848 revolution in Paris from the perspective of three contemporaries, Marx, de Tocqueville, and Flaubert. I found this a stimulating distraction from the daily gloom of looking after my father in his deteriorating condition. A couple of months later, after Dad had died, Austin Gough and I would discuss the similarities and differences between events in May and June 1968 and May and June 1848.

On April Fools' Day, 1968, Abraham Frankel, my father, was close to death. He had turned all yellow from the cancer spreading to his liver. He was unable to eat, and in a grim irony, looked like a concentration camp skeleton with a stomach full of fluid. I called a taxi and warned the driver not to get a fright from Dad's jaundiced appearance. I took him to the Alfred Hospital for admission. He died six days later on April 7, 1968. We all came to see him before he fell into a coma, for the last few days of his life. There was such a disjunction between his life of action and the miserable last months of his life.

* * *

I have often wondered whether my father looked back on his active political life as a deluded subservience to the 'god that failed' or whether at the end of his life, he was still proud of his campaigning for peace and social justice. All of us rely on certain illusions and delusions about our lives or about the larger world. Without them, many of us would not get out of bed in the morning as the harsh reality, unadorned and stripped bare, would be too difficult to confront. Without hope and illusions, many political activists of all political persuasions and colours would not exist.

Dad never quite recovered from his delusions about Soviet Communism. His reaction was not unusual as he fell into one of three common responses of people who have lived under Communist regimes. Firstly, there are those who became active anti-Communists in a zealous manner, either in politics and business or in private life but were happy to tolerate and accept major injustices in Australia and the rest of the world. Secondly, like my father, those who became deeply disillusioned often emotionally exited or turned away from political participation and immersed themselves in all kinds of private activities from music to tending their own garden. One strand of political disillusionment was represented by writers such as Milan Kundera, a conventional body of conservative literature celebrated in the West. According to these now 'mature' adults who accepted the status quo, dreams of revolution were simply products of the youthful 'immature lyrical age' but were lies. While Dad rejected the lies propagated by the Soviets, he did not become a political conservative. Finally, a minority of people, including my mother and her children, belonged to those who managed to develop a more complex and richer understanding of politics and society after learning from our life-changing experiences in the authoritarian Soviet Union.

These three general responses to Communism had less to do with the age of the person and were more connected to their individual experiences and psychological capacities to move on from their former views of the world. Apart from my father, our family made the transition beyond old Communist beliefs to a broader and more radical critique of both capitalism and Communism. We did not become pro-capitalist just because Soviet Communism was a mockery of socialist values. Instead, we recognised that the profound inequalities in Australia and other capitalist societies required supporting new anti-authoritarian parties and new social movements. My mother rejected and outgrew many of her old Stalinist views. She took great interest in radical 1960s and 1970s politics and culture, attended many protests, and was an avid reader and supporter of her children's social, artistic, and political activities.

By contrast, my father's disillusionment with Communism left him emotionally drained. This was compounded by the trauma he experienced when separated from his family and facing the genuine possibility that he would never see us again. Once back in Australia, he remained politically trapped in a bygone era, continuing to despise those on the political Right but also full of contempt for the myopia of the old Communist Left. Crucially, he did not seek out political alternatives. In this respect, he continued to live his remaining years still immersed in the social reality of an earlier era without transitioning to the contemporary political world. My father's reaction remains quite common. Today, it is possible to see generations of former or current activists, who not only cling to the past (whatever their beliefs) but fail to develop an alternative politics that is appropriate for new national and global socio-political and environmental realities. I discussed these political positions in *Zombies, Lilliputians and Sadists: The Power of the Living Dead and the Future of Australia,* a book I published in 2004.

Our direct experiences of both Soviet and Australian bureaucracy and security forces, meant we became acutely aware of the degree to which governments not only paid lip service to democracy but also presided over outright violations of human rights. Also, our political and social education in Russia made us different from most Australians who have lived relatively affluent but parochial lifestyles. These differences made me sometimes feel at odds with even those with whom I shared political positions, such as radical New Left students or those in social movements of recent decades. I was particularly conscious that many fellow radicals had either very abstract concepts of communism or were mainly focused on philosophical and cultural issues rather than practical everyday problems. For many, it is still easier to simply oppose capitalism than to also work out ways to avoid repeating the institutional and organisational mistakes of Soviet and Chinese Communism. Nearly all Left radicals today proclaim their anti-Stalinism but only a minority are sensitive to the complex problems of developing an environmentally sustainable and democratic political economy.

As to conservatives and liberals, who are so quick to condemn and dismiss socialism, this condemnation is often accompanied by a defence of the most disastrous environmental destruction and social inequalities arising from capitalist market societies. These can be the same people who mouth platitudes about individual freedom but promote, and still defend most forms of social inequality or offshore detention centres for refugees. By contrast, our experiences of being deliberately isolated and ignored by both the Australian and Soviet governments taught us to be extremely sensitive to the plight of thousands of helpless victims. These languishing victims, such as refugees and discriminated minorities, are caught in the maze of secret and unaccountable bureaucratic practices that hide behind the veil and excuse of 'national security'. I know what that feels like.

In recent years, the focus on children needing to develop resilience has become either an almost empty cliché, or a quick cure-all panacea for deep-seated social inequalities that have little to do with a person's psychological strength. Our experiences in the Soviet Union were, by contrast, not a mere ideological demonstration of so-called resilience. They were genuine psychological, social, and political struggles that helped us to develop patience, strength, and courage against considerable odds. For all of Abrasha Frankel's blind spots and dogmatism, and for all of Tania Frankel's stubborn pigheadedness, we children were extraordinarily lucky to be showered with such profound love by our parents. Importantly, they provided the vital support and enriching family atmosphere that enabled the three of us to learn from our traumas and collective struggles.

Among the many things that our parents taught us were lessons on how to speak up for ourselves, and to call out lies and abuses. We were also taught why it was important not to succumb to whatever views were popular simply because they were uncritically accepted by the majority. Although we were made by ASIO into a Cold-War caricature of what were considered to be 'subversives', there was also another conception of 'subversive' during the Cold War. The radical philosopher, Herbert Marcuse, wrote in *One Dimensional Man* (1964) that: "remembrance of the past may give rise to dangerous insights, and the established society seems to be apprehensive of the subversive contents of memory." As a 'family of subversives' shaped by love and care, we also learnt lessons in moral courage and resistance which were genuinely subversive of social and political conformity and complacency. These lessons became the basis of my social and personal formation and remain an integral part of who I am today.

SELECT BIBLIOGRAPHY

While this book is not written as an academic text with detailed footnoting, readers may refer to the following books and articles and files from the national archives for additional material and background on some of the events, persons and topics covered:

The National Archives of Australia contains hundreds of pages on members of our family. These files are listed under the following numbers: Attorney-General's Department/ASIO's files on Frankel/Frenkel/Frankl aka 'Sasha', NAA A6119, 7534, 7535; Department of Immigration, A6980 61-17433, 201205 and 61-6515, 201206; Prime Minister's Department, 59/491; and External Affairs Department 1453/4137.

Newspapers used include *The Age, The Argus, The Herald, The Sun* and *Canberra Times*.

Other sources:
Leonard Broom, F. Lancaster Jones and Jerzy Zubrzycki, *Opportunity and Attainment in Australia*, Canberra, Australian National University Press, 1976
Musa Budeiri, *The Palestine Communist Party, 1919–1948: Arab and Jew in the Struggle for Internationalism*, London: Ithaca Press, 1979
Brian Costar and Paul Strangio, 'B. A. Santamaria: 'A True Believer'?' *History Australia vol.*1, no.2, 2004, pp.256–78
Phillip Deery, 'Menzies, the cold war and the 1953 convention on peace and war', *Australian Historical Studies*, vol.34, no.122, 2003, pp.248–269
Isaac Deutscher, *The Non-Jewish Jew and other Essays*, London, Verso, 2017

Gary Fields, *Enclosure: Palestinian landscapes in a historical mirror*, Berkeley, University of California Press, 2017

Sheila Fitzpatrick, *White Russians, Red Peril: A Cold War History of Migration to Australia,* Collingwood, La Trobe University Press/Black Inc., 2021

Sheila Fitzpatrick, *Everyday Stalinism: Ordinary Life in Extraordinary Times: Soviet Russia in the 1930s*, Oxford, Oxford University Press, 1999

David Horner, *The Spy Catchers: The Official History of ASIO, 1949–1963*, Sydney, Allen & Unwin, 2014

Max Kaiser, 'Jewish Culture is Inseparable from the Struggle Against Reaction': Forging an Australian Jewish Antifascist Culture in the 1940s', *Fascism*, no.9, 2020, pp.34–55

John Kimsey, '"The ends of State" James Angleton, Counterintelligence and the New Criticism', *International Intrigue: Plotting Espionage as Cultural Artifact*, vol.13, 2017

Andrew Moore, *The Right Road: A History of Right-wing Politics in Australia*, Oxford, Oxford University Press, 1995

Gail Warshofsky Lapidus, *Women in Soviet Society: Equality, Development, and Social Change.* Berkeley, University of California Press, 1978

Moshe Lewin, *The Soviet Century*, London, Verso, 2005

Stephen Lovell, *The Soviet Union: A Very Short Introduction*, New York, Oxford University Press, 2009

Stuart Macintyre, *The Party: The Communist Party of Australia from Heyday to Reckoning*, Sydney, Allen & Unwin, 2022

Robert Manne, *The Petrov Affair: Politics and Espionage*, Sydney, Permagon, 1987, and second edition, Melbourne, Text, 2004

David McKnight, *Australia's Spies and their Secrets*, Sydney, Allen & Unwin, 1994

Philip Mendes, 'The Melbourne Jewish Left, Communism and the Cold War. Responses to Stalinist Anti-Semitism and the Rosenberg Spy Trial', *Australian Journal of Politics and History*, Vol. 49, No. 4, 2003, pp. 501–516

Samuel Moyn, *Liberalism Against Itself: Cold War Intellectuals and the Making of Our Times*, New Haven, Yale University Press, 2023

Bob Santamaria interviewed by Robin Hughes, *Australian Biography*, National Film and Sound Archive of Australia, April 1997

SELECT BIBLIOGRAPHY

Mark B. Smith, 'The Withering Away of the Danger Society: The Pensions Reforms of 1956 and 1964 in the Soviet Union', *Social Science History*, Vol. 39, no.1, 2015, pp. 129–148

Ronald Taft and John Goldlust, 'The Current Status of Former Jewish Refugees in Melbourne', *Australian and New Zealand Journal of Sociology*, vol.6, no.1, 1970, pp.28–48

Richard Teese and John Polesel, *Undemocratic Schooling: Equity and Quality in Mass Secondary Education in Australia*, Carlton, Melbourne University Press, 2003

Benjamin Tromly, *Cold War Exiles and the CIA: Plotting to Free Russia*, Oxford, Oxford University Press, 2019

Gleb Tsipursky, 'Worker Youth and Everyday Violence in the Post-Stalin Soviet Union', *European History Quarterly*, Vol. 45, no.2, 2015, pp. 236–254

Michael Tubbs, *ASIO: The Enemy Within*, Croyden Park NSW, Michel Tubbs, 2008

Patrick Wolfe, *Settler Colonialism and the Transformation of Anthropology*, London, Cassell, 1999

Peter Yule (ed.), *Carlton A History*, Carlton, Melbourne University Press, 2004

Arnold Zable, *Wanderers and Dreamers: Tales of the David Herman Theatre*, Melbourne, Jewish Cultural Centre & National Library, 'Kadimah', 1998

www.ingramcontent.com/pod-product-compliance
Lightning Source LLC
Chambersburg PA
CBHW030250010526
44107CB00053B/1656